**IN MEMORY OF
HELEN "ROSIE" MAGEE**

Bach for a Hundred Years

Bach for a Hundred Years

A Social History of the Bach Choir of Bethlehem

Paul S. Larson

LEHIGH UNIVERSITY PRESS
Bethlehem

Published by Lehigh University Press
Co-published with The Rowman & Littlefield Publishing Group, Inc.
4501 Forbes Boulevard, Suite 200, Lanham, Maryland 20706
www.rowmanlittlefield.com

Estover Road, Plymouth PL6 7PY, United Kingdom

British Library Cataloguing in Publication Information Available

Library of Congress Cataloging-in-Publication Data
Larson, Paul, 1932–
    Bach for a hundred years : a social history of the Bach Choir of Bethlehem / Paul S.
Larson.
        p. cm.
    Includes bibliographical references and index.
    ISBN 978-1-61146-094-0 (cloth : alk. paper) — ISBN 978-1-61146-095-7 (ebook)
    1. Bach Choir of Bethlehem (Bethlehem, Pa.)—History. I. Title.
    ML28.B196L37 2012
    782.506'074827—dc23   2011034849

♾ ™ The paper used in this publication meets the minimum requirements of American
National Standard for Information Sciences—Permanence of Paper for Printed Library
Materials, ANSI/NISO Z39.48-1992.

Printed in the United States of America

To my wife, Jan; to Jack, my friend; and to Judi, my reader.
They sustained me in a variety of ways.

The notion of community is one of the most characteristic, one of the most important, yet one of the least noticed American contributions to modern life.

—Daniel Boorstin, Hidden History

Let people judge by what standards they will; but to us whose eyes and feet and hearts turn annually towards old Bethlehem, to find here the high moment of the whole year, this city wears a special and enduring distinction. To her belongs by peculiar right the music of Bach.

—Charles Osgood, Going to Bethlehem

Contents

Illustrations

Acknowledgments

I am indebted to many people who shared their stories with me. They are Barbara Stout, Susan Sommers, Dorothy Ferguson, Mary Meilinger, Tom Church, Kathy Link, Greg Funfgeld, Jan Bonge, Bridget George, Jack Jordan, Howard Cox, Ellis Finger, Ed Young, Charles Holdeman, and Martha Luckenbach, now deceased. Linda Lipkis prepared the discography. As archivist and curator of The Bach Choir, I have attended meetings of the Board of Managers and have been influenced by the skill and understanding of the present president, Dr. David Beckwith. Watching the Board process has been an inspiration to me. Edith Laver and Jack Jordan critiqued numerous versions of the manuscript. Evelyn Miller offered me unexpected riches about J. Fred. Wolle's time in California. John Roach did a total editing out of goodwill. I was most fortunate in his interest in The Bach Choir and in his desire to make my telling clear to readers regardless of their musical backgrounds. Christy Roysdon found whatever I needed in the Lehigh University libraries and on the World Wide Web and critiqued the manuscript, as did Annette Benert. Many, many thanks to them both. Also, my thanks Mr. George Myers for technical assistance. Many thanks to Mrs. Judith Mayer of Lehigh University Press for her patience, understanding, and expert exactness and guidance. John Spadaccia's friendly assistance in photography is much appreciated. Finally, untold thanks to Scott Paul Gordon. Without his commitment to academic scholarship and to the Lehigh University Press and without his interest in this story, this book would not have been possible.

Author's Note

The group of singers and instrumentalists whose musical home is Bethlehem, Pennsylvania, and who specialize in the music of Johann Sebastian Bach and those his music influenced has been variously called the Bach Choir, The Bach Choir, the Bethlehem Bach Choir, The Bethlehem Bach Choir, and presently The Bach Choir of Bethlehem. These changes are found in the chronology of this history. However, I felt that The Bach Choir of Bethlehem was too cumbersome considering the many times it appears in the text. When writing of its present activities, I used either The Bach Choir, or often simply The Choir if there was no ambiguity.

The same circumstance applied to festival references: first, simply the festival, then the Festival, The Festival, The Bach Festival, The Bach Festival of Bethlehem. Again, I used The Bach Festival in the last section of the text when there was no ambiguity.

An identical situation arose when writing about The Choir's first conductor. He preferred J. Fred. Wolle. However, others wrote of him as J. Fred Wolle, Mr. Wolle, Professor Wolle, and Doctor Wolle, or called him simply Fred. After the first reference, usually I chose to use the last name only, but all of the above are in quoted references.

Two archival collections formed the basis of this volume, Archives of the Bach Choir of Bethlehem (ABCB) and Archives of the Moravian Church, Bethlehem (MABC). Their abbreviations appear universally throughout the notes.

Bethlehem, Pennsylvania
2011

xii

Introduction

The Bach Choir's Wreath on Bach's Tomb

On 27 March 1900, in Bethlehem, Pennsylvania's Central Moravian Church, the city's Bach Choir gave its first public concert, presenting Johann Sebastian Bach's *Mass in B Minor* in its entirety for the first time in the United States. J. Fred. Wolle, the brilliant young choirmaster of Central Moravian, conducted. The church itself was the center of a vibrant tradition of choral music reaching back more than 150 years to a time contemporary with Bach (1685–1750) himself. This American premiere of the *Mass* began at once to carve a significant place for Bach, and for Bethlehem, in the history of American musical culture.

Settled by Moravians in 1741, Bethlehem was, except for a few years, the lifelong home of J. Fred. Wolle, its most prominent musician, professor of music at Lehigh University, and nationally known concert organist. With a deep passion to conduct the music of John S. Bach (as English speakers called him in 1900), Wolle infused the community through his charm, confidence and courage, ancestry, and profound musicianship, with his devotion to Bach's music.

Many American churches had enthusiastic choirs in 1900, in cities with thriving industries, wealth, institutions of higher learning, dedicated singers, and talented musicians. But in Bethlehem a quite unusual spirit forged a close connection among industrial and religious leaders, academicians, social elites, and people of all classes to foster high musical choral art. This history is an account of that nexus.

In his teens Wolle had studied Bach's organ music with Dr. David Wood of Philadelphia, himself a renowned interpreter of Bach's work. Wood encouraged Wolle to go to Europe to study with Joseph Rheinberger, one of the most prominent European organists and composers of his time. In Munich in 1885, Wolle heard his first large Bach choral work, *The Passion According to St. John*, in a performance celebrating the bicentennial of Bach's birth.

Wolle returned to Bethlehem fired with the desire to perform that same work with the Choral Union, the community chorus he conducted. Two years later, the group performed the American premiere of the *Passion According to St. John* on 5 June 1888. The performance was part of the broadening public reception of Bach's music that had begun in Europe, and by 1900 had taken root in the United States. Composers, conductors, music historians, critics, and performers were awed by the vast scope, superb skill, and the emotional depth of Bach's compositions.

After Bach's death in 1750, the first center for performances of his choral and instrumental music was Berlin. Many who knew Bach's sons and students began promoting Bach performances, and at the end of the eighteenth century, a number of people there were collecting his manuscripts and printed music. Karl Friedrich Christian Fasch, a member of this Berlin circle, organized a singing society that rehearsed in the home of one of the female singers. The society grew rapidly and was given rehearsal space in the Prussian Academy of Art. In 1793, the *Singakademie* was founded. The next year Fasch noted in the attendance book, "Today we began studying Bach's *Motetta Komm, Jesu, komm* BWV 229.[1] Karl Fredrich Zelter, Fasch's assistant, continued the rehearsals and in April the society sang the motet from "beginning to end." The group learned *Singet dem Herrn*, BWV 225 and another motet after that. By 1816, Bach's motets were frequently sung.[2]

Karl Fredrich Zelter succeeded Fasch as conductor, added an instrumental group, the *Ripienschule*, which practiced weekly, and began studying the "Kyrie" from the *B Minor Mass* with the chorus in 1811. Apparently, the choir found the music too difficult. Wolle would have the same experience a century later, but unlike Wolle, Zelter retreated to less demanding Bach vocal pieces, at which the singers were successful. In September 1813, he began rehearsing the *Mass* again and by the end of the month "the *Singakademie* went through the whole Mass under Zelter's direction."[3] A variety of sacred and secular cantatas, arias, and instrumental works by Bach followed. Two years later Zelter began rehearsing Bach's much larger choral work, *The Passion According to St. John*. Using Bach's manuscript as his reference, Zelter apparently conducted the work on Good Friday 1822. "During these years, no other chorus sang so many Bach pieces as the *Singakademie* and no instrumental group played as many pieces by Bach as the *Ripienschule* during their Friday rehearsals."[4]

Zelter's music students, Felix Mendelssohn and his sister, Fanny (both of whom for family reasons used the surname Mendelssohn-Bartoldy after 1812), joined the *Singakademie* at the beginning of October 1820. In addition to their early piano and organ instruction in Bach's instrumental solo works under Zelter, both became immersed in Bach's vocal music. Soon Zelter organized a group in his home to learn Bach's massive choral work, *The Passion According to St. Matthew*. To celebrate Bach's birthday on 21 March, Mendelssohn-Bartholdy conducted the work in the hall of the *Singakademie* using a manuscript score given to him by his grandmother, who had studied with one of Bach's students. The prominent Bach scholar Peter Wollny wrote about this performance: the "early phase of the Bach Renaissance . . . culminated in 1829 in the famous centennial performance of Bach's *St. Matthew Passion* by the Berlin Singakademie under the direction of Felix Mendelssohn."[5] Zelter then directed the singing society in performances of the work in 1830, 1831, and 1832. As a mentor of Mendelssohn, he served to introduce Bach to the romantics. Mendelssohn eagerly picked up the torch.

Mendelssohn's own compositions were frequently and directly influenced by Bach, whose music he played often. Like Bach, he became the leader of music in Leipzig, where he conducted the orchestra and was active in founding the conservatory. He also promoted the publication of Bach's works in both Germany and England.

Zelter and the Mendelssohns were members of a "Bach Cult" flourishing in Berlin around 1800. It was centered in the music-literary Salon of Sara Levy, Mendelssohn's great-aunt and a very talented pianist and daughter of a member of the Prussian court, who had studied for ten years with Bach's son Wilhelm Friedmann Bach. Levy was a member of the *Ripienschule,* where she frequently played Bach's keyboard concertos. Following her husband's death in 1806, she invited friends every Thursday and Sunday to her mansion in Berlin. There were cultivated conversations, and performances of music by the Bach family, and by contemporary composers. In addition to owning many Bach family manuscripts, including a number of Bach's own, Sara Levy was an active subscriber to editions of published music. Similarities between the "Bach Cult" in Berlin and the one that developed in Bethlehem are described later in this history.

In Vienna, another group loosely connected with Sara Levy also met regularly to study Bach's works. At various times Wolfgang Mozart, Joseph Haydn, and Ludwig van Beethoven participated. Conductors of choral groups in other German-language cities were slowly introducing Bach's large choral works to audiences.[6]

Music printing played an increasing part in promoting the availability of Bach's music. He published few of his compositions during his lifetime, and at his death most were still manuscripts. Within a short time many were lost, including more than half of the cantatas. The *Well-Tempered Clavier* (two volumes of preludes and fugues in all keys for keyboard) was published in 1754 in Leipzig by the prominent music publisher Breitkopf and Son. Numerous instrumental works followed. However, the vocal works, cantatas, passions, and the *B Minor Mass* were printed much later. An exception was the complete motets published in 1802 and 1803, again in Leipzig. These works were the favorites of the *Singakedemie.* Though the scores had been published earlier, the individual parts for the singers of The *St. Matthew* and *St. John Passions* were not published until 1834.[7]

Publication of Bach's choral works increased greatly after mid-century. In Bethlehem, Wolle's Choral Union, church choir, and later Bach Choir, were totally dependent upon music published in England in English by Vincent Novello. Wolle used Novello's editions in every Bach performance before the Bach Choir was founded, and of the twenty-seven different choral works Wolle did with the Bach Choir from 1900–1905, twenty editions were printed by Novello. Later the Bach Choir of Bethlehem furthered the publication of editions of Bach's cantatas in English prepared by Ifor Jones, The Bach Choir's third conductor.

The first biography of Bach appeared at the beginning of the nineteenth century, written by Johann Nikolaus Forkel.[8] Serious, methodical Bach scholarship had begun and continues unabated. By the end of the century two monumental studies of Bach's life and music had appeared: *Johann Sebastian Bach* by Phillip Spitta (1873 and 1880) and *Bach* by Albert Schweitzer (1905). J. Fred. Wolle owned both books.

In 1850 the centenary of Bach's death and the "Bach movement," as it was often called, was so firmly established that an organization called the *Bach-Gesellschaft* was formed to publish Bach's extant works. There was general agreement that his music must be accessible to the world, so all the works known at the time were organized and printed handsomely in German and the cost of the enterprise was borne by subscriptions. The volumes, to appear annually from 1851, were instrumental and vocal scores not individual parts. Ten cantatas were included in the first complete volume. *The Passion Music from St. Matthew* was published in 1854, the fourth year, the *Mass in B Minor* in the sixth year, and *Passion Music from St. John* in 1862. The final volume was printed in 1900, and the original association was replaced by the *Neue Bachgesellschaft*. J. Fred. Wolle owned a complete set and used these scores frequently.

Highly significant for Bach research in the twentieth century was the formation of an American chapter of the *Neue Bachgesellschaft* in 1972. The center of that group for a number of years was The Bach Choir of Bethlehem. Alfred Mann, The Choir's fourth conductor, initiated the organization of the new society and brought it to Bethlehem. Mann's many contributions to Bach scholarship are discussed in the chapters devoted to his tenure with The Choir.

The promotion of Bach's music was the absorbing goal of Samuel Wesley (1766–1837), the great Bach disciple in England. He formed the "Sebastian Squad," a group of four musicians including the British music publisher Vincent Novello, to promote Bach's music through regular recitals. Mendelssohn, who traveled to England a number of times, added fervor to the growing interest in Bach's music.

In 1850, The Bach Society had its first rehearsal in London on Bach's birthday. One of its primary purposes was "the furtherance and promotion of a general acquaintance with the numerous Vocal and Instrumental works of this great and comparatively unknown Master, chiefly by performance."[9] The premiere of the *St. Matthew Passion* in England used some of the "actual vocal parts (all in manuscript) which Mendelssohn [had] used for the revival of the 'St. Matthew Passion' in 1829, at Berlin."[10] Two more performances followed, then eleven movements of the *B minor Mass* in 1860, and the *Christmas Oratorio* the next year.

If there were an English language antecedent for The Bach Choir of Bethlehem, it was the choir formed in London in 1875 "for the production of the Mass in its entirety."[11] The next year the group gave the first performance of the *Mass* in England. Like the singers in Bethlehem, those in London rehearsed for a year in the homes of members. Notable women musicians were prominent in both groups, Jenny Lind Goldschmidt (the Swedish singer had married Otto Goldschmidt in 1852) in London and Ruth Doster in Bethlehem. Both Bach Choirs initiated annual Bach Festivals, one or more days of afternoon and evening concerts devoted to a series of Bach's works on a particular theme. On 21 March 1885, The Bach Choir in London commemorated the bicentenary of Bach's birth. Unlike the performance in Bethlehem, the orchestra and chorus in London had 600 performers, instruments no longer in use were manufactured for the occasion, and a player was "fetched from Berlin" to play the high trumpet part. The next year Sir Arthur Sullivan conducted the *B Minor Mass* at the Leeds Festival.[12]

The purposes of these two English musical activities discussed above are remarkably similar to those of The Bach Choir of Bethlehem. The London Bach Choir (1875) "was formed . . . with the desirability of keeping together a trained body of singers as a permanent association . . . having for its object the study and production . . . of choral works of excellence of *various* schools."[13] Both singing groups were for amateurs, and were initiated to commemorate events in Bach's life as well as to study and promote his liturgical choral works independent of the Lutheran liturgy and the Church Year. Bach Festivals were given in Berlin in 1901, Leipzig in 1904, Eisenach in 1907, and Duisburg in 1910.

Wolle was surely aware of these festivals if for no other reason than that he used the English-language editions they generated, but he made no comment about where he got the idea for a Bach Festival in Bethlehem. He would have been well aware of what was happening in Germany because of his Moravian connections there and his own personal associations with other musicians. Much later, conductor Alfred Mann hypothesized that Wolle had been "[a]dapting the pattern of the English Choral Festivals," and that The Choir had "established American Bach Festivals with the American premiere of the *B Minor Mass* in 1900."[14]

The London Bach Festival brought four fundamental musical performance issues to the fore: the appropriate size of a Bach choir; the kinds of instruments in a Bach choir orchestra and how they should be played; what instruments should be used to accompany solo passages; and whether changes in volume and tempo should be present in performance even though they had not been indicated by Bach himself. Conductors' solutions to these issues and the responses of music critics to their solutions still persist. Bach scholars continue to adjust Bach's notation, requiring newer editions of his works. Also, until fairly recently, the cantatas and passions had not been translated into English, raising issues of matching the English text closely with Bach's music. After 1970, The Bach Choir of Bethlehem began singing all Bach works in German.

A further problem involved the performance of Bach's many church cantatas, about one third of his surviving works. Over one hundred had been published by 1900 in score, along with a fair number of editions in which the voice parts were printed above a keyboard reduction of the instrumental parts. Albert Schweitzer clearly articulated the problem in his book *Bach*:

> Even where the Passions are regularly given, there are certain difficulties in the way of producing the cantatas. It looks as if their title were against them. Many conductors who have vowed themselves to the service of Bach think it injudicious to place cantatas on their programs, with the exception of the one or two that have become classics. They do not strike these people as sufficiently decorative . . . afraid that the programme will not draw, or that it offers too little variety.[15]

Schweitzer offered a musical compromise that could be sung in sanctuaries and secular halls alike:

> The ideal for the present day is really a sacred concert, composed of three or four Bach cantatas, selected for the appropriateness of their text to the ecclesiastical season. Pure Bach services of this kind should have the preference over the liturgical celebrations that are grouped around Bach cantatas . . . It should be observed, however, that under these circumstances the church must no longer be regarded as a sacred place. If the church, for any reason, is not available, the performances can be transferred to the concert room without their obvious character being affected thereby . . . The great point is that Bach, like every lofty religious mind, belongs not to the church but to religious humanity, and that any room becomes a church in which his sacred works are performed and listened to with devotion.[16]

Summarizing the increasing performance of Bach's choral music in Germany and in England, a prominent German musicologist wrote:

> Performance of the vocal works greatly increased in number since the 1860s. The concert hall remained the home of the Passions, Masses, and cantatas, just as it had since 1800. The choruses that performed them were not church choirs but the civic societies. After William Sterndale Bennet founded his Bach Society in London (1849) and William Rust his Bachverein in Berlin (1853), the number of choirs that dedicated themselves principally to the cultivation of Bach grew enormously: beginning in the 1860s, the Singakademie in Halle, under Robert Franz, became a center for the cultivation of Bach in Germany.[17]

There was no "Renaissance" or "Renewal" of Bach in nineteenth-century America. His music was imported, chiefly by American musicians studying music in Germany. The two most important of these American musicians were organists John Knowles Paine (1839–1906) and Dudley Buck (1839–1909). These New Englanders (Paine from Maine and Buck from Connecticut) were the first generation of Americans to study music in Germany and return to teach at home. Paine became Harvard University's first professor of music, and Buck assumed a teaching post at the New England Conservatory of Music, becoming one of the era's most important composers. These men made Boston a center for Bach performance, and "the pattern of spreading the gospel of Bach was thus established at Harvard."[18]

Lowell Mason and Theodore Thomas were of the same generation, performing Bach throughout the East in recitals, in the case of Mason (1829–1908), and instrumental performances, in the case of Theodore Thomas (1835–1905), a German-born conductor.

"Compared with Bach's keyboard and ensemble music, serious performances of his choral works came relatively late to American concert life," wrote Barbara Owen.[19] The entire *St. Matthew Passion* was first performed in America in 1879 by the Boston-based Handel and Haydn Society, founded in 1815 and now one of the oldest musical organizations in the United States. That Society performed an abridged version of the *B Minor Mass* in 1887. The Bach Society of Cleveland (Ohio) was organized around 1878, the first Bach Society in America. While the Cincinnati May Festival performed choral music by other composers, under the direction of Theodore Thomas, the group sang *The Magnificat* in 1875, Bach cantata BVW 11 in 1882, and sections from the *B Minor Mass* in 1886. Thus, a Bach Society preceded The Bach Choir of Bethlehem, and a May Festival—not devoted entirely to Bach—preceded the one in Bethlehem. An earlier annual music festival had begun in 1858 in Worcester, Massachusetts, where in 1870, an entire festival was devoted to "vocal, organ, and chamber music by Bach and Handel."[20]

Music critics and music publishers played an essential role in the Bach Movement in America as they had in Europe. John Sullivan Dwight, who published critical music reviews from 1852–1881 in *Dwight's Journal*, took a positive view of Bach's music. The Boston music publisher Oliver Ditson printed the *Passion Music According to the Gospel of St. Matthew* with both German and English text in 1869. G. Schirmer of New York published keyboard works later in the century, a time when "Bach assuredly had arrived in America."[21]

Bach's vocal, organ, and instrumental works were known and fairly regularly performed in Boston, New York, Philadelphia, Cleveland, Cincinnati, and Chicago. However, "the most important impetus to the performance of Bach's choral works in the United States was provided by an American Moravian, J. Fred. Wolle."[22] His achievement must first be considered in the light of the European Bach Renaissance. However, that "impetus" took place in Bethlehem, where Wolle was able to build upon a long association. A description of that tradition and Wolle's interaction with it follows.

NOTES

1. Georg Schünemann, "Die Bachflege der Berliner Singakademie," in *Bach-Jahrbuch* (1928): 151.

2. Ibid., 151.

3. Ibid., 146.

4. Ibid., 157–58.

5. Peter Wollny, "Sara Levy and the Making of Musical Taste in Berlin," *The Musical Quarterly* 77 (1993): 657.

6. See *Bach-Jahrbuch* (1960): 65–66 for a list of some of these conductors.

7. Max Schneider, "Verzeichnis bis zum 1851 gedruckten Werke v. Bach," *Bach-Jahrbuch* (1906): 84–113.

8. Hans T. David and Arthur Mendel, eds., *The New Bach Reader: A Life of Johann Sebastian Bach in Letters and Documents* (New York: W. W. Norton, 1998).

9. *A Dictionary of Music and Musicians, 1879,* 1st ed., s.v. "The Bach Society."

10. Ibid.

11. "Bach's Music in England," *The Musical Times and Singing Class Circular* 37, no. 646 (Dec. 1, 1896): 800.

12. "Bach's Music," *The Musical Times*, no. 645 (1 September 1896): 585–87; no. 644 (1 October 1896): 652–57; no. 645 (1 November 1896): 722–26; no. 646 (1 December 1896): 797–800.

13. *Dictionary of Music and Musicians, 1879,* 1st ed., s.v. "The Bach Society."

14. "Bach's Music" *The Musical Times*, no. 646 (1 December 1896): 800.

15. Alfred Mann, "Review," *American Choral Review* (Winter/Spring 1990): 34–35.

16. Albert Schweitzer, *Bach* I (New York: Macmillan, 1905), 262–63.

17. Friedrich Blume, "Bach in the Romantic Era," *Musical Quarterly* 50, no. 3 (July 1964): 301.

18. J. Bunker Clark, *American Musical Life in Concert to 1865*, James R. Heintz, ed. (New York: Garland, 1994), 342.

19. Barbara Owen, "Bach Comes to America," in *Bach in America*, Stephen A. Crist, ed. (Urbana: University of Illinois Press, 2003), 11.

20. Ibid.

21. Matthew, Dirst, "Doing Missionary Work: Dwight's Journal of Music and the American Bach Awakening," in *Bach in America*, 15–35.

22. Ibid., 14.

Chapter 1

Bach, Bethlehem, and Wolle

1733–1897

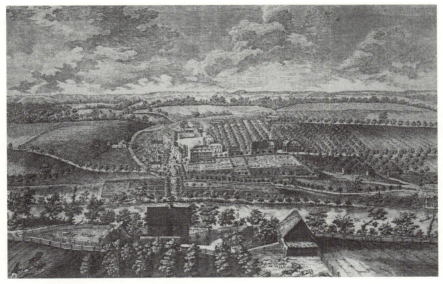

View of Eighteenth-Century Bethlehem

Without J. Fred. Wolle, Bethlehem would not have become a national center for Bach performance. Without Bethlehem, Wolle would not have become a great American Bach conductor. As Carl Friedrich Zelter and the city of Berlin had worked together; Felix Mendelssohn-Bartholdy had focused Leipzig again on Bach; and later composer and conductor William Bennett, founder of London's Bach Society, and singer Jenny Lind Goldschmidt and her pianist husband, had promoted and performed Bach's choral works in London;

1

so too, Wolle and Bethlehem had to work together as a cohesive musical organization for the Bach Choir to emerge in December 1898. This chapter is an account of the pervasive, intricate interplay between Wolle and Bethlehem that prepared for that event.

Christian Pietists called United Brethren or Moravians founded Bethlehem in 1741, seventy miles north of Philadelphia on the frontier of the English colonial empire. With origins in Central Europe, the group (persecuted, displaced, and dissatisfied) was sheltered and consolidated under the leadership of Count Ludwig von Zinzendorf, a Saxon noble. Intending to reestablish Pietistic ideals in the New World, they founded Bethlehem as a theocratic community. With all property held in common, there was no direct aristocracy. Christ was the chief elder, and everyone worked ambitiously and skillfully to build a congregation that was worthy of Him, acting as witnesses to all who desired knowledge of Christ. In a short time large buildings were constructed in the Provincial German Baroque style that Bach would have found familiar. Many remain today virtually unchanged in Bethlehem's historic district.

H. E. Krehbiel, music critic of the *New York Tribune*, who became a formidable force in the early Bethlehem Bach festivals, drew a subtle connection between Bach and Bethlehem in a review that appeared on 12 May 1901. He recounted how the founding group had gathered in a log house to celebrate Christmas Eve in 1741. There the name of the new settlement emerged:

> Toward midnight he [Count von Zinzendorf] led the worshipers through the house and the stable, and there started the old hymn, with a verse as follows
>> Nicht Jerusalem, sondern Bethlehem,
>> Aus den kommt, was uns frommt,
>> Nicht Jerusalem.
> The hymn is still sung by the congregation in a translation made in 1890 by C. S. Chitty, the verse quoted running thus.
>> Not Jerusalem—lowly Bethlehem
>> 'Twas that gave us Christ to save us.
>> Not Jerusalem.
> It was this incident that suggested the name for the settlement and the tune that was to be. The hymn, however, is not Moravian, though pietistic. It was composed, words and music, by Adam Drese (1670–1718), who was court chapelmaster at Arnstadt where Bach was organist.[1]

As Bach would have found the buildings in Bethlehem familiar, he also would have felt at home in its musical landscape; the practice that would have touched him particularly directly was the presence of a *Collegium Musicum* (community orchestra). Its founder in Bethlehem was Johann Christopher

Prylaeus (1713–1785), who had studied theology at the University of Leipzig. Lawrence W. Hartzell, the historian of Moravian Music in America, described Prylaeus in Leipzig during the time of Bach:

> From a musical point of view, Leipzig was an excellent city for a young musician studying to be a pastor. It is highly likely that Pryrlaeus attended the Thomaskirche or Nicolaikirche during his student years [also probably the University church that Bach was connected with]. The cantor of these churches Johann Sebastian Bach was the leading representative of the German high baroque. Bach was also director of the *Collegium Musicum.* It is likely that Prylaeus provided himself with many opportunities to observe Bach's work with this group . . . The young pastor was to become the direct link between the *Collegia* of the old world and the new.[2]

The Leipzig *Collegium* consisted mainly of university students. Prylaeus certainly knew of this highly visible musical group; with his musical talent and ability, it is difficult to imagine that he would not have joined them. Hartzell concluded his article:

> Prylaeus' most significant contribution to American music was the establishment of America's first *Collegium Musicum* on December 13, 1744. This group consisted of various wind and string instrumentalists whose purpose was to accompany hymn singing and other types of vocal music . . . One can assume that Prylaeus was attempting to follow the practice he had observed [or participated in] in Leipzig.[3]

Count Zinzendorf also knew Dresden and Leipzig well and would "have been familiar with this [*collegium musicum*] tradition, and is believed to have employed instrumentalists at the chapel in his own relatively modest . . . residence, built in 1721 in Berthelsdorf."[4] Zinzendorf encouraged a *collegium musicum* in Bethlehem, and within three years of the founding of the community, Prylaeus was leading one there. By 1744 a cantata written for the laying of the foundation of the Single Brethren's House in Herrnhaag in September 1793 was performed three times by the *Collegium musicum* with Prylaeus as the solo singer.[5] Arias, recitatives, duets for soprano and bass, and hymns sung by the residents were all present in the work accompanied by two violins, viola d'amore, flauto dolce, and keyboard. Though the group was modest, this cantata was a fully developed composition that Bach would have recognized.[6] Soon every Moravian community in America had a *Collegium* with its members proficiently performing concert music, often of extreme difficulty. The group served as an inspiration for highly gifted Moravian composers residing in America. By 1748 the Bethlehem *Collegium* was made up of fourteen players and practiced an hour each day.[7]

One piece by Bach is in the library of the Bethlehem Philharmonic Society, a group that grew from the *Collegium* as well as a number of pieces by one of Bach's sons. Two symphonies and two trio sonatas by Johann Christoph Friedrich Bach survive only in this collection.

As with the Moravian Trombone Choir, a line can be drawn to The Bach Choir of Bethlehem from the *Collegium Musicum*, through the Bethlehem Philharmonic Society, to the Choral Union in Wolle's time and to the choir of Central Moravian Church. Without question, the American Bach premieres that took place in Bethlehem before 1900, described later in this chapter, would certainly not have been possible without the body of seasoned singers and instrumentalists living in Bethlehem.

There is proof that Bach was known as early as 1823 in Bethlehem, and the first performance of a Bach choral work in America may well have taken place there.[8] Two years earlier, the cantata "Ein feste Burg ist unser Gott," BWV 80, had been published in score (all the choral and instrumental parts together on a page) in Leipzig. In 1823 the Bethlehem Moravian Congregation paid the church organist John Christian Till (1763–1844) to copy the vocal and instrumental parts of this cantata. Till also created a keyboard reduction of the full musical score that could be used for rehearsals and performance. "In 1829 Zelter writes Goethe that they [the publisher Breitkopf] regarded the work as a 'drug.' Such was the fate of the first cantata of Bach's that was offered to the German public."[9]

The Bethlehem Congregation, however, was clearly interested in the work. While there is no direct proof that the cantata was performed in Bethlehem, circumstantial evidence suggests that it probably was. The cantata is at least a twenty-minute work. The effort involved in copying the individual parts certainly indicates an intention to perform the work, and there was a longstanding tradition of singing and playing such works in Bethlehem. In addition, a new concert hall in Bethlehem was opened in 1823, requiring a special musical dedication. That "Ein feste Burg ist unser Gott" was sung and played by members of the Philharmonic Society is a reasonable assumption. The manuscript shows no wear, but that can be expected. Seldom were pieces repeated frequently enough to cause wear on the parts.

To give this a mark of great significance, in a chronology of the English Bach Awakening from 1754–1829, there are only two references to Bach's choral music performed in America: "in 1806 Boston publication of the polonaise from his French Suite No. 6 (BWV 817/5) . . . and an 1823 manuscript of Bach's cantata 'Ein feste Burg ist unser Gott' (BWV 80) in the Moravian Archives at Bethlehem, Pennsylvania."[10]

There is no account of Bach in Bethlehem for the next fifty years, though performances of major choral works by other composers were given frequently by the Philharmonic Society and the Moravian Young Ladies' Seminary.

On 15 January 1874, however, there was a spectacular musical event in Central Moravian Church in which two of Bach's most extraordinary organ works were performed "for the citizens of the town" in a "Grand Organ Concert."[11] This concert introduced the newly built Central Moravian Church organ, which Theodore Wolle, the church organist and J. Fred. Wolle's cousin, had designed. Two of the finest organists in the United States had been asked to dedicate the instrument: David Wood, the blind Philadelphia organist, and G. W. Morgan, organist at two of the most prominent Episcopal churches in New York City. David Wood, an early exponent of Bach's organ music, began the recital with the "Passacaglia and Fugue in C Minor," BWV 582. Morgan played the "Toccata and Fugue in D Minor," BWV 565.

While no document confirms J. Fred. Wolle's attendance at this concert, it is difficult to imagine he would not have been present at such an important musical event. He was twelve, old enough to appreciate the importance of the occasion and the power of the music played that evening. And he lived just across the street from the church. If he was present, it would have been the first time he'd heard Bach's organ music, and the importance of the evening for his whole musical career can't be underestimated. In addition, at this concert Wolle could have learned of Dr. Wood, his future organ teacher, organist of St. Stephen's Episcopal Church in Philadelphia. Dr. Wood had been blind from the age of two, yet was "Philadelphia's greatest organist in the mid-nineteenth century, particularly excelling in the interpretation of the organ works of Bach, many of which he played for the first time in Philadelphia."[12] The concert established that Theodore Wolle knew of Wood.

Bethlehem Female Seminary, ca. 1860

Wolle had not only been born into a community with a 150-year history of dedicated highly skilled singing of sacred choral music with instrumental accompaniment; he had, in effect, been born and raised in a music conservatory, the building housing the Moravian Young Ladies' Seminary. The school had a national reputation, and parents who wanted the best in music instruction for their daughters sent them to Bethlehem. Francis Wolle, his father, was its headmaster and Elizabeth, his mother, was headmistress. From his father, a well-known published botanist, he experienced greatness based on the persistence and exactness of science. Wolle himself had a lifelong scientific interest in spiders and roses. His mother was a well-educated, charming, very devoted spiritual person with Moravian mystical beliefs. He was well prepared for the world he was about to enter: the world of eminent musicians, conductors, teachers, industrialists, wealthy patrons, and the works of Bach.

The first connection with Bach recounted by Wolle himself involved a music dictionary. He told the story in his introductory speech to the faculty of the University of California in 1905, when he was invited to found a department of music and to establish a Bach choir. Wolle graphically expresses his immediate attraction to Bach:

> In 1879 appeared the first number of the dictionary of music; musicians, edited by Sir Geo. Grove. One of the teachers of the Seminary [Wolle's home] subscribed to this then modern work . . . Knowing well my tastes, she kindly offered to let me read the parts as they were received. [J. Fred was 17 years of age.] Beginning at the beginning I eagerly learned A . . . Then came the B's . . . and the name B-A-C-H, of which I had heard little, and knew less. There was a whole family of them . . . and there was Johann Sebastian, "to whom," in Schumann's words, music owes about as great a debt as a religion owes to its founder: I read his biography. His life, simple and uneventful was like that life in my native town. As a boy he learned to play the violin, so had some of us boys, though crudely, indeed—as a youth he was a singer. My church is a church of song. Even as a young man he was master of my chosen instrument [the pipe organ]. I read on; on and found that he was imbued with the gift of the stately chorale, the very melodies on which I had been raised. He intensified the meaning of the hymns in his harmonizations of those chorales in ways then unattempted . . . These stately melodies which the people of my church had been singing from the cradle to the grave he had invested with fresh charm, new interpretation, deeper meaning [note the connection Kriebell made in his account above]. On those rocks of Gibraltar he had built his noblest cantatas and planned his greatest fugues—from them he had evoked his stupendous passion music; I read; reread again; again. I went no further . . . I stopped at Bach.[13]

Like other Moravian boys, Wolle had to continue his schooling or become an apprentice. His father said that he could enter Lehigh University, just across the Lehigh River from Moravian Bethlehem, or apprentice with Mr. Rau, the local pharmacist. Wolle chose the pharmacy because it would give him time to devote to music. He began transcribing manuscripts from the massive collection of the *Collegium Musicum* in the church attic.

His apprenticeship did not work, however. He had no interest in becoming a pharmacist. But he did love mathematics almost as much as he loved music, so he joined the faculty of the Moravian Parochial School, teaching mathematics and geometry. Very soon he was provided with two musical opportunities that led to his becoming a self-supporting musician, which he was determined to be. The first opportunity was a full-fledged theater production, and the second was a position as an organist of a newly built Episcopal Church of the Nativity in South Bethlehem.

In 1882 when Wolle was twenty, he conducted "The Flower Queen," a cantata by George F. Root. He shaped every element of the performance. He provided "alterations, additions and improvements . . . [and] of course there will be full orchestral accompaniment composed and arranged by Prof. J. Fred. Wolle [the title stemmed from his position at the Parochial School] leader and director of the whole affair."[14] This production was the first test of his organizational ability. He created a chorus "of a large number of Bethlehem's fair young ladies," and then brought together some of the best voices in the town drawing from community churches and the Bethlehem Philharmonic Society. A long newspaper review of the performance closed with a request for more performances:

> On the whole the cantata was a grand success, and the performance of the girls reflected great credit on themselves and on their instructors. Bethlehem has always had the name of being a musical town, but lately it had depended upon a reputation won long ago. The event of Saturday night had made a break, now let the ball be kept rolling. Let the next thing be the production of some grand chorus from the masters:[15]

Buoyed by the success of "The Flower Queen," Wolle organized the Choral Union, a group of community singers to perform major choral works. *The Moravian*, the church newspaper, found this newly formed chorus newsworthy, and reported:

> Friends of music will be glad to hear of the organization of the Choral Union, which will be conducted by Prof. Fred. Wolle, the rehearsal to be held in the Hall of the Parochial School. Considerable enthusiasm was manifest at the first

meeting . . . We hope the new Society will be a worthy successor of the old Philharmonic.[16]

Within a few months the Choral Union performed sections from Haydn's *Creation*. Other performances followed rapidly, and the editor of *The Moravian* expressed his pleasure. "Under the efficient management the Union had made rapid progress, and its concerts are highly appreciated by the lovers of music in Bethlehem."[17] Thus Wolle continued the line from the *Collegium Musicum* through the Philharmonic Society, and building in the direction of The Bach Choir.

His reputation spread beyond Bethlehem as he assumed the leadership of the choral society of nearby Easton. Again, *The Moravian* reported, "under the efficient leadership of J. Fred. Wolle . . . This society has made rapid progress[;] one of the choruses will be sung by 150 voices.[18] At twenty-one, J. Fred. was the conductor of two large community singing groups.

Because his love for Bach was already widely known, one of the groups gave him the Peters Edition of Bach's complete organ works. In two years he had become a notable musician in the area, and *The Moravian* printed a summary of Wolle's achievements, "Mr. Wolle has done much to develop and regulate the musical taste and ability of Bethlehem. His greatest success so far has been the development and training of the Choral Society of Bethlehem and Easton."[19]

Simultaneously, his career as organist began. He was nineteen years old when he took the organist's position at Nativity Church, where he was introduced to the Episcopal musical tradition, very different from that practiced by Moravian Pietists. This new position brought him into contact with many of the South Bethlehem elite who would heavily support his musical activities in years to come.

The Episcopal organ position was another connection with his next Bach organ teacher, Dr. David Wood, the same organist who had played at the dedication of the new organ at Central Moravian Church when Wolle was twelve. A major figure in the American Bach Movement, Wood owned the first set of Bach's organ works brought to Philadelphia,[20] and on 8 May 1894, he gave the first all-Bach organ program in Philadelphia. During the thirty years he taught organ at the Philadelphia Musical Academy, he introduced a number of generations to Bach's music. When he was asked to instruct J. Fred. Wolle, he agreed. Wolle could not have been more fortunate, as Wood could teach him exactly what he most wanted and needed to learn. Wolle later described that experience with Wood in a newspaper interview in which there are distant echoes of Wolle's mother's Moravian mysticism:

> I began to study organ. My first lesson was on a little fugue of Bach's. For some reason or other this piece took hold of me, and I asked my teacher [Wood] to give me Bach compositions entirely . . . I seemed to feel that I was coming back to something that I had known or heard before.[21]

Wolle studied with Wood for only a short time, but the lessons had a profound effect on him. He never forgot the debt he owed Wood. After Wood had attended the premiere of Bach's *B Minor Mass* conducted by Wolle, he wrote his congratulations in a letter now lost, but Wolle's response remains:

> Your kind note touches me too deeply for expression. Coming from you who embody Bach's spirit, and have Beethoven's head, the letter is the greatest treasure I possess. . . . It was your masterful inspiration which led me to study Bach.[22]

Many years later, Wolle wrote to Wood's widow, "If I have accomplished anything, or if I ever do anything worthwhile, may it reflect all the glory back to my dear old friend and teacher."[23] Wood had surely been involved in the decision Wolle made to go to Munich to study organ and composition with Joseph Rheinberger. The preparatory lessons with Wood had expanded young Wolle's organ technique and clearly solidified his devotion to Bach, making him ready for successful music study in Munich.

J. Fred. Wolle was a member of the second generation of American musicians studying in Germany. His oldest brother Hartley, an administrator in the newly formed Bethlehem Iron Works, had offered to pay for a year's study abroad, and Wolle left for Munich in July 1884. He chose Munich because Joseph Rheinberger was director of the conservatory there and in charge of music in the royal chapel. He held two of the highest musical positions in the German-speaking nations, he was recognized as one of Europe's finest organists and most prolific composers, and he was a Bach specialist. With the encouragement of Dr. Wood and the superior background of his Moravian upbringing in Bethlehem, Wolle set off confidently for Germany.

Rheinberger accepted only four organ students each year. Following a rigorous examination, he selected J. Fred. Wolle as one of them. Acceptance by Rheinberger attested not only to Wolle's musical superiority, even genius, but affirmed the superiority of the Moravian organ tradition, still vital enough in the late nineteenth century to have enabled him to move immediately into the highest musical circles.

When asked to characterize his organ lessons with Rheinberger for the press, Wolle said, "I asked him . . . to give me only Bach compositions."[24] However, "there was a fundamental difference in temperament and viewpoint between a teacher who regarded the organ as strictly an ecclesiastical instrument to be played without emotion and a pupil whose thought was, and is, that the organ—and all music—would express human feeling."[25] In contrast to the organ technique he had learned from Rheinberger (which must have been superb), Wolle became convinced that he did not want to play Bach the way Rheinberger did.

At the time that Wolle was in Munich, two schools of taste and composition contended for supremacy in German music. The conservative school believed that because Bach had included few expression markings, his music was objective. It had no deviations in volume and tempo. The aesthetics of the other, the "New German School," was embodied in the romantic works of Wagner, Liszt, and others.

Rheinberger himself was a musical conservative. However, "[i]t was typical of his generous nature that, although he himself did not like the work of Wagner and Liszt and was not a partisan of the New German School, he never tried to influence the young artists in his care through his personal views."[26] Wolle benefited greatly from his teacher's tolerance. He not only studied music by Bach and Rheinberger, he came to know Wagner's music, and on his return to Bethlehem began playing Wagner's works in recitals.

In 1885, Wolle's cousin Theodore died. The Elders offered Wolle the organ position of Central Moravian Church if he would return home. The pastor recorded the invitation in the church diary.[27] Wolle accepted, though he would remain in Munich until the year of study was completed.

Wolle's decision to remain longer in Munich was life changing, for on 5 June 1885, he heard a performance of Bach's *Passion According to St. John*. The music stunned him. Though overall he did not care for the performance by the singers of the Munich Opera, his best expression of the effect the *Passion* music had on him was a quote from Keats:

Then felt I like some watcher of this skies,
When a new planet swims into his ken.[28]

Wolle's vision for his life's work had developed in Munich—to conduct and play Bach's music for Americans. When he left Rheinberger, Wolle had become an organ scholar, capable of working independently to perfect his artistry. His rapid rise to fame as an American virtuoso was the result of his successful synthesis of talent, excellent training, and a rare but convincing view of the organ as an instrument for the expression of human feeling. His formal education was now complete.

Despite their short time together, Rheinberger remembered Wolle well. A Bethlehem choral conductor, Richard Schantz, emeritus professor of music at Moravian College, told this anecdote of an American musician who went to Munich to study Bach with Rheinberger: "You could have saved yourself the trip. The person who knows the most about Bach lives in Bethlehem, Pennsylvania. His name is J. Fred. Wolle!"

When he returned to America, Wolle resumed conducting The Choral Union, taking the first step in sharing Bach with the music lovers of Bethlehem. In 1887–1888, Wolle proposed a season of large choral works to prepare the group for Bach. In the fall they presented Mendelssohn's *Elijah*; on February 7, Handel's *Messiah*. The season concluded with *The St. John Passion*. He concluded the season with the American premiere of *The Passion According to St. John* with volunteer singers, soloists, and orchestra.

Mendelssohn's *Elijah* went well, but the performance of *Messiah* was harshly criticized in the *Bethlehem Daily Times*. The organ in the Episcopal Church of the Nativity [now Cathedral] was pitched "outrageously low . . . and is voiced in a most aggravatingly harsh and strident manner." The accompanist "was so ragged and uneven. . . .The strings were too loud in all the solo numbers." One of the singers sang flat. A baritone sang the bass part. Mrs. Estes (who later played a decisive role in the founding of The Bach Choir) did not put enough "soul in her work . . . The Chorus did not come up to its standard set in earlier efforts." However, "We trust . . . the last oratorio of the series . . . may . . . by its excellence, undo in large measure the impressions made by the 'Messiah' last night."[29]

Wolle began rehearsals of the *St. John Passion*, and in the end of April wrote Mrs. Estes asking her to be a soloist:

> The Bethlehem Choral Union has been working hard ever since its last concert of Bach's Passion Music according to St. John, trying to conquer some of its almost insurmountable difficulties. It is with some hesitancy that I again venture to trouble you with a request but I cannot help writing to ask you whether you would be willing to help us once more . . . there are two beautiful solos in which we would be delighted to hear you. The first is "From the bondage of transgression"; the other, "It is finished" . . . Notwithstanding the unjust and even ridiculous criticism which followed our recent concert, I hope you will find it within your power to give us your consent, as it is a long time since you have favored an audience on this side of the river. The concert will be given in Parochial Day School Hall, in about five weeks from the date.[30]

A date was set for a performance in early June 1888. The announcement in *The Moravian* was brief; the event was clearly a concert and not a sacred service:

> At some date in June next, the members of the Bethlehem Choral Union have decided to present to the music-loving people of the Bethlehems Bach's "Passion, according to St. John. [*sic*] This fact will, no doubt, be hailed with much pleasure, and the efforts of the Choral Union—which always mean a most enjoyable treat—will be rewarded by a well-filled house of those who can appreciate such performances.[31]

The performance was in English; "[t]he text is obviously the translation of Troutbeck found in Novello Edition (1872)."[32]

While the national importance of the performance was not mentioned by *The Moravian*, the *Daily Bethlehem Times* was eager to determine if the Choral Union would in fact premiere the *Passion*. New York critics were invited, and the staff of the paper "awaited [their responses] with interest."[33] One critic mentioned the conductor of Boston's Handel and Haydn Society, who said that he himself had performed only a section of this "masterpiece" in concert. As far as he was aware, the Bethlehem performance would be the American premiere. The announcement "brought forth much applause."[34] There was a current of Bach performance moving through the United States, and Bethlehem was swelling it.

With civic pride abounding, a reporter wrote "A Successful Rehearsal" a week before the concert. The music truly had excited him, and he wrote not only of the high quality of the composition but of the importance of Bach's music in general. "We feel no hesitation in assuring the public that they will be fully repaid for their attendance . . . with the breadth and dignity of style possible with music of so elevated and a sacred character."[35] He pointed out the difficulty of learning the work, "one of the severest tests of the capabilities of the chorus, whose powers of execution it tasks to the utmost . . . prepared not without strenuous effort by our ambitious and painstaking singers."[36]

The reporter was correct. The Bethlehem Choral Union possessed no singers who had sung Bach. Everyone was moving in uncharted waters under J. Wolle's youthful direction. The independence of the voices, the density and complexity of the sound, the often tortured quality of the harmony and dissonance, the emotionally charged Baroque asymmetrical melodies with unusual accompaniments, the difficult rhythms and entrances all made the undertaking tremendously challenging.

In addition to teaching the chorus the vocal parts, other musical difficulties arose that must have come as a shock. No wind and brass parts were available in America. The *Daily Bethlehem Times* reported:

So rarely is the St. John "Passion" performed in this country that after several unsuccessful attempts to procure the orchestral parts the directors [officers] of the Choral Union were obliged to send to England for them, and could even then procure only the stringed quartette [*sic*], the other parts existing only in manuscript.[37]

This lack of parts is puzzling, for the score had been printed a number of years before in the *Bachgesellschaft*, the complete edition of Bach's works. However, it must be taken as further evidence of how avant-garde this enterprise was for the time.

There were more difficulties. Wolle not only had to play the missing wind and brass parts on the organ; at the same time he had to improvise from Bach's organ part which was only the bass. Above the part for pedal, Bach had written only indications of the chords that were to be used, leaving but one hand occasionally free to conduct. In addition, he lacked enough string players to balance the size of the chorus. The paper reported "the orchestra did its duty quite satisfactorily, even though weak in numbers."[38] Finally, no soloists had experience singing the recitatives, an art in itself. As a result, many of the recitatives were not sung at all but were read "very expressively." A further major alteration was the performance of the chorales. They were sung without accompaniment, though Bach had clearly indicated parts for the orchestra. Wolle, like all of his predecessors, adjusted Bach's music to fit the musical circumstances. Zelter, Mendelssohn, and Goldschmidt had also altered Bach, often in major ways. Current music performance practice did not exist. The review of the American premiere of the "Passion" according to St. John observed:

From the sweet strains of the orchestral prelude to the majestic chorus which marked the end of the work the audience was rapt in wonder as the exquisite beauty of the composition and the skill with which the large body of singers and players rendered the work under the magic influence of Prof. Wolle's baton.[39]

The reviewer felt pride that this premiere had taken place in Bethlehem:

In short, Bach's "Passion," as rendered by the Bethlehem Choral Union, was a thorough success and Prof. Wolle and his faithful assistants can feel very proud of the first rendition on the continent of this magnificently set story of the "Passion" of our Lord Jesus Christ.[40]

The Moravian pastor modestly recorded the event in the church diary:

On Tuesday Evening the "Choral Union" gave the first rendition in America of Bach's "Passion" according to St. John, and succeeded remarkably well.

The difficult choral sections and the magnificent chorales were especially well rendered. Some of the longer recitatives were read by Prof. E. G. Klose instead of being sung. The audience was not very large.[41]

There was no mention of the performance in *The Moravian*, but a notice appeared in the *Musical Courier* [New York], 13 June 1888.[42]

What had Wolle demonstrated? Bach's monumental choral works could be performed in a small American community without the musical resources and experienced professional musicians available in a European city like Munich. Unlike the practice in Europe, the performance was given without financial backing from aristocratic or church patronage, and Wolle now knew he had the musical understanding, the teaching and conducting skills, and the managerial savvy demanded for the preparation and performance of such a complex artistic undertaking. As a twenty-five-year-old, he had made his first contribution to the Bach Movement in America.

To place Wolle's premiere in its broader context requires noting other similar choral societies and Bach performances. Ten years before the 1878 Bethlehem Choral Union's Bach performance, "The Bach Society" had been organized in Cleveland, Ohio. The Society, with seventy-five active members, had two purposes: "to provide the church services with the choicest music and being composed of those whose taste and ability are musical, the society is devoting much and patient attention to a superior art culture."[43]

A Society concert in 1881 included but one Bach motet. The next year the *Cleveland Herald* reported, "The only criticism that can be ventured is that made by one of the hearers in passing out of the church: 'It was a Bach Society concert, with Bach's picture adorning the platform, but without a selection from Bach on the whole program.'"[44] A concert a year later again contained only a single Bach motet. This Society never performed large Bach choral works. Theodore Thomas, one of America's most prominent conductors, did conduct the Bach *Magnificat* in 1875 and sections of the *Mass* in 1886, but while the Cincinnati May Festival was the most important festival in the Midwest by the 1870s, the works of Bach were still only occasionally performed.

The Oratorio Society of New York was founded in 1873 and was contemporary with Bethlehem's Choral Union. Andrew Carnegie served as its president from 1888 to 1919 and financed the building of Carnegie Hall in 1891 specifically to showcase the Society. The Society was not devoted solely to singing Bach, but a performance of the *Mass* conducted by Frank Damrosch came only a month after Wolle's American premiere in Bethlehem. However,

"Where Wolle had given all twenty-four numbers, he [Frank Damrosch] cut the work to nineteen, two hours being all he dared venture with his public."[45] Other outstanding performances of Bach's works followed. The Oratorio Society continues to perform, and has received many honors for its contribution to American music and to the music of the City of New York.[46]

A number of Choral Union musical seasons followed that were designed for audience building and securing funds. *Messiah* was sung during the Christmas season with a much smaller orchestra. The soloists and instrumentalists were probably all volunteers, resulting in a concert that not only cost much less but included more neighbors and friends, which assured a larger audience. Of greater importance in this history is the fact that the concert was held in the Fountain Hill Opera House rather than in the Moravian Parochial School. Most of the newly wealthy rail and iron industrialists, engineers and managers were building their mansions in Fountain Hill, which adjoined South Bethlehem. These people had no direct roots in Moravian culture. At this time the Choral Union also became independent of decisions made by the Moravian Church Elders. Furthermore, the music lovers among the industrial families were supporting the performances. Concurrently Wolle was deepening the social connections that would prove essential to later Bach projects. A number of years later these music lovers would ensure the founding of The Bach Choir, its survival, and, after a hiatus, its revival as The Bach Choir. The Bethlehem Choral Union now resembled Zelter's Berlin *Singakademie*.

Wolle's desire to conduct large Bach works stirred him again, and he was about to begin his next Bach project—a performance of *The Passion According to St. Matthew*. He wanted the performance held in Central Moravian Church, not in the school and not in the Fountain Hill Opera House. When he requested permission to use the sanctuary, past problems arose with greater urgency. The church diarist wrote that the Board of Elders, after some discussion of the case, "concluded to grant the petition of our organist" on two conditions.[47] The first was, "if they succeed in the effort to master it." This was surprising, for it might imply that the previous Bach performance had been considered so poor with all its compromises that the capability of the Choral Union and J. Fred. Wolle were being questioned. The situation was awkward.

The second condition was even more limiting and was ultimately fatal to Wolle's plan. The Elders greatly tightened their restrictions involving financing sacred concerts in the sanctuary. They stated emphatically, "No selling of tickets or taking money at the doors will be permitted. The money will be raised by special subscription and tickets will be issued to subscribers only."[48]

As the performance date neared, there was not enough money to sign the contracts. The telling question was raised in a newspaper interview with Wolle himself. Was there an audience to support Bach performances? Appeals for subscribers appeared in the paper. A concerned reader wrote to the editor, "Does this subscription price of five dollars for the series seem too high? We have heard the idea expressed."[49] In response, he directly addressed the public perceptions of Bach's music that he must have heard after *The Passion According to St. John.* The music was not "dry and abstruse," he insisted. It was lucid and simple, accessible to all and well worth the subscription price.

> While, undoubted to many minds the name of Bach carries with it the idea of dryness and abstruseness, Bach's biographer, Spitta, says in a few words enough to dispel such an impression. Here it is: "St. Matthew Passion," as a whole, is . . . a popular work.[50]

The interviewer added, "The present status of the Choral Union and the "Passion" music is rather precarious. I believe Professor Wolle's enthusiasm, if nothing else, will carry both of them through."[51]

For reasons that are unclear, the Choral Union split in two, and the wealthy part of town founded the Bethlehem Oratorio Society, which rehearsed in South Bethlehem. The other half of the Choral Union continued to rehearse in North Bethlehem. Wolle conducted both groups. The Oratorio Society sang a successful concert in the Fountain Hill Opera House. The group often rehearsed in the home of Mrs. Estes, who now became much more than Wolle's contralto soloist. Her home was already a major center for the industrial, academic, banking, professional elite, resembling closely Zelter's Berlin singing society. "The success of the Bach Choir . . . was built on the foundation of these two earlier organizations." Robin Leaver, a major Bach historian and yearly author of the program notes for the contemporary Bach Choir, concludes "both of these choral societies must be considered forerunners of The Bach Choir of Bethlehem."[52]

The Bethlehem Oratorio Society was actually small, but among its members were Mr. and Mrs. Albert Cleaver. Albert Cleaver held large mining and manufacturing interests. He was a trustee of Lehigh University and secretary of the Board of Trustees of St. Luke's Hospital, where Mrs. Estes's husband was the chief surgeon. Cleaver and his wife were prominent members of the Episcopal Church. This couple became absolutely essential to the upcoming sacred performance of *The Passion According to St. Matthew.*

On the other hand, the Choral Union's complete season was in danger. The initial concert was first postponed, then canceled entirely. Its Bach performance was subsequently abandoned. However, Wolle saw another opportunity as 1892 (the 150th anniversary of the founding of Bethlehem) drew near. With characteristic ingenuity and enthusiasm, he used the celebration to revitalize his plans to perform Bach's *Passion According to St. Matthew*. What better way for the Moravian congregation to celebrate its musical heritage than by sponsoring a community performance of Bach? All parties readily agreed that this anniversary was the appropriate time for such a grand undertaking, and J. Fred. Wolle began preparing for a performance during the Easter season. It would be a sacred service in the sanctuary with no applause.

However, Bethlehem was not the site of the American premiere. That had taken place in Boston with the Handel and Haydn Society in May 1874. There were six hundred in the chorus, an orchestra of ninety, and a boys' choir of sixty. The Oratorio Society of New York sang it next in 1880 with Leopold Damrosch conducting. Walter Damrosch, Leopold's son and Frank's brother, conducted two performances in 1884 and 1888. Two performances during the Cincinnati May Festival were directed by Theodore Thomas in 1882 and 1890. The first (*St. Matthew Passion*) in Philadelphia was sung in 1885.[53] As Wolle was planning his performance of *The Passion According to St. Matthew* for April 1892, Walter Damrosch conducted the work in New York a month before.

In Bethlehem the Moravian Elders remembered that their decision for a season subscription had destroyed the "Passion" performance two years before, causing the collapse of The Choral Union's season, and modified their position, allowing the sale of advanced subscriptions to apply to this performance alone and not the entire season. Each subscriber "invited" a certain number of "friends." Tickets were not mentioned.

Since the 150th anniversary was to be a community-wide celebration, Wolle selected instrumentalists only from Bethlehem and neighboring Allentown. Two of the vocal soloists were popular area singers. Mrs. Estes was of course one of them. In addition one hundred children were selected from the Lehigh University Chapel Choir and the Moravian Parochial School. The two Choral Unions rehearsed separately and combined for the performance.

Wolle shrewdly added a chorus of children as concrete proof that this music was for everyone. Like the two Choral Unions, the two children's choruses were rehearsed separately and then combined just before the performance. The addition of children greatly increased the monumentality of the production at no additional cost, and the size of the audience was immediately enlarged by the children's families and by many who would not otherwise have attended a Bach performance.

On the Monday before the performance, the Moravian pastor recorded the coming together of all these forces:

> Monday evening the two large choruses of the augmented Choral Union, one of Bethlehem and one of South Bethlehem, which have been practicing the great masterpiece of sacred music, The Passion according to St. Matthew, by John Sebastian Bach, under the leadership of our organist, Brother J. Fred. Wolle, with a view to its rendition in our church, had their first rehearsal in the church:[54]

The pastor was filled with pride. Though this was an important community musical event, it was also a Moravian one, and there was no question that Bach's music was a "masterpiece." They were performing the very best sacred music. When he later described the performance, he was overwhelmed by the "achievement" and by the "devout spirit" of the listeners. It was without doubt a sacred service:

> It was a magnificent success and a fitting introduction to the Holy Passion Week. This 150th Anniversary year of Bethlehem, crowning a century and a half of music fame with the greatest achievement yet reached. The church was entirely filled . . . and the devout spirit in the church the noble composition listened to was like that which pervades the congregation during the solemn liturgy of Good Friday. It was felt that such a thing as applause would be profanation. It was a privilege to be present.[55]

The *Bethlehem Daily Times* agreed with the pastor. This was the "most impressive Lenten service ever held in Bethlehem . . . a triumph thoroughly worthy of the gold of the sesquicentennial years."[56] The reporter went on to describe the ideas held by the public prior to the service and the significance of the performance. Many of the listeners had gone to the service with misgivings, fearing:

> The effort [was] too great, the undertaking too ambitious. The identical "Passion Music" had been rendered but twice or thrice before in America, and then only by large thoroughly drilled, semi-professional city choruses. For a place of Bethlehem's size to undertake it they deemed altogether too audacious. They dreaded the possible result. And with their acute critical faculties sharpened to the excitement they awaited the denouement with fear and trembling . . . But they need not have quaked . . . . novices could enter into it [Bach's music] with keen delight and the only regret was that it was too brief. It lasted exactly two hours.[57]

J. Fred. Wolle made this Bach performance work in every way. He confidently moved ahead, having the Choral Union, the Moravian Church, and the music-loving residents of the Bethlehems join forces in the American premiere of Bach's most colossal choral work, *The Mass in B Minor*. An entirely unexpected reaction from his singers awaited him.

Rehearsals began. Yet within a few weeks fewer and fewer singers came to practice. When asked why they were losing interest and why others were no longer coming to rehearse, they said they "got stuck in so many places and the music sounded so awful . . . they would not take his [Wolle's] reproving, nagging session any longer."[58]

"The Mass or nothing," he proclaimed again and again and continued rehearsing until he was practically alone in the hall. Wolle's nephew recounted how "[t]he director in grief and disappointment broke his baton—and never thereafter did he use one in directing."[59] More than ten years later, Wolle gave his account of this crucial event during a newspaper interview. He simply wanted nothing to do with music as entertainment, he said:

> Several times rehearsals were taken up, but for one reason or another had to be dropped. At last I washed my hands of the whole movement, declined to have any part of any musical entertainment until the mass should be produced.[60]

Mrs. Ruth Doster, secretary of the Choral Union, was the third woman to play a decisive role in the formation of a Bach Choir in Bethlehem. As his friend and neighbor, she approached Wolle with the singers' complaints. She pleaded with him, "Please, please do give in, Fred., for this season at least do something just a little less difficult."[61] Six months after the successful performance of *The Passion According to St. Matthew*, the Bethlehem Choral Union ceased to exist. Wolle had moved too far, too fast, and too stubbornly.

Bethlehem Moravians made no move to save the Choral Union. However, showing the spirit encompassing South Bethlehem, "the general opinion of the Fountain Hill people was that the entire abandonment of a musical organization would be a kind of stigma on Bethlehem."[62] Those who were recent citizens of Bethlehem were feeling a great sense of cultural pride. Wolle proposed a plan to the most influential new industrialist and business leaders.

William Sayre, an owner of the Lehigh Valley Railroad, one of South Bethlehem's many philanthropists, and a collector of rare books, chaired the meeting. Wolle "gave a short account of the rise and fall of The Choral Union" and "deplored the lack of interest that caused its downfall and rejoiced that the entire extinction of musical enthusiasm would not be permitted."[63] He would organize a new chorus. Sayre was elected president, and Wolle was appointed music director. He held the first rehearsal that evening in a room in the administrative building of the Lehigh Valley Railroad, at the time one of the most important rail lines in America.

The Bethlehem Oratorio Society was a fundamentally different singing group. It was a secular group, not an organization of singers from local churches. The new group rehearsed and performed where the industrialists worked and lived. The center of musical patronage had shifted, and a concert was now a social event for the Bethlehems. On the Moravian side of the river, Wolle was insisting on "the Mass or nothing," yet his singers were refusing to perform what they saw as complicated music; on the South side, which provided the support for his new chorus, he was rehearsing for a program of popular musical entertainment for the Fountain Hill Opera House. While Wolle was driven to perform Bach, he had no chorus; while he was driven to be a choral conductor, the chorus that he had was rehearsing lighter music.

The newspaper headline of the review of the first concert read, "The Wealth, Beauty and Fashion of the Bethlehems Grace the Fountain Hill Opera House."[64] The social attributes of the audience were expanded into a full paragraph. People were attending with their own kind and to be seen doing so as much as to be among the critical-music-loving social set:

> The audience was one of the most select, cultured, and critical that the opera house has ever contained. All of the Fountain Hill and Bethlehem society was there. Nearly everyone in town who understands and appreciates music of a high character was there and many out of town people attended. The auditorium was completely filled and there was a generous sprinkling in the balcony.[65]

Mrs. Estes, Mrs. Doster, and the Cleavers were all directly involved in the performance. Wolle's response to the concert is astonishing. He told the newspaper, "This chorus is the best music ever undertaken by any society in Bethlehem and all the parts won for every member of the society new and fresh laurels."[66] For the next concert, this "most select, cultured, and critical audience" was promised a performance of *Faust* (*Scenes from Goethe's Faust* by Robert Schumann) "which has hitherto been heard but once in this country."[67] In fact *Faust* had been performed three times in America: once in Boston, once in Cincinnati, and once in New York.

A new building was under construction in the center of Bethlehem where the Oratorio Society was going to rehearse. Because the structure was not complete when the chorus was ready to move from the Lehigh Railroad building, the group approached the Board of the Moravian Parochial School with a request to use the school hall until the new building was finished. The board was composed entirely of members of the Moravian Church. Permission was granted, but the report by the pastor in the church diary concluded with a statement that expressed what was felt when the society was founded, "Like some other organizations in this town it finds it of advantage or even necessary, after experiments in other quarters, to come back to the Moravian Church for aid and comfort." The diarist stressed that the Oratorio Society "is under the directorship of Bro. Fred. Wolle, our organist."[68]

It is true that Brother Wolle had successfully maneuvered a difficult political situation, but still the performance never took place. It appeared that his conducting of community choral groups had ended.

He now concentrated his attention on a performance with the Central Moravian Church choir of Bach's *Christmas Oratorio*, easier to sing than the *Mass*. It contained many familiar chorales that would be sung in English as a sacred service. The pastor noted it "suitably introduced the Christmas season."[69] The Elders were willing to have the expenses met by "a collection, entirely voluntary and without appeal" during the intermission.[70] The problems that had plagued Wolle were for the moment sidestepped.

This was not a premiere; it would not be sung in its entirety in America until Wolle premiered it in Central Moravian Church during the 1903 Bach Festival. For now, Wolle would conduct Parts 1 and 2 only, but they had been heard just three times before, twice conducted by Theodore Thomas.

The pastor recorded the event in a long entry in the church diary:

> At 8 o'clock in the evening the church choir and orchestra, assisted by a few friends, [Mrs. Estes was one.] rendered in Bethlehem for the first time John Sebastian Bach's Christmas Oratorio Parts 1 and ll, under the direction of the organist Bro. J. Fred Wolle. The Passion Music according to St. John by Bach, has been rendered in Bethlehem, June 5, 1866, and the Passion according to St. Matthew, by Bach has been given in Bethlehem, April 8, 1892; and this evening worthily to follow the Christmas Oratorio. A program containing the words of the oratorio was in the hands of the audience. The body of the church was densely filled; and the galleries were crowded as far back as a view of the singers could be obtained. The people who had gathered for the occasion represented all the churches of the town, and those who make any pretense to musical attainment, or to love music: and everybody was deeply interested throughout and all thoroughly enjoyed the rare treat . . . The oratorio introduced the Christmas season.[71]

A brief account in *The Moravian* concluded, "Mr. Wolle has again placed the people of this community under obligation for an evening of delightful and inspiring enjoyment."[72]

Mr. Wolle had held firm. "The Mass or nothing." Four years after the *Christmas Oratorio*, the desires, wills, and events in the community coalesced to favor Bach again in Bethlehem.

NOTES

1. H. E. Krehbiel, "Supplement," *New York Tribune*, Sunday, 12 May 1901.

2. Lawrence W. Hartzell, "Musical Moravian Missionaries, Part 1, Johann Christopher Prylaeus," *Moravian Music Journal* (Winter 1984): 91–92.

3. Ibid.

4. Carol Traupman-Carr, ed., *"Pleasing for Our Use": David Tannenberg and the Organs of the Moravians* (Bethlehem, PA: Lehigh University Press, 2000), 50.

5. Nola Reed Knouse, ed., *The Music of the Moravian Church in America* (University of Rochester Press, 2008), 281.

6. Robert Steelman, "A Cantata Performed in Bethlehem in the 1740s," *The Moravian Music Foundation Bulletin* 20, no. 2 (Fall/Winter 1975): 2–7.

7. Hans T. David, *Musical Life in the Pennsylvania Settlements of the Unitas Fratrum* (Winston-Salem, NC: Moravian Music Foundation, 1954), 15–16.

8. See Ralph Grayson Schwarz, *Bach In Bethlehem* (Bethlehem, PA: The Bach Choir of Bethlehem, 1998), 9–13.

9. Schweitzer, *Bach* 1, 250.

10. Owen, "Bach Comes to America," 2–3.

11. "Diary of the Bethlehem Congregation," (hereafter "Diary"), 24 December 1873, Moravian Archives of Bethlehem Pennsylvania (hereafter MABP).

12. Robert Gerson, *Music in Philadelphia* (Westport, CT: Greenwood Press, 1970), 106.

13. J. Fred. Wolle to the students and faculty of the University of California at Berkeley, speech, 1905, ABCB.

14. *Bethlehem Globe Times*, 28 and 31 August 1882.

15. *Bethlehem Daily Times*, 4 September 1882.

16. *The Moravian*, 4 October 1882.

17. Ibid., 12 December 1882.

18. Ibid., 28 November 1883.

19. Ibid., 25 June 1884.

20. *Dictionary of American Biography* 4, (New York: G. Scribner's Sons, 1928–1970), s.v. "David Wood."

21. "How Wolle Came to Take Up Bach," n.d., n.p., scrapbook newspaper item, Archives of the Bach Choir of Bethlehem (subsequently abbreviated as ABCB).

22. Program Book no. 6:107, ABCB.

23. Ibid.

24. "How Wolle Came to Take Up Bach," n.d., n.p. ABCB.

25. Ibid.

26. Stanley Sade, ed., *The New Grove Dictionary of Music and Musicians* 15, s.v. "Joseph Reinberger," 791–92.

27. "Diary," 2 October 1885, MABP.

28. Raymond Walters, "Bach at Bethlehem, Pennsylvania," *The Musical Quarterly* 21, no. 2 (April 1935): 184.

29. *Bethlehem Daily Times*, 1 February 1888.

30. Robin A. Leaver, "The Revival of the St. John Passion, History and Performance Practice," *Bach Journal of the Riemenschneider Bach Institute* 20, no. 3 (1989): 21.

31. *The Moravian*, 30 May 1888.

32. Leaver, "St. John Passion," 22.

33. *Bethlehem Daily Times*, 1 June 1888.

34. Ibid., 4 June 1888.

35. Ibid.

36. Ibid.

37. Ibid.

38. Ibid.

39. Ibid., 6 June 1888.

40. Ibid.

41. "Official Diary of the Moravian Church of Bethlehem, Pa. 1888–1895," (hereafter "Official Diary"), 5 June 1888.

42. *The Musical Courier*, no. 435 (12 June 1888): 404.

43. *Cleveland Herald*, "The Bach Society Its Fine Work, History and Prospects," 15 November 1881.

44. Ibid., 18 September 1882.

45. Lucy P. Stebbins, *Frank Damrosch, Let the People Sing* (Durham, NC: Duke University Press, 1945), 192.

46. See www.oratoriosociety.org for further information about the history of the Oratorio Society of New York (accessed April 22, 2010).

47. "Official Diary," 8 July 1890, MABP.

48. Ibid.

49. *Bethlehem Daily Times*, 18 November 1890.

50. Raymond Walters, *The Bethlehem Bach Choir* (Boston: Houghton Mifflin, 1918), 42.

51. Ibid.

52. Robin A. Leaver, "New Light on the Pre-History of the Bach Choir of Bethlehem," *Bach, The Journal of Riemenschneider Bach Institute* 22, no. 2 (Fall/Winter 1991): 33.

53. See H. Earle Johnson, *First Performances in America* (Detroit: The College Music Society, 1979) for these performance dates.

54. "Official Diary," 4 April 1892, MABP.

55. Ibid., 8 April 1892.

56. *Bethlehem Daily Times*, 8 April 1892.

57. Ibid.

58. Francis Wolle, *A Moravian Heritage*, (Boulder, CO: Empire Reproduction; Printing Co., 1972), 41.

59. Ibid.

60. *(Philadelphia) North American*, 11 May 1903.

61. Ibid.

62. *Daily Bethlehem Times*, 16 November 1892.

63. Ibid.

64. Ibid., 14 April 1893.

65. Ibid.

66. Ibid.

67. Ibid.

68. "Official Diary," 13 November 1893, MABP.

69. Ibid., 18 December 1894.

70. Ibid.

71. Ibid.

72. *The Moravian*, 26 December 1894.

Chapter 2

Creating an American
Bach Choir

1898

The choir that was to make J. Fred. Wolle world famous was organized by Mrs. W. E. Doster, the young bride of a wealthy Civil War general. She was eighteen when she came to Bethlehem in 1888; he was fifty-one. As the General's second wife and as stepmother of his nearly grown children, she took up residence in his grand house just around the corner from the Wolles'. Immediately Ruth Doster assumed membership in Central Moravian Church and joined the church's choir conducted by her neighbor.

William E. Doster was a prominent member of the Bethlehem Moravian community. He had attended Yale University as an undergraduate and had received his law degree from Harvard. He then matriculated at the University of Heidelberg, Germany. Doster had served with great distinction in the War, including the battle at Gettysburg, and President Lincoln had commissioned him a Brigadier General. He later wrote a history of the Fourth Pennsylvania Veteran Cavalry. When Doster returned to Bethlehem, he became the legal counsel for the Moravian Congregation and for the prosperous individuals creating Bethlehem's various new industrial enterprises. It was Gen. Doster who prepared the title abstracts for Charles Schwab when he assumed leadership of the Bethlehem Steel Company.

Ruth Doster (née Porter) was a wealthy heiress of two elite Boston and Manhattan families. Her father, Gen. Josiah Porter, commanded the New York State Militia. Because she was so highly gifted in music, her parents had sent her to Germany to study the piano at the age of twelve, and at sixteen she was transferred to a Moravian school for girls in Monmirail, Switzerland, to complete her education.[1] There she became a friend of Gen. Doster's daughter and met General Doster when he visited his daughter. Ruth herself was deeply in love with Count D'Alorso, a Romanian aristocrat. They had planned to marry, but her family opposed the marriage, and made her return to the United States. "Years later he [the count] visited Ruth in Bethlehem," one of her in-laws related. "She never conquered her feeling of having been cheated of happiness, and was always very bitter on the subject."[2]

Soon after Ruth returned to America, she married Gen. Doster "against the wishes of her family. Ruth and her father never got on well," reported her brother-in-law. "She had his quick and fiery temper."[3] In addition Gen. Porter and Gen. Doster disliked one another.

While the Bach Choir might have come about at some later date without the efforts of Ruth Doster, the Choir's history would have been very different had she either married the count or not married General Doster. As Mrs. Doster, she was immediately in the social center of Bethlehem, in which she assumed a position of cultural leadership. Her elite family background, the refinement of a European education, and her highly developed musicianship were all qualities everyone admired. Thus, Ruth Doster was able to fulfill the desire for beauty, refinement, and the prestigious cultural activity that added to her social status. Catherine Drinker Bowen (a writer and daughter of Lehigh University president Henry Drinker) related visits with Ruth Doster:

> Mrs. Doster was beautiful and talented and played magnificently; my mother used to drive across the river to sit and listen. Sometimes I went along. Mrs. Doster's husband, General Doster, many years older than his wife, had made a considerable fortune in the law, and built a big house behind the beech trees on Lehigh Street. My father spoke of him as a man of ability, my mother said he was a cantankerous old curmudgeon. Whether the general was jealous of his wife's music, I did not know, being too young to think about it. But one day Mrs. Doster went out of town to visit, and when she came back, there sat her Steinway grand out on the lawn, where the general had it carried. "And it was raining!" my mother told my father furiously. "Oh Harry, these people are all border ruffians!"[4]

Ruth Doster was also a fine singer. She became the musical director of the Moravian Sunday School and part of the innovative church and community musical performances Brother Wolle was undertaking. She graciously gave free piano lessons as well.

However, Doster opposed his wife's love of music at every turn. Had she allowed the General to have his way, as a proper upper-class wife was expected to do, her involvement with music would have ceased completely. Fortunately for the Bach Choir, she continued her musical activities and expanded them by forming a unique musical salon, which Bowen

Ruth Doster

remembered attending, made up of amateurs interested in music who met to study music by singing it rather than passively listening and discussing it, which had usually been the case. The General's jealousy of his wife's musical interests, including organizing the Bach Choir, continued to grow and contributed to their eventual divorce.

Mrs. Doster had sung in the Choral Union that had failed. She hoped Brother Wolle would lead her own group of singers. Repeatedly, she asked him to lead the group, but he refused. Only if they agreed to study Bach's *Mass in B Minor*, he kept saying. Fortunately, she shared his love of Bach.

Wolle's nephew recounted that in 1898, Ruth Doster's small group came to him and said, "'Fred. . . . we will try to sing anything you want, if you'll direct us.' 'Well then, the Mass in B Minor,' he said; and they acquiesced with misgivings." About thirty singers agreed to undertake the assignment.[5] "Fred, teach us the Mass," was Ruth's masterstroke. Her request ignited her friends' imaginations, energized their musical minds, and created a conduit through which all of their energies, ideas, and skills could flow. A newspaper reporter later described this turning point:

> She gathered a group of women interested in meeting regularly to study music and persuaded Wolle to guide them. Then she and her friends began to canvas the area for singers interested in performing the "Mass." Catasauqua, Hellertown and Schoeneck were close by, even allowing for the needed travel time.
>
> Soon Wolle was able to announce that after Central Church's regular choir rehearsal those who wished to stay for a study of the "Mass in B-minor" would be joined by a group of "outsiders," some of whom were willing to come an hour's journey for the rehearsals. He found he could count on at least 80 singers.[6]

Using her music study group as a nucleus, Ruth Doster organized interested area singers and choir members from Central Moravian Church in Bethlehem into a group of "about 80 singers."[7] Thus, the first choir in America devoted to studying and performing the works of Bach was founded in Bethlehem, Pennsylvania.

The pastor of Central Moravian Church recorded the first rehearsal in the church diary:

> Monday evening the augmented choir organized Dec. 5, 1898 under the direction of Brother J. F. Wolle, as the "Bach Choir," to learn the Mass in B minor by John [*sic*] Sebastian Bach, had the first rehearsal of the new year in the church.[8]

J. Fred. Wolle gave her a photograph of himself and wrote across the bottom, "To the organizer of the Bach Choir Mrs. W. E. Doster from its leader, J. Fred. Wolle"[9] Later, Raymond Walters wrote in *The Bethlehem Bach Choir* that "Dr. Wolle . . . and others have always paid tribute to Mrs. Doster as being the immediate organizer."[10]

Ruth Doster was elected secretary of the Executive Committee of the Choir, a post she held until the first Bach Choir dissolved in 1906. Years after her death, her daughter Dorothy wrote a moving imaginary letter to her deceased mother describing her mother's role in organizing the Bach Choir:

> Then, mother, your deep conviction that the Bach Mass in B Minor could and should be sung in America as it had never been before. It was your continued enthusiasm and tireless efforts with the others that finally brought about the accomplishment of your dream and the establishment of that first Bach Festival which this year [1938] will present the B Minor Mass for the 34th year. Mother, I go to the festival every year, my annual pilgrimage, and this I do in

remembrance of you without whose inspiration this beautiful musical event would not exist today.[11]

Wolle took his place in the arena created by Ruth Doster's cultural and organizational ability and enthusiasm. He could now begin to flourish and realize his desire to teach Bach's *Mass* to community amateur singers who were prepared to experience their learning of this work as a spiritual activity.

NOTES

1. Nelson James Newhard, Sr. *The Newhard Piano Quartette of Bethlehem, Pennsylvania* (Allentown, PA: Lehigh Printing Company, Inc., 1946), 160.

2. "Family Anecdotes of Uncle Charlie Robinson," TS in the author's possession.

3. Ibid.

4. Catherine Drinker Bowen, *Family Portrait* (Boston: Little, Brown, 1970), 25.

5. Raymond Walters, *The Bethlehem Bach Choir: A Historical and a Critical Compendium* (New York: Houghton Mifflin, 1923), 44–45.

6. "Area Communities Aided Formation of Bach Choir." *Bethlehem Globe-Times,* 24 December 1976.

7. Porter Cole to Dorothy Doster Cole, 10 February 1973, letter in the author's possession.

8. "Official Diary," 1 January 1888; 9 January 1888.

9. Photograph, ABCB.

10. Walters, *Bach Choir*, 45.

11. Dorothy D. Cole to Ruth Doster (dec.), 1939, "To My Mother," letter copy in the author's possession.

Chapter 3

A National Success

1899–1900

"A Typically American Organization"

—Charles Schwab

The nation was growing faster than anyone could have imagined as it moved to center stage in the world. British historian, Paul M. Johnson, wrote:

> In 1840, the United States ranked fifth in output among the world's manufacturing countries. By 1860 it was fourth. By 1894, it had taken the first place. By that time America produced twice as much as Britain, the previous leader in manufacturing, and half as much as all Europe put together. By the turn of the century, the United States' imports of manufactured goods were insignificant and it was already exporting them to all the world.[1]

The Spanish American War in 1898 had established the United States as a dominant military and political world power. By 1900, it had surpassed every country in industrial innovation and production, a fact that at the time, played an essential role in the founding of The Bach Choir.

In 1899, John Dewey, the American philosopher and educator, described the forces of applied science, industry, commercialism, and world communications:

> The change [that] . . . overshadows and even controls all others is the industrial one, the application of science resulting in the great inventions that have utilized the force of nature on a vast . . . scale; the growth of a world-wide market as the object of production, of vast cheap and rapid means of communications and distribution between all its parts . . . One can hardly believe there has been a revolution in all history so rapid, so extensive, so complete.[2]

The growth of The Bethlehem Steel Corporation was the result of scientific industrial innovations. Soon it exported steel worldwide; and Bethlehem became a major manufacturing center. It remained so for the first seventy-five years of The Bach Choir.

Much of America's new wealth was used to purchase and transport from Europe nearly every piece of art that could be bought. Not only material objects were imported; European institutions for the performing arts were established on American soil as well. However, those art works and performance institutions were assembled in characteristically American ways. Immensely wealthy individuals founded democratic cultural institutions for the education and pleasure of the general public. Exactly one hundred years after Dewey wrote of the changes in American markets, historian Paul Johnson's overview of the era from 1860 to 1900 makes clear how intimately we still share the legacy of those who lived then:

> By the end of the Civil War, the United States and its people were beginning to take on the characteristics with which we are familiar at the end of the 20th century; huge and teeming, endlessly varied, multicolored and multiracial, immensely materialistic and overwhelmingly idealistic, ceaselessly innovative, thrusting, grabbing, good to get rich, to make everybody happy. All the great strengths of the mature republic were already appearing, and the reactions of those who lived there, and those who visited it, were the modern mixture of admiration, astonishment, and shock.[3]

American culture at the beginning of the twentieth century has been described as the Gilded Age or the American Renaissance, characterized by strong social strains of nationalism; a philosophy of idealism that aimed to elevate the individual the national spiritual life through the arts; and cosmopolitanism, the nation's growing awareness of the world.

Each characteristic emerged as a strong, even guiding force in the founding and the continuity of The Bach Choir. Because of Wolle's early Bach premieres and a number of greatly successful Bach festivals, national music critics asserted that an American school of Bach performance would arise in Bethlehem. Singing, playing, and listening to Bach was a spiritually ennobling force for those who participated in the festivals. In the mind of Charles Schwab, The Choir's first major benefactor and president of The Bethlehem Steel Corporation, The Bach Choir would be a major force transforming Bethlehem into "a new Athens," interconnecting music, industry and academia. When Schwab accepted the presidency of The Bach Choir, he told the public:

> It has been my conviction that music should be a part of every well-rounded human life. Our Bach Choir supplies this need in ideal fashion for its members,

for our citizens of Bethlehem and for our many friends from far and wide who enjoy the spring festival and the choir's concerts in New York. I am happy to accept the Presidency of a typically American organization that is upholding the best standards in choral music.[4]

Other civic leaders agreed with Schwab and immediately supported The Choir. Thus, The Bach Choir mirrored the American Renaissance, and mirrored the Bethlehems, as the communities stretching along both sides of the Lehigh River came to be called. Bethlehem was named the American Bayreuth because it focused on the music of a single composer as Bayreuth in Germany focused on the music of Richard Wagner. It was also likened to Oberammergau, for the whole Bethlehem community was engaged in a festival.

Ruth Doster and J. Fred. Wolle put forth the Bach Choir as an American singing group, superior to similar groups in Europe. Wolle recited a poem he wrote to the members summarizing the feelings of the era. After chastising Germany for its "ignorance" in its neglect of Bach and his widow, Wolle praised America:

America, less old in years, but wiser in detection,
of the gems of art which Germany so long refused to hear,
is rising in her youthful strength to show her real affection
for the stirring proclamation of a prophet [Bach] and a seer.[5]

Catherine Drinker Bowen vividly described Bethlehem at the beginning of the nineteenth century in her autobiography *Family Portrait*:

Bethlehem had a population of about twenty-five thousand people, divided down the middle by the Lehigh River and the old Lehigh Canal which ran along side. North of the river lay the Moravian settlement with its church . . . the ancient tree-shaded graveyard and the Seminary for Young Ladies . . . Southward [lay] the steel company's great sheds, belching fire and smoke, stretching beside the water for nearly a mile. Lehigh University perched serenely on a hillside—we called it a mountain—far above the river, the steel mills and tangled railroad tracks where the three lines met.[6]

But the concentration of natural resource and human power that merged Bethlehem into one pattern drew, as the Bach Choir would, from a wide area. Drinker wrote of that amazing coalescence:

Bethlehem, with Easton and Allentown, was indeed the focus of an industrial complex that reached into the mountains as far as Wilkes-Barre and Scranton. From these towns came the entrepreneurs, the management men, most of them self-made, out for profits and frank about it in a booming laissez-faire economy that put no limits on a free marketplace. And into South Bethlehem, on our side of the river, poured the immigrant labourers, ignorant, unorganized, fated to be blocked for years in any attempt at union or betterment.

Nobody talked about conditions in the foreign part of town, or suggested they be improved. What people talked about was *opportunity*. Had not Asa Packer been a poor boy, and Charles Schwab begun as a stake-driver? . . . Iron and the H-beam dominated our town. Mill whistles waked the valley at early morning, below the noon hour and closed the shops at sundown. Imperious, relentless, they called the tune.[7]

Wolle exemplified the philosophy of *opportunity*. Anyone who wished could and should be in the Bach Choir. Anyone and everyone who wanted to hear the glories of Bach but didn't have the money for a ticket could sit on the lawn during the festival and listen. The Bach Choir came to express this cultural laissez-faire philosophy; the belief in unlimited *opportunity* as well as the belief in the virtue of the enterprise, the superiority of the western world, America, its economy, its industry and culture.

As the Moravians had done, other ethnic groups built churches, churches that gave Bethlehem the appearance of a "medieval" city to visitors who came to hear Bach, sung in an American copy of a French Gothic cathedral.

Rehearsals of the *Mass* began in early January1899. The busy Christmas and New Year seasons, a time when singers are always fully occupied, were past, and interested singers were now free to begin rehearsing with the newly organized Bach Choir. Ruth Doster's study group and other area singers met with members of the Central Moravian Church Choir after their weekly choir rehearsal. J. Fred. Wolle and the singers of the first Bach Choir in America began studying Bach's *Mass in B Minor* as a community.

Wolle sat on the organ bench. Each singer held a thick copy of Bach's music. Except for the "Crucifixus," which the members of the Central Moravian Church Choir had already sung a number of times, the music was strange to everyone. Singers waited expectantly for their conductor to begin.

The singers regarded Dr. Wolle differently from when they had been members of the Choral Union attempting to sing the *Mass*. He was now a Lehigh University professor of music, but more importantly recognized as one of the most prominent Bach interpreters in America. His most recent triumph was his unique organ recital at the St. Louis World's Fair. There he played an all-Bach program and gave the American premiere of Bach's *Goldberg Variations* before an audience of hundreds of people. Wolle's expertise as conductor of Bach's choral works was beyond question as well. He had already directed a number of the greatest works and two were American premieres (*The Passion According to St. John* and *The Christmas Oratorio*).

It was a privilege to have him be their teacher and to be studying the *Mass* with him.

With the memory of his prior failure to teach the *Mass* to members of the Bethlehem Choral Union still fresh, Wolle prepared himself thoroughly for the first rehearsal. He had carefully thought out every detail, and he brilliantly designed an ingenious new way to teach his singers the *Mass*.

"Turn to the final page. Count back four measures from the end." There were questioning glances, and a buzz went through the room. The Bach Choir learned the last four measures of the Mass. The singers were singing the magnificent conclusion of the *B Minor Mass*. With no apparent effort, each person was successfully singing music that just a few moments ago had seemed impossible. "Count back eight measures from the end. We'll learn this section. Now sing to the end." His nephew remembered how his uncle

> frequently told me with glee, 'I taught them the Mass backwards.' He started four bars from the end of a great chorus. Then eight, and so on. Thus, he se-cured the beautiful, impressive climaxes first, and so built on them. He sold the singers on the greatest parts first. Also they always knew the end before they went further back; so they made no stops in the middle to spoil the mood. From wherever they started they could go on to a glorious finish.[8]

Singers reported that Wolle commonly used this strategy. Many sing-ers sang the *Mass* and other works by Bach from memory—an extraordi-nary achievement, and one largely the result of "teaching them the Mass backwards."

This teaching method was not his only innovation. It was usual for him to conduct from the organ in both Central Moravian Church and in Lehigh University's Packer Memorial Church. But the choral music in both places was much simpler than Bach's complex polyphony. Conducting the *Mass* this way was very difficult, but he had not yet trained any organist to take his place.

The difficulty for the organist lay in the fact that Bach wrote only the bass notes for the organ. The organist had to improvise the additional organ voices using numbers printed below the bass notes as guides, notation called "figured bass." Wolle was well trained in "realizing the figured bass," having learned it as a child from his Moravian uncle Theo. However, the harmonic and rhyth-mic complexity of Bach's music made playing the organ for the *Mass* much more daunting than usual. However, as a renowned organ virtuoso Bach's bass part on the pedals and filled in the required chords with one hand.

With the other hand Wolle conducted. Having a hand free was abso-lutely necessary. The singers required complex entrance cues and continual expressive gestures. The entrance cues were complex because of Bach's continuous many-voiced, polyphonic musical texture. Expressive gestures were necessary because Wolle's aesthetic demanded frequent subtle changes in dynamics and tempo. His interpretation might even change from one rehearsal to another. To make matters more difficult, the Central Church organ console was in the back of the choir loft, so he could not easily see the choir and the orchestra. However, his teaching strategy and his unusual approach to conducting The Bach Choir using small gestures assured that the singers knew their parts very well and were able to realize his musical interpretation. Each person was securely independent and soon had his/her part memorized. Wolle successfully solved these seemingly insurmountable problems, making the rehearsals each Monday evening a success.

Conductor Wolle confidently announced his plan for singing the *Mass* to the musical world to the editor of the *Musical Courier*, a widely read New York music journal. When the *Musical Courier* attributed the American premiere of Bach's *St. John Passion* to a Boston choral group in 1899, he reminded the editor of his Bethlehem premieres and performances of Bach's choral works, and he unveiled his plans for the Bethlehem premiere of Bach's *B Minor Mass*:

> Bethlehem, Pa. April 15, 1899 . . . On June 5th, 1888, it was my privilege to conduct Bach's Passion Music according to St. John, here for the first time in this country. . . . The Passion Music according to St. Matthew we performed in the Moravian Church on Friday, April 8th, 1892, with a chorus of 200 and orchestra . . . It is not the intention of the writer to detract in the slightest degree from the credit due the conductor and singers who undertook the recent production in Boston further than to claim priority in the order of performance in this country. Nor would the writer dare to appear to be laying too much stress upon mere precedence, at the possible risk of haste and carelessness in preparation. The "Christmas Oratorio," Parts I and II, were given on December 18, 1894, and unless prevented by unforeseen circumstances, or anticipated by some other conductor, I shall have the extreme pleasure, some time during the present year, of inviting you to attend the first complete production in America of Bach's great Mass in B Minor.
>
> J. Fred Wolle[9]

It is interesting that Wolle expected to premiere the *Mass* in 1899. To use 1900, the anniversary of Bach's death, for the premiere apparently was not his initial plan.

Following the summer break, a local paper announced the Bach Choir would resume rehearsing on 4 September 1899 at 8 o'clock, and Wolle warmly invited anyone else interested to join them. They "will please communicate at once with J. Fred. Wolle. This invitation holds until Oct. 2, after which date no new members will be admitted without special action of the chorus membership."[10] All were welcome, and there was no cost. "Neither initiation fee nor dues are required."[11] One singer, Gertrude Hafner, recalled, "You never made another engagement. We were so interested, we wouldn't think of being absent. Well, you just wouldn't be able to sing that kind of work if you weren't present. The person aside of you would hear."[12]

A few weeks later Wolle followed up with a personal invitation. He described the excitement everyone was already feeling, the "singers' thrill." He also made clear the intensity of the commitment he required from all members of the Choir. This premiere would be a heroic undertaking:

> The question whether in any sense it pays to devote oneself so thoroughly to the performance of a work beset with obstacles can best be answered by those members of the chorus who, since last December, with genuine heroism, have braved the difficulties, and who, with keen artistic insight, doubtless, ere this, have had revealed to them unsuspected beauties in unlooked for places in this veritable masterpiece of unspeakable power and imperishable glory.
>
> J. Fred Wolle[13]

Gertrude Hafner also recounted:

> Nearly everybody who sang in the choir had a voice. They sang in their own church choirs. I knew everybody . . . Lucy Brickenstein, she was Moravian. Mabel Cope was Grace Lutheran. Annie Stein, Episcopalian. Sarah Litch, the Presbyterian minister's daughter . . . There were many from the Christ Reformed Choir and from Salem Lutheran and Grace Lutheran. Most of them were teachers and students.[14]

Wolle announced 27 March 1900 as the date for the premiere. He was well aware of the national importance of the event he was creating. "The choir is thoroughly prepared to appear even before a most critical musical audience."[15] The public had been informed that the format of the performance would be a unique one "on account of the magnitude of the work and to permit of its thorough enjoyment, there will be two sessions."[16] The *Musical Courier* described what Wolle had designed. "The first section of the performance of the *Mass* will begin at 4 o'clock in the afternoon, when the 'Kyrie' and 'Gloria' will be sung. The work will be resumed, commencing with the 'Credo,' at 8 o'clock."[17]

Finally, Wolle's activity with The Bach Choir became national news with a straightforward, factual announcement in the *New York Times*, 18 March 1900. The same day, the *New York Tribune* expressed a more personal reaction, comparing Bethlehem with New York and recognizing Wolle's achievement in conducting from the organ:

> It would seem as if the distinction of being the first city or town in America to hear the complete performance of Bach's Mass in B minor was to fall to Bethlehem, for more than a century a particularly active little musical center, thanks to the Moravians, their zeal and culture . . . The Oratorio Society of New York will produce all the numbers of the work next month . . . Mr. J. Fred Wolle, organist of the Moravian Church, in which the performance will take place will not only conduct the performance, but also play the organ part. A musician who is willing to attempt that must feel that his forces have a firm seat in the saddle.[18]

Wolle announced the soloists: Miss Katharine Hilke, St. Patrick's Cathedral, New York; Miss Lucy A. Brickenstein, musical instructress of the Moravian Seminary and College for Women in Bethlehem and recently returned with a music degree from the University of Leipzig; Mrs. W. L. Estes, Fountain Hill, who had sung in all of Wolle's Bach performances; tenor, Nicholas Douty, Philadelphia; and bass, Arthur Beresford, Boston. "An orchestra of thirty-one people will assist in the rendition, consisting of the best talent of Bethlehem, Allentown, Easton and Reading in the string and flute parts, the oboes, bassoons, French horns, trumpets and drums coming from Philadelphia."[19] Thus began a long Bach Choir association with the Philadelphia Orchestra.

In early March, Wolle assembled his orchestra of local musicians and began rehearsing. As was the case with all important sacred events in Bethlehem, the Moravian Trombone Choir would announce the beginning of the two sessions from the tower of Central Moravian Church. The editor of *The Moravian*, the official church newspaper, reminded its readers why the church Elders had agreed to have a Latin Mass by a Lutheran composer performed by a non-Moravian chorus and orchestra. "The Central Moravian Church has been kindly placed at the disposal of Mr. Wolle and his Choir, an eminently fitting courtesy in view of the deeply devotional character of the music and the long association of this church with everything that is best in the annals of Moravian, not to say American, church music."[20] This was a sacred service. Concerts were not allowed in the sanctuary. Tickets had to be purchased at the neighboring Moravian Book Store.

A week before the premiere, and contrary to Moravian practice, members of the Choir presented their conductor "with a purse of money . . . as an indication of appreciation of his efforts in preparing for the production of Bach's masterpiece."[21] When the week of the premiere arrived, there were almost daily newspaper accounts of the preparations. The "handsome program" was described. "The sale of tickets, which has been very encouraging up to this time, indicates a large audience."[22] Two open rehearsals for ticket holders were announced.[23]

One paper reported a humorous exchange with a caller in a neighboring community:

> Telephoned from Stockertown. "Hello! Is this you Free Press?" "Yes." "How about that B Minor thing at Bethlehem next Tuesday? Is it one of Harry Miner's plays? Some of us boys want to go up if it is." "No, we judge not; the advertisement says it's by Mr. Bach, and some people think his pieces are better than Harry Miner's. There are said to be over 700 seats sold, and we think you'll find it all right." "Guess we'll have to take it in. Much obliged. Good-bye."[24]

The day of the performance began with a salute to Bach by the students of the Moravian Seminary and College for Women in Bethlehem situated across the street from Central Moravian Church and the birthplace of J. Fred. Wolle:

> The memory of John Sebastian Bach is held in grateful memory today at the Moravian Seminary and College for Women. At the rising of this morning's sun Old Glory was unfurled from the flag staff on the balcony of old Colonial Hall and soon thereafter the Seminary colors . . . were seen waving a welcome to the National colors from the roof top of west annex . . . The Seminary will be represented at the Bach Festival this afternoon by the attendance of over 30 of the inmates, including members of the faculty, teachers and pupils.[25]

This news item is the first time the name "Bach Festival" had been used.

Ticket holders, including many guests and out-of-town music critics, attended an open rehearsal in the morning. All day, people arrived to attend the premiere, including a "committee of the managers of the New York Oratorio Society." "Prominent New Yorkers . . . arrived on the Black Diamond Express this afternoon and were at once driven to Mr. Wolle's cozy home on Church Street, where a reception was held from 2:30 to 3:30 P.M. . . . There are many eminent newspaper critics here and all say the rehearsals bespeak a fine performance."[26]

Wolle was well aware that this was an opportunity to expand his national reputation. He personally invited important critics from various metropolitan presses, assuring national press coverage. The critics did not disappoint him. Because they recognized immediately the musical importance of the event, they came, and they were charmed by the Wolles and by Bethlehem. The *Philadelphia Press* told its readers the performance was not solely for trained musicians, "Professor Wolle . . . wants the general public to learn to love and appreciate the great composer."[27]

FIRST COMPLETE AMERICAN PRODUCTION.

The Mass in B Minor,

COMPOSED BY

John Sebastian Bach.

First public performance by

The Bach Choir,

Mr. J. FRED. WOLLE, Organist and Conductor.

Soloists.

Miss KATHRIN HILKE, New York City, Soprano.
Miss LUCY A. BRICKENSTEIN, Bethlehem, Soprano.
Mrs. W. L. ESTES, South Bethlehem, Contralto.
Mr. NICHOLAS DOUTY, Philadelphia, Tenor.
Mr. ARTHUR BERESFORD, Boston, Bass.

Moravian Church,
Bethlehem, Pennsylvania,

TUESDAY, MARCH 27, 1900.

Afternoon, four o'clock,   Evening, eight o'clock.

Mass Premiere Program

Promptly at 3:00 p.m. Wolle politely excused himself from the people gathered at his home and walked briskly, as was his manner, two blocks to Central Moravian Church where the musicians were already in place. Eleven trombonists stood in the church belfry ready to announce the beginning of the service, a tradition that still continues during each Bach Festival. Eighty singers had arranged themselves on both sides in the choir loft. Said one singer, "I certainly remember that first festival. The girls wore white dresses with high collars. And the men wore dark suits."[28] Thirty orchestra members waited before the organ console.

As ushers directed tickets holders to their assigned seats, they gave everyone an eight-page program. A portrait of "John Bach" was on the front cover, with a view of the Central Moravian Church belfry on the back. Bach's birth and death dates were inside, connecting Bach to the Moravian musical tradition, making clear that the "First Complete American Production" was a triple anniversary: the month and week of Bach's birth and the 150th year of Bach's death. The printed program contained the text in Latin and in English, the names of "The Chorus. The Orchestra. The Trombone Choir" and "Notes," in which Ruth Doster's importance was emphatically stated. "The choir was organized by Mrs. W. E. Doster, December 5, 1898."[29]

The church was filled to capacity; everyone now waited for the trombones to begin their sacred announcement. Wolle had chosen two Moravian chorales, "Vater Unser im Himmel Reich" and "Sei Lob und Ehr dem Höchsten Gott," to open the service. The trombone choir pierced the silence from the belfry to notify all of Bethlehem that the *Mass* was about to begin. As the echoes of the second chorale, a song of praise to the "Highest God," died away, the trombone choir descended the belfry stairs. The men walked gently through the great beamed church attic, then appeared behind the choir, and intoned the third chorale, Martin Luther's Protestant hymn "A Mighty Fortress is Our God." When the trombones played the final chord, the Bach Choir, already standing, the orchestra, and the organ sounded the first chord of the Mass. By connecting the final chord of a Lutheran chorale played by the trombone choir with the first chord of the *B Minor Mass*, Bach's *Mass* flowed as if directly from God. In addition, Wolle had brilliantly melded the *Mass* with the liturgy of the Moravian Church, as had been done visually on the program cover. "The effect was grand," the pastor wrote.

Years later, four singers left accounts of that day. In 1978, the only surviving member of the original choir, then ninety-two years old, remembered when she had joined the Bach Choir at the age of fifteen with other members of her Presbyterian Church choir. "I was tremendously thrilled by the whole thing, as any young girl would be," she said.[30] A ninety-one-year-old who sang second soprano recalled, "It was so inspirational, so wonderful . . . But of course we

never knew it was going to be [recognized] like that years and years after.
Who ever thought of such a thing? . . . We felt it was an honor to study Bach
and it wasn't easy. The performance must have been rather impressive. People
talked about it for months. As a result, the festival became a tradition."[31] A first
alto, a member of the Central Moravian Church Choir, recalled:

> A first bass wrote in a letter to the Editor of *The Bethlehem Globe-Times* after
> 14 months of preparation, Mr. Wolle said the choir was ready, and in the
> evening after the performance, what thrills we all experienced. There were just
> 80 of us then, and to think we had sung the entire Mass in B Minor in the Central
> Moravian Church for the first time in America. We had been truly singing this
> difficult music with almost unsurpassed religious feeling and spirit.[32]

Reflecting the importance of the event to the Moravian Congregation, Pastor
Joseph Levering summarized his reaction in a lengthy entry in the church diary:

> Tuesday, the most notable musical event in the history of Bethlehem took
> place—the rendition in the church of John Sebastian Bach's famous and
> exceedingly difficult Mass in B minor under the direction of Br. J. Fred. Wolle,
> organist and choir-master. It was given without any omissions—the first time
> this has been undertaken and accomplished in America. It was rendered in two
> parts—the first 4 to 5:30 P.M. and the second 8 to 9:40 P.M. Both sections were
> introduced by the performances of three chorales by the trombones, two from the
> belfry and the last in the organ loft, closing with the key of the opening chorus
> which broke forth with the last note of the trombone. The effect was grand. A
> great many people were present from neighboring-towns and from the large
> cities, for the performance of a colossal master work created a real sensation.
> The city newspapers with scarcely an exception bestowed an enthusiastic praise
> on the splendid work of the big chorus which was made up entirely of non-
> professional local talent. It was a grand success crowning the assiduous efforts
> of more than a year and reflected immense credit upon the accomplished and
> Daring Leader, making his name famous among musical circles throughout the
> country . . . Every available seat in the church was occupied.[33]

Reactions of the local press were unanimously ecstatic: "A Glorious Triumph,
Unsurpassed in Its Character in This Country"[34] and, "Brilliant Lustre Added
to the Old Town's Finest Traditions."[35] National papers and magazines carried equally complimentary congratulations. The *Boston Evening Transcript*:
"excellent work of the chorus and splendidly thorough knowledge evinced
by their conductor."[36] The [New York] *Musical Courier*: "It is a great honor
to have heard it."[37] *Harper's Bazaar*: "the peculiarly romantic conditions
under which it had been produced in Bethlehem gave the event unusual

significance."[38] The (Philadelphia) *North American*: "One of the greatest events in the music world occurred here [Bethlehem] tonight."[39] *Philadelphia Times*: "Notable Event in Music."[40] The *Philadelphia Press*: "a community well grounded in Bach has laid the broad and enduring foundation of true musical culture."[41] The *New York Tribune*: "A more delighted audience never came away from a similar performance in Bethlehem."[42] The same paper quoted a reader, "Perhaps I am over enthusiastic, but I don't see how I can be when I recall the splendid way they sang that extremely difficult music . . . I shall never forget the wonderful beauty of the Crucifixus."[43]

Wolle was praised personally from every corner, and no one questioned the import of this premiere. The *Boston Evening Transcript*'s accolade was typical: "Too much praise cannot be awarded to Mr. Wolle, whose splendid musicianship and whole-hearted enthusiasm have alone made the giving of the work possible, and incidentally spread the name and fame of his town far and wide."[44]

Perhaps the most knowledgeable and genuine praise came from Wolle's esteemed colleague, Frank Damrosch. Wolle called Damrosch "the greatest choral missionary alive." His good will was clearly expressed in a letter to the *Times* written when he returned to New York City after hearing Wolle conduct the *Mass* in Bethlehem. Much of the letter is quoted here because it expresses so eloquently his admiration for Wolle's achievement and the sense of aspiration of American culture of the time:

> It has been claimed that Americans as a race are not musical. It was also formerly believed the prairies were deserts. When they were watered by irrigation, their latent fertility brought forth the richest crops. Similarly the experience of those who have brought musical culture within the reach of the people has been that the response is immediate and wonderful in its result.
>
> Until Mr. Wolle succeeded, by his perseverance and enthusiasm, in inspiring the people of Bethlehem to attempt the tremendous task of producing those large and difficult works, no one in Bethlehem or elsewhere had supposed them capable of accomplishing it. He with rare single-mindedness and devotion to a high ideal, set to work to move an inert mass, a mass which, eight years ago, absolutely opposed his efforts to cultivate the study of Bach's greatest choral works, succeeded in kindling an enthusiasm and love for the highest and best in choral music which have resulted in one of the most beautiful and inspiring festivals of music ever heard in this country . . . [T]he lesson I wish to draw from this festival is this, that what has been done in Bethlehem may be done almost everywhere, to a greater or lesser degree.[45]

Though metropolitan music critics were not unanimous in their praise, one critic did appreciate the chorus and the soloists, "The care and earnestness of their work, coupled with the tonal beauty of their voices, is due to the large measure of success achieved." He did not care for the orchestra, "Its [the performance] shortcomings were principally due to the scratch orchestra . . . and the attempt of the organist to play his instrument with one hand and conduct with the other. So long as the choir were singing, the vagaries of the orchestra were to some extent covered up, but in the solo passages their shortcomings were very much in evidence."[46]

A few days after the premiere, the *Bethlehem Times* reported, "The concert was a financial as well as a musical success."[47] A national newspaper reported, "It was decided to continue the choir under the name of the Bach Choir and in the future to produce other masterpieces of the world's best composers."[48]

The Bach Choir had learned the *Mass* and loved it. Wolle held the first Bach festival in America in his Bethlehem, his birthplace, and the festival had been a national success. One music critic went so far as to connect Bethlehem and Bayreuth, the German shrine of Richard Wagner (a particular favorite of Wolle), and asked, "Is Bethlehem destined to become the Bayreuth of Bach?"[49]

In *The Moravian* a writer pointedly answered why the Bethlehem premiere was interesting and important to so many people and why the efforts of Ruth Doster, J. Fred. Wolle, and The Bach Choir were given such high praise:

> There are many ways in which a community benefits by the production within it of such a work as the B Minor Mass. It imparts a new stimulus toward aesthetic ideals. A music loving people must needs be a refined people, and a town where such a performance can be made an artistic and financial success has given the best proof of the genuineness of its culture. Praetorius [*sic*] long ago wrote: "Experience teaches that music does not remain where the devil rules, for the wicked are not worthy of the art." May it never lack promoters among those of our own spiritual household.[50]

Many held that fine art improved people. In essence, music was spiritual, and singing and appreciating music created cultivated individuals. Cultivated surroundings were proof to oneself and to others that one was culturally refined, had "cultural capital." Plato expressed this philosophy in *Symposium*, "For he who would proceed aright in this manner should begin in youth to visit beautiful forms; and first, if he be guided by his instructor aright, to love such form only—out of that he should create fair thoughts."[51] Dr. Wolle had fused numerous needs and desires with his own vision of bringing Bach's music permanently to America.

A month after the premiere, Wolle announced that the Bach Choir would continue and invited the community to join in the "work" of studying Bach's music:

The Bach Choir, which so successfully rendered Bach's Mass in B Minor March 27, has now formally organized for the purpose of still further studying the works of this great composer. Numerous applications have been made for membership in the newly organized choir, it is now announced that any person desiring to become a member must apply before May 15 to J. Fred. Wolle, Director, who may be seen at his home No. 148 Church Street, any day between the hours of 1 and 2 or 6 and 7 pm. Applications must be made by the date named, in order that work may be begun at once with full attendance.[52]

As Wolle and the members of the Bach Choir proceeded with plans to create a permanent Bach festival in Bethlehem, they were straining their aesthetic ideal to its limits. The Moravian Congregation in Bethlehem would soon begin to question whether Bach festivals were really sacred services and, as such, an appropriate use of their sanctuary. Were these possibly performances and social events for many who attended, rather than sacred services? Such a question would soon threaten the festivals and the Bach Choir itself.

NOTES

1. Paul M. Johnson, *A History of the American People* (New York: Harper Perennial, 1997), 530.

2. Reginald D. Archambault, ed., *John Dewey On Education* (New York: Random House, 1964), 297.

3. Johnson, *History*, 512.

4. *Bethlehem Globe*, 8 January 1921.

5. "My Bach Choir," poem, Wolle papers, ABCB.

6. Bowen, *Family Portrait*, 21–22.

7. Ibid., 22–23.

8. Francis Wolle, *A Moravian Heritage* (Boulder, CO: Empire Reproduction; Printing Co., 1972), 41.

9. Wolle scrapbook 1, 4. ABCB.

10. "The Rehearsal of the Bach Choir," *Daily Times*, 2 September 1899, Wolle scrapbook 1, 2, ABCB.

11. Ibid.

12. "First U.S. Performance of Bach *Mass* Recalled by Bethlehem Choir Member," *Morning Call*, Allentown, 15 May 1972.

13. "A Laudable Undertaking," *Bethlehem Times*, 22 September 1899.

14. "First U.S. Performance," *Morning Call*.

15. "The Bach Choir Concert," *Globe*, 2 March 1900.

16. "The Bach Choir," *Bethlehem Times*, 5 March 1900.

17. *Musical Courier*, 14 March 1900.

18. *New York Tribune*, 18 March 1900.

19. "Unusual Musical Event," scrapbook 1, 4, ABCB.

20. *The Moravian*, 14 March 1900.

21. "Efforts Warmly Appreciated," *Bethlehem Times,* 14 March 1900.

22. "The Bach Choir," *Bethlehem Times*, 23 March 1900.

23. "Bach;s *B Minor Mass*," *Bethlehem Times*, 26 March 1900.

24. "Telephoned from Stockertown," scrapbook 1, 7. ABCB.

25. *Bethlehem Times*, 27 1900.

26. "Bach Festival Notice," *Bethlehem Times,* 27 March 1900.

27. "Bach Festival in Bethlehem," *Philadelphia Press*, 26 March 1900.

28. "1st Bach Festival Holds Fond Memories," n.d., n.s. newspaper clipping, ABCB.

29. All quotes are from the 27 March 1900 program of the American premiere, ABCB.

30. *Bethlehem Bach Choir News* 10, no. 1 (Winter 1978).

31. *Morning Call*, 15 May 1972.

32. *Bethlehem Globe-Times*, 6 May 1959, reprint.

33. "The Official Diary of the Moravian Congregation of Bethlehem, Pennsylvania, 1 January 1888," 190, AMCB.

34. "The Johann Sebastian Bach Festival," *Globe*, 28 March 1900.

35. "Production of Bach *Mass* Proves an Unqualified Success," *Bethlehem Times*, 28 March 1900.

36. "Production of the Bach *Mass in B Minor* at Bethlehem, Pa.," *Boston Evening Transcript*, 31 March 1900.

37. "Bach's *Mass in B Minor* Sung," *Musical Courier*, 4 April 1900.

38. "America's Musical Shrine at Bethlehem," *Harper's Bazaar*, 7 April 1900.

39. "Bach Music Festival Grand Success," *North American*, 28 March 1900.

40. "Bach's *Mass in B Minor* Sung," *Philadelphia Times*, 28 March 1900.

41. "Editorial," *Philadelphia Press*, 28 March 1900.

42. "Bach's *B Minor Mass* at Bethlehem," *New York Herald Tribune*, 28 March 1900.

43. "Comments on the Bach Concert," *Bethlehem Times*, 2 April 1900.

44. "Production of the Bach *Mass in B Minor* at Bethlehem, Pa.," *Boston Evening Transcript*, 31 March 1900.

45. Stebbins, *Frank Damrosch*, 190–92.

46. "Bach's *B Minor Mass*," *Public Ledger*, 28 March 1900.

47. "Bach Choir Meeting," *Bethlehem Times*, 2 April 1900.

48. "To Continue Bach Choir," *The Press*, 3 April 1900.

49. *Music Courier*, 11 April 1900.

50. "Bethlehem's Latest Music Achievements," *The Moravian*, 4 April 1900.

51. Rollo May, *The Courage to Create* (New York: W. A. Norton, 1975), 140.

52. *Bethlehem Times*, 25 April 1900.

Chapter 4

Becoming International

1901

Three days after the American premiere of Bach's *B Minor Mass*, the pastor of Central Moravian Church wrote simply in the church diary, "The Bach Choir which resumed its weekly practicings after Easter met on Monday evenings."[1] A Choir ledger dated April 1900 contains the names of the people who made up the organizational structure:

> Director—J. Fred. Wolle President—R. R. Hillman Vice president—W. L. Franklin—Treasurer M. J. Shimer—Recording Secretary H. J. Wiegner— Corresponding Secretary Mrs. W. E. Doster—Librarian Clinton Zerweck— Membership committee Miss Brickenstein MissWunderling Miss Chandler Miss Shields Mr. Wilhelm Mr. Knauss Mr. Sterling Mr. Hammar.[2]

The Bach Choir, which quickly grew from eighty to 110 singers, assembled with Wolle to continue the study of Bach. The group soon learned of his colossal plan to present a three-day festival in late May 1901 in Central Moravian Church. Wolle's design was straightforwardly simple, yet innovative. The Choir already knew the *Mass*. Sections of *The Passion According to St. John* and of *The Christmas Oratorio* were familiar to many singers from Central Church, and Wolle added many youngsters from his Lehigh University choir to form the core of the boy singers. To that group, he added many youngsters from the community for a total of one hundred boys. In the service they joined the congregation singing the many chorales Bach had included in both works. Twelve adult soloists were required. Eleven were from out of town.

The Bach Choir would sing *The Christmas Oratorio* and *The Passion According to Saint Matthew* in English. Singing the entire *Oratorio* would be another American premiere, as Wolle had previously conducted only sections of it. The *Mass* would close the festival, establishing a precedent that continues to the present. Wolle doubled the orchestra by adding thirty instrumentalists. T. Edgar Schields, Wolle's organ student, would be the organist, leaving Wolle free to conduct the entire work from a podium.

In no way was the festival a series of Bach's choral works performed for a concert audience. Its design was profoundly sacred. With Dr. Wolle as teacher and spiritual guide, the festival mirrored the life of Christ musically and compressed the Christian church year into three days of six sacred services.

Such an expanded second Bach Festival could only be managed with the help of the community. Bethlehem had a number of large hotels, and many supporters of the Choir promised to host Festival guests in their homes. The Lehigh Railroad and the Philadelphia and Reading Railroad agreed to run special trains to Bethlehem during the Festival.

Central Moravian Church interior, 1867

Only after heated debate did the Central Moravian Church Elders grant permission to use the sanctuary. This concession was made reluctantly, as the pastor summarized in the official diary, "The monthly meeting of the Board of Elders was held at 7:30 and several important decisions were made. The use of the church was granted to the Bach Choir for another possible festival, under very rigid restrictions, however."[3] They also agreed to permit the sanctuary to be reorganized to accommodate more people, and the pastor notes, "The Board of Elders [gave] permission to place chairs on the pulpit; platform and adjacent spaces facing the gallery and commanding the highest price towards helping to cover the enormous expense of the undertaking."[4] The Elders worried about the increased cost, because the expense of accommodating a second festival would be much greater.

Moravian architects had originally placed the choir gallery in the back of the church so the congregation's attention would not be drawn aside from the spiritual message of the sacred music. It was a concern that pews reconfigured at the front of the sanctuary would make it a concert hall, though by now the Bach festival was in fact becoming a concert more than a sacred service. In addition, the sanctuary would be used for three days and three evenings in a row. A further complication was the expansion of the choir gallery to accommodate the large boys' choir.

The Elders made another highly unusual decision to permit the church to underwrite the cost of a number of public services. Through long practice, money collected in the sanctuary had been spent only for church purposes. In this case, possibly, they felt raising money to pay for Bach festivals could be considered missionary outreach. However, no tickets were available at the church. They were sold prior to the services in the Moravian Publication Office.

In an unexpected move two months before the festival, Wolle increased the number of rehearsals. In March, the pastor recorded in the church diary that "the vocal and instrumental practicing at intervals day and night" was disturbing the "mental labor" of the archivist, Brother Levering, who was writing his monumental history of Bethlehem.[5] Soon the rehearsal disturbances went far beyond perturbing Brother Levering. The "practicings" began attracting "considerable audiences to the church each evening." As the festival neared, Wolle took over the sanctuary entirely and the pastor reported, "vocal and instrumental practising [*sic*] in the church almost continually day and evening."[6] To his great dismay, he eventually was forced to hold Sunday services in the Old Chapel, a much smaller building near the main church. The Congregation had lost its sanctuary.

Preparations also spread throughout the town. Ruth Doster conducted sectional rehearsals across the street in the Women's Seminary building. Singers gathered in groups to practice Bach's *Mass* in their homes. There was time only for Bach. Wolle and Doster had turned Bethlehem into a center for Bach study, just as they had wished.

The day before the festival, four highly important critics—W. J. Henderson, of the *Sun (New York)*; H. E. Krehbiel, the *New York Tribune*; Reginald Jones, the *Public Ledger (Philadelphia)*—and a nationally recognized academic; and Albert A. Stanley, contributor to the *Zeitschrift der Internationalen Musikgesellshaft (Leipzig)* arrived in Bethlehem. The presence of these critics stamped this festival as an international musical event.

In addition to the critics, famous and influential musicians arrived. Walter Damrosch, conductor at the Metropolitan Opera House in New York City, was accompanied by his brother Frank, conductor of the New York Philharmonic Orchestra. Frank Damrosch would conduct the *Mass* just one month after Wolle's premiere. In the corridor of the Sun Inn, Walter Damrosch said graciously to someone nearby, "Mr. Wolle is most certainly a genius. To think of undertaking such a great task in so small a town is wonderful. My brother and I have come on from New York to give him the happy hand."[7]

Bethlehem music lovers were flattered that these musical notables who had chosen to attend their Bach festival could make thousands aware of Bethlehem's growing "luster and fame." Many out-of-towners bringing their own musical scores joined local enthusiasts, prepared to follow the performances note by note. W. J. Henderson, of the *Sun (New York)*, predicted, "Those who have come to this festival will go away refreshed and strengthened in their musical faith, and there is no reason why the Bach performances here should not become an annual feature." No group so illustrious had assembled in Bethlehem since members of the Continental Congress had listened to the Moravian Church choir and orchestra during the Revolutionary War. The morning of the festival the local newspaper announced that "Music loving people from far and near are arriving in town by the score." Four news columns of "Visitors To The Festival" followed.[8]

Like the first festival, the second began with the trombone choir playing chorales from the belfry of Central Moravian Church. The adults' and boys' choirs, soloists, and orchestra were crammed into the choir gallery, and Wolle stood on the podium. The women were dressed in white for *The Christmas Oratorio*; in black, "with ecclesiastical propriety" according to the Moravian pastor, for *The Passion*; and in a variety of colors for the *Mass*. The men wore black suits throughout the festival. The boys wore choir robes with white surplices.

One of the boys was thirteen-year-old R. Fred. Mease, who many years later remembered the event:

Dr. Wolle made us feel important. We were so fond of him, we used to wait for him . . . and walk to church with him . . . I can vividly recall his waving his arms around energetically as he conducted. . . . I guess I was too young to really appreciate Bach at the time . . . but it did impress me for I was inspired to sing with the church choir . . . and even joined the trombone choir, playing in it for 39 years. My days with the choir were the happiest of my life.[9]

Ushers opened the doors at 3:30 p.m. All ticket holders were in place by 4:00. Most had purchased programs containing the English texts and the printed music for each chorale. This was clearly intended to be a sacred service in which everyone was expected to sing the chorales with the Moravians.

The Moravian Trombone Choir announced the beginning of the festival. The strains of the chorales were heard throughout the town, and as the trombones ceased, in stunning contrast the full chorus, organ, and orchestra burst forth with the opening of Bach's *Christmas Oratorio*:

Central Moravian Church exterior, 1867

Christians, be joyful, and praise your
salvation, Sing, for today your Redeemer is
born.

Three days later the final powerful *Dona Nobis Pacem* from the *Mass*
completed the festival. Henderson reported to his *Sun (New York)* readers:

> At the end of the last chord of the work the entire chorus pelted Mr. Wolle with
> flowers, and the audience, not to be restrained any longer, burst into prolonged
> applause. The tribute was well earned and to be forgiven even within the walls
> of the historic church.[10]

The second Bach festival was over. The pastor recorded rather abruptly
that "a hired company of men; boys set to work immediately after the
close of the final performance to get the church in readiness for Sunday.
Everything was gotten into perfect order and the church locked at
3:30 A.M."[11]

The Central Church pastor expressed the pleasure of the Moravian
Congregation in a three-page diary account of the event. "The achievement was
a splendid triumph of the daring, the ability and the indefatigable industry of the
Director, our famous organist and choir master, Brother J. Fred. Wolle." Then,
he added "Scarcely less credit was due to Mrs. W. E. Doster, an accomplished
scholar in severely classical music . . . who by her warm support and persistent
industry in encouraging the singers; helping to drill them by sections; groups
did very much to insure the eventual success . . . of this occasion has given
Bethlehem a unique celebrity throughout the United States; has called forth
admiring attention; comment in European musical centres."[12]

In addition to the unique celebrity of Bethlehem created chiefly by
New York City music critics W. J. Hendersen and H. E. Krehbiel, it was
Albert Stanley, writing for an important German music journal, who had
made the second Bach festival an international event. There were three
lasting achievements of the second Bach festival: the American premiere of
Bach's *Christmas Oratorio*; the expansion of the festival to three days; and
Henderson, Krehbiel, and Stanley's support.

Responding to the interests of their Bethlehem readers, the editors of
the local papers gave their columns over to quotations from the *New York
Times* and the *New York Tribune* written by Henderson and Krehbiel. Each
held that the festival was an extraordinarily worthwhile undertaking. All
three praised the singers, and Henderson observed, "What will dwell in
the memory of every visitor . . . [is] the wonderful achievement of the
chorus."[13] Describing the impact of the performance taking place in a
sanctuary, Hendersen wrote "the performance in this revered temple has
had such a potent effect."[14]

Krehbiel wrote, "A share [of the success] is due to the handsome encouragement given to the enterprise by the music-loving people of Bethlehem."[15] He gave high praise to the director, "To Mr. Wolle is due the success of the festival," and to the choir, "which he has nourished and stimulated till it has become akin to an artistic rapture."

However, the orchestra and the soloists were far from perfect. Stanley, writing for European readers, was the most direct in pointing out their deficiencies. "Little of the solo work was on the same high plane of excellence as the chorus singing, and most of it was in no sense adequate."

Equally important were issues of interpretation and of Bach scholarship. The constant slowing of the tempo in the chorales and inconsistencies in the execution of ornaments were mentioned in every review. Though all the critics agreed "that these criticisms were offered with hesitation and would not have been made if not for the fact that they sink into insignificance when compared with the transcendent merits of these productions."[16]

In light of present day interest in authentic performance practice, the way Wolle dealt with pitch and orchestration is important. In the final months of preparation for the festival, the organ was tuned to "international pitch," as noted in the church diary. He accompanied the recitatives on a "Steinway Grand." The oboe d'amore, which had fallen out of use, was used in recognition of the original instruments. Wolle borrowed two of them from Frank Damrosch, who had used them in his performance of the *Mass* the previous year. An official circular included further information that reveals that other changes could be made when the music of Bach was still "new." "In the Christmas Oratorio and the Mass the instrumentation will be followed excepting the trumpet parts which have been rewritten by Mr. J. Fred. Wolle. In the Passion Music the Franz score will be used to a large extent."[17] Albert Stanley commented on the trumpet rewrites, "Aftermath of the Bach Festival." The trumpets and horns "failed to produce anything but a feeling of trepidation . . . Mr. Wolle by rewriting many of the parts reduced these disasters to a minimum, but further revision would seem necessary if they are to be effective."[18]

Though the critics gave high praise to Wolle and to the chorus, the quality of the orchestra, the soloists, and Wolle's interpretation was not acceptable. Future Bethlehem Bach Festivals would be scrutinized in every detail and would be judged as a standard for the performance of Bach's choral music in America. Few realized at the time that what the "big city" critics had done was destroyed Bethlehem's innocence. No one, fortunately, knew how painful this loss of innocence would be.

The Wolles left town for a brief but well-deserved rest. When they returned, they found their home, now called *Bachheim* (Bach's Home), "festooned with ferns. Huge bunches of American Beauties filled big vases." Wolle sent a letter of thanks to each Choir member in which he expressed his feelings about the festivals:

> To my Bach Choir:—Can you adequately appreciate the overwhelming sensations of a man, who, after long years of waiting and many a heart-ache, finds himself on the threshold of unfolding plans: co-workers and friends upholding him with unexampled fortitude and enthusiasm, his every wish fulfilled, and finally crushed with inexpressible kindness?[19]

The singers were eager to begin studying and learning whatever work their admired director wanted to teach them. People associated with the festivals expected the Bach Choir to continue, and felt certain that there would be a third Bach festival.

NOTES

1. "Official Diary," 30 March 1900, 195, MABP.
2. Choir Ledger, April 1900, ABCB.
3. "Official Diary," 4 November 1901, 280, MABP.
4. Ibid., 20 May 1901, 243.
5. Ibid., 13 March 1901, 242.
6. Ibid., p. 243.
7. "Preparations Completed for the Opening of the Bach Festival," *Bethlehem Times*, 24 May 1901.
8. "Fine Performances at Bethlehem's Festival," 24 May 1901, Wolle scrapbook, item no. 7. ABCB.
9. N.d., unidentified newspaper article, ABCB.
10. "The Bach Festival Ends," 25 May 1901, Wolle scrapbook, item no. 11, ABCB.
11. "Official Diary," 20–25 May 1901, 245, MABP.
12. Ibid., 243–46.
13. "Close of Famous Bach Festival on Saturday Afternoon; Evening," *Bethlehem Times*, 27 May 1901.
14. Ibid.
15. Ibid.
16. "Aftermath of the Bach Festival," miscellaneous scrapbook, ABCB.
17. "Second Bach Festival Third Official Circular, Beth., Penna.," miscellaneous scrapbook, 8, ABCB.
18. Miscellaneous scrapbook, ABCB.
19. J. Fred. Wolle to Bach Choir, 15 June 1901, album, vol. 1, 1900–1901, ABCB.

Chapter 5

The Bach Festivals Questioned

1902

Photograph of J. Fred. Wolle

Rehearsals had begun the previous September; the Festival would again portray the life of Christ musically with the *Christmas Oratorio*, the *Passion According to Saint Matthew*, and the *Mass* as the centerpieces. In addition, cantatas associated with events of Christ's life depicted in the three major works would be added. The Festival would last three days.

The *Christmas Oratorio* would be preceded by the chorale cantata, "Sleepers Wake," telling of the need to be prepared for the coming of Christ. The *Magnificat*, Mary's praise to the Lord, would follow. The evening before the *Passion According to Saint Matthew* would consist of the "Second Brandenburg Concerto Grosso," for instruments only "as an interlude," and two solo cantatas, "Strike, Oh Strike, Long-looked for Hour," for alto solo, and "I With My Cross-Staff Gladly Wander" for bass voice. Both are somber cantatas that describe following Christ into "eternal rest." The *Mass* would be preceded by two cantatas, "The Heavens Laugh, the Earth Itself Rejoices," and "God Goeth Up With Shouting." Both are joyous reactions to Christ's resurrection. Keeping with his desire to continually introduce Bach works unfamiliar to American listeners, most of these cantatas were American premieres. Wolle's plan was a brilliant application of the Moravian *Singstunde,* the Moravian "hour of singing," affirming that the Festivals were sacred services.

Wolle planned to hold another Bach Festival in Central Moravian Church. Accordingly he sought permission from the church Elders to use the sanctuary for "future renditions of the Bach Choir." In spite of the international success, possibly even because of it, some Elders "opposed the use of the church for such programs under any conditions."[1] Others "favored the granting of the request under certain stipulations."[2]

Because of their deeply contrary views, the group referred the question "to a committee to report at the next meeting."[3] If there had been doubts about the sanctity of the Festivals before, Wolle's colossal plan for a Third Bach Festival only aggravated the question of using the church sanctuary for public musical performances.

The burden of the new performances would fall on the soloists and orchestra already criticized in the press. The critics were unhappy with the quality of both groups, and the Elders were disturbed at the use of out-of-town singers and instrumentalists.

A major reason the Elders had sanctioned previous festivals had been to enhance local sacred music. More fundamentally, the Moravian musical tradition, stretching back over 150 years, was one of skilled amateurs giving their talents freely as worship, not for payment. In addition the previous Festival had disrupted Sunday services, which had to be held elsewhere. What disruptions would be caused by a festival a week long? Finally, when, where, and under whose direction would the Central Moravian Church choir rehearse?

For a month the strain on Wolle and on the singers had been intense. The special committee was strained as well. Whether or not an international musical event would take place was in their hands. Since Bethlehem was a tightly knit community, people knew the conflicting views held by members of the Moravian Congregation and by the community. In November the special committee delivered its report, and the pastor recorded the result in the church diary: "The use of the church was granted to the Bach choir for another festival, under very rigid [conditions]."[4] In the spirit of compromise severe problems could be accommodated, but clearly had not been reconciled.

Presumably, the Bach Choir continued its rehearsals, but the crucial months of March and April passed without promotional notices for the upcoming Festival, even though the Elders had granted their reluctant permission in November. Exactly why the year passed without a Festival in spite of the Elders' approval is not known. A Baltimore reporter wrote, "The organist and the authorities of the church fell into disputes and other difficulties arose."[5] What the "other difficulties" were, the reporter did not say. The Central Church pastor made no mention of "disputes and difficulties" in the church diary.

Though the Bach Choir, the Bach Festivals, the Central Moravian Church Elders and Congregation, and the Bethlehem community were interconnected, such an enterprise could not continue without everyone's collaboration.

NOTES

1. "Church Diary," October 1901, 276, MABP.
2. Ibid.
3. Ibid.
4. Ibid., November 1901, 230.
5. *(New York) Sun*, 12 April 1903, Scrapbook #2, ABCB.

Chapter 6

Bach Festivals as an Idea

1903

The Bach Choir on the Steps of Central Moravian Church, 1903

March 1903 arrived. J. Fred. Wolle had not requested permission from the Moravian Church Elders for a Festival, and the pastor became surprisingly candid, "Practically, since the beginning of the year Bro. Fred Wolle has been on the edge of nervous prostration."[1]

Wolle's illness, his "nervous prostration," was probably what doctors at the time called neurasthenia or nervous exhaustion. The causes were overwork, emotional stress, and chronic illness as the sufferer lost all interest in work, family, and avocations. A present day diagnosis would probably be depression as a result of stress. His doctors recommended rest and healthy food.

Wolle's workload had become overwhelming. He was the organist and choir director of Central Church. His Lehigh professorship meant daily chapel services, chapel choir rehearsals, and assisting university singing groups. The Bach Choir rehearsed. He was studying vast amounts of music, much of it new to this country, and bore the responsibility of national and international prominence. If the Festivals failed, that prominence might be lost. The Bach Choir was totally dependent upon him to resolve disagreements over Festival arrangements. Then, his only daughter became extremely ill.

T. Edgar Shields, the Festival organist, could have stepped in, but Shields apparently made no move to assist. In fact, he contributed to Wolle's difficulties. In October 1902 Shields resigned from Central Church and became organist and choir director of The Episcopal Cathedral Church of the Nativity, South Bethlehem. It was the most prestigious church in the area, and one would not have expected him to refuse the position. Musical conditions in the Moravian church were not going well as a result. The pastor recorded that the problem could not be resolved until Wolle had recovered. The matter of an assistant organist was not solved until the following March.

Ruth Doster surely assisted Wolle, but she could not replace him. It would have been impossible for a woman to take over the Bach Choir directly. She, herself, was under severe strain. Her husband was totally against her musical activities, particularly those involving the Bach Choir. Her marriage was failing.

Finally, the Central Moravian Church pastor was able to report that the illnesses of Wolle and his little girl were nearly over. Wolle resumed his church duties and began rehearsing the Bach Choir regularly. Near the end of March he asked the Moravian Elders' permission to hold a Third Bach Festival. Had he waited longer, another year would have passed. His preparations for the Third Bach Festival moved ahead, and by the early spring of 1903 he had averted the collapse of the whole Bethlehem-Bach enterprise.

The Board of Elders met in April. The pastor's report of 11 April 1903 specified that Brother Wolle had made two requests, both of them problematic: that the first fifteen center pews be removed from the sanctuary; and that pews be replaced with chairs facing the choir gallery at the rear of the church. He also needed additional rehearsal time in the sanctuary. There was agreement to have the pews removed. Settling the issue of extra rehearsals required a joint meeting with the executive committee of the Choir, "the object being to safeguard the musical work of the church during the period."[2] The Elders quickly notified the press of their decision. "Again this year it was very doubtful whether there would be a festival, but there is to be one and so Bethlehem is preparing to receive visitors in larger numbers than ever before."[3]

Arrangements for the third Bach Festival began. Seven choral works and a difficult orchestral concerto would be performed in the most audacious and arduous Bach Festival yet. The plans were national news:

> New York: "Another Bach Festival . . . which is even more ambitious in plan than the affair which excited the interest of the entire musical world two years ago."[4]
> Pittsburgh: "Bethlehem Bayreuth of Bach . . . There is probably no other place where such a volunteer chorus could be persuaded to work so steadily in rehearsal for such a series of difficult works."[5]
> Philadelphia: "A Great Undertaking."[6]
> Allentown: "That Bethlehem will be the Mecca of all the high priests of the synagogue of music . . . is not the slightest doubt and that Prof. Wolle will achieve another triumph is the wish and hope of his many friends throughout the entire [Lehigh] valley."[7]

On 11 May 1903, the first day of the Festival, workmen were busy removing the pews. They enlarged the platform below the pulpit and numbered the seats.[8] In the church diary the pastor noted, "The town begins to show the great number of visitors who have come to enjoy the musical activities of the week."

Bro. J. Fred.Wolle intended a Bach Festival with noble, religious, and musical aims. All the participants were eager for its success, and he was well aware that he and his Choir were working to achieve his goal within a highly critical arena. In fact he had invited "the best critics in the world" to attend. They were given free passes on the Lehigh Valley Railroad. He expected the critics' approval, yet he knew they would tailor their critical reactions to their broad readership.

Townspeople had similarly high regard for Professor Wolle and for his choir. Businessmen and the local press told Choir members repeatedly that singing in the Bach Choir was an important civic duty.

Finally, the metropolitan music critics arrived with more in mind than reporting on the performances. They had broad agendas. Krehbiel of the *New York Tribune* had the most comprehensive and clearly formulated, which he wrote about in "Reflections on the Bach Festival":

> For three years past I have dreamed a beautiful dream whenever the thought of Bethlehem and its Bach festival presented itself to my mind. It was a dream of the establishment of a center of Bach culture in Bethlehem . . . which should set

a standard for concert room and church, to which singers should repair to learn the correct manner of singing the old music, and musicians to hear authoritative readings. If Bach is to become a really living work for the people of today such a "Stylbildungschule" as Wagner wished to see established for his art is a necessity.[9]

Krehbiel granted that Bethlehem was possibly already "set apart as the fountainhead of a cult, rare, elevated and pure, protected from the common place, selfishness, and pretense by the festival's surroundings."[10] Krehbiel made a musical requirement of "such a measure of excellence in the performances as to set a standard for future readings of Bach's works."[11] He wanted no less than that the world standard for Bach performance be set in America and centered in Bethlehem under the leadership of Mr. Wolle. While no other critic articulated a vision as precisely or as dramatically, most held similar expectations of America becoming a world leader in the arts.

These critics were promoting the Bethlehem Bach Festivals even though they had raised questions of performance quality and of interpretation. They were again in Bethlehem to hear if Wolle had heeded their critiques.

For many visitors to Bethlehem, the Bach Festival was not a religious service at all. It was a series of concerts for music lovers who enjoyed being in rural industrial steelmaking Bethlehem, away from the hustle and bustle of the city. Religious surroundings were a pleasant bonus.

Festival goers clustered around Central Moravian Church listening to the trombone choir announce the beginning of the Third Bach Festival. As the last chorale sounded, ticket holders moved into the church. For those without tickets, a critic observed that it "seemed as if half of the young people of the town must have assembled around the church to hear the music without charge."[12]

The pastor declared, "The long anticipated Bach Festival opened with the cantatas "Sleepers, Wake! for the Night is Flying," and "Magnificat."[13] The critics and other musically schooled listeners sat with scores, matching what Bach had composed with the sounds Wolle's ensemble produced.

Following the performance the critics telegraphed reviews to their newspapers. Two facts were clear. Different groups had very different expectations, and their expectations conflicted.

Krehbiel fired the first salvo. "There is only one thing wanting to make Bethlehem Bach Festivals ideally beautiful, and that is perfection of performance."[14] Why had there been no improvement in the performances he asked, when the Bach Choir was willing to rehearse "twice, thrice, even six times a week," and most of the music already known to the Choir? "It appeared reasonable to expect . . . that the period of preparation for the third festival would be devoted largely to making the performances as unique in character as the programs." Visitors, "who had come from distant places, attracted by the fame achieved by Mr. Wolle and his singers" had a right to expect a better performance than the one they had heard on opening night.

Henderson fired the second salvo. "It is not possible to indulge more than moderate praise of tonight's concert. The beauties of 'Sleepers Wake' were interpreted very imperfectly."[15] The tenors made a false entrance, attacks were generally uncertain, and in several sections the full chorus had difficulties.

Henderson expressed openly what other critics had sensed, "It seemed as if everyone were suffering from nervousness, the conductor most of all." But he offered an excuse to Wolle and to the singers. "Why not be nervous?" The audience was filled with "musical prominence," with musicians holding scores in full view of the performers. However, to Henderson's ears, while there was not evident growth from the last Festival, "This concert fairly maintained the singular excellence of the Bethlehem festivals." In the end he forgave Wolle, because he'd provided the "musically elect" with an opportunity "to hear works of wonderful beauty." "It was worth the longest journey . . . to hear the 'Miserecordia' in the Magnificat."

Henderson's readers could take consolation in the realization that Bethlehem was no "less favored" than other towns in lacking tenors that were "sufficient," though the basses "have an immense vigor and energy." He explained that even though Wolle rewrote the trumpet parts for performance on modern instruments, Bach's notes were actually too high. It was not Wolle's fault that modern instruments were not designed to play Bach's music. Every conductor had that problem with Bach. Yet, Wolle's players still had difficulty even playing the parts Wolle had rewritten.

The pastor also expressed concerns. Attendance was "rather small" in comparison to other Festivals. The congregation worried they might not be able to meet the expenses because of the high cost of outside musicians. Also, "the chorale did not engage the effort of the audience to the degree that will doubtless be the case later."[16]

Few were happy as the Bach Festival approached midweek. Bethlehem was reeling, and angry debates became commonplace. On Wednesday evening the pastor responded in the diary with uncharacteristic anger:

> The metropolitan newspaper critics continue to be very severe, particularly upon the single performers. But an indignant reaction has begun to set in against this spirit of criticism, and many murmurings are heard against those who have been robbing the Festival of its devotional aspect and making it a bid for public musical approval.[17]

The "many murmurings" erupted when Bethlehem residents went to press themselves. The *Bethlehem Times* printed letters to the editor that were critical of the critics:

> To the Editor of the Times, would it not be wise and courteous and eminently more judicious to call attention to Mr. Wolle personally to any shortcomings, without rushing into print? . . . I thank God I am enabled to hear Bach in such placid historical surroundings and that Mr. Wolle will repeat the same program.[18]

Another reader attempted an impartial view and pointed out the positive results from the negative critiques. After agreeing with the critic of the *New York Stats Zeitung* regarding the orchestra a reader wrote:

> The unfortunate conditions under which Mr. Wolle worked during he last few weeks are unknown to most people, and to those who know he is certainly considered a genius. However, the critics make no allowance. The lack of practice of the orchestra was probably more undesirable to Mr. Wolle than anyone else, and the nervous strain under the conditions to which he was subjected by the various accidents which he must tolerate would render any other than a master of the art totally unfit for further work. Taken all in all, there is no question but that the criticisms have aroused the choir, orchestra and soloists to do their very best and instead of it being a secondary production, the severe criticisms have placed it unwillingly or unconsciously in the very first class.[19]

The debate in the press was not without humor. "Professor" made a clever wordplay on Bach's name, which means spring or stream in the German language:

> Sir: The bacteriologists have condemned the spring and also found microbes in the river. During the past week certain music bacteriologists have discovered that even the Bethlehem Musical Brooke "Bach in German" is polluted with the germ "Bachillius Prodigiosus." Professor.[20]

With the Festival "nearing its climax," Wolle's energy and concentration were taxed to the utmost, when the emergency that conductors most dread occurred. The tenor for *The Passion According to Saint Matthew* was taken ill. At a time when these works were new, there were few singers who could sing the solos. The tenor from the previous day agreed to learn the role. He and Wolle worked every moment between other performances rehearsing the tenor part in order to save the *Passion*. He learned his part in two days and was ready for the performance.

Krehbiel reported, "The conviction is written down with keen regret that Bethlehem cannot rise to its lovely mission." That "lovely mission" required Wolle to make a study "of contemporary records and traditions which is essential to a truly artistic and historically correct performance of the music of Bach and his period." The choices were clear. "If the Bethlehem festivals are to remain only devotional functions," they will become like the seasonal performances of *Messiah* found in every city. "If the festival is to become a fetish," not open to criticism and directed by firm scholarship, "it will soon lose all interest so far as musicians and music lovers–to whom Bach's music is neither novelty nor fit subject for seasonal exploitation–are concerned."

Krehbiel repeated the problems with ritards, musical ornaments, and the accompaniment of recitatives. For the first time he stated specific authorities for historic performance practice with specific applications of the ideas from historic sources as well as instances of Wolle's noncompliance. Why did the results of his conducting not square with the known information? Were there reasons he did what he did other than his personal self-expression? If there were reasons, what were they? After all, by his own admission, the Bach Choir was a scholarly pursuit, rooted in Ruth Doster's study group. Wolle always said the purpose of the Bach Choir was to "study the music of Bach." Krehbiel, in the role of a responsible critic and music educator, was pointing the way to Professor Wolle.

Though local reporters must have pressed him to respond, Wolle chose not to enter the debate. It would have been helpful if he had, for he owned a copy of Carl Philip Emmanuel Bach's *Treatise* containing all the appropriate ways to perform Baroque ornaments.[21]

Though Krehbiel's critique of the program was brief, for the first time his comments went beyond those expected of a music critic, showing the vengeful side of his personality:

> The performance presents many questions for the discussion of musicians (who, by the way, have been invited to leave the town, if they find themselves in disagreement with local opinion touching Bach's music, every Bethlehemite having received a gift of plenary inspiration in this matter).

Another critic, also perturbed by Bethlehem's reaction to musical criticism, reported

> indignation reached its climax today, when a prominent musician among the visitors was told by a person high in authority that if he did not like the performances he should go home and his railway fare would be paid . . . They [Wolle and the Bach Festival] must improve, because they have attracted the attention of the country . . . It is unfortunate that the conditions of the festival two years ago cannot longer satisfy, but they cannot.[22]

The final day of the Festival every seat was filled, except space remaining in the pulpit area. Wolle, exceeding his power, permitted chairs to be placed there. Even the pastor reacted sarcastically with a thinly veiled jab:

> This carried a little indignation and has taught the Board of Elders hereafter not to trust anything to the charge of those who cannot be held more definitely responsible than this shadowy Executive Committee which it now comes to light, had scarcely any existence or power at all.[23]

The *Mass* was sung in two sessions, as previously. When the evening was concluded, all traces of the performance were quickly wiped from the sanctuary:

> Immediately upon the leaving of the audience the Head Sacristan, Bro. C.H. Eggert, had a corp[s] of workers ready to restore the Church to its usual conditions for Sunday, and at 10:15 pm. This had been accomplished and the lights went out.

In the fall, Wolle requested permission from the church elders to hold a "Bach Cycle" performing "selected works" in the church celebrating the Birth, Death, and Resurrection of Christ "as nearly as possible at the times for which they were written."[24] Vocal and instrumental works expressing the meaning of each event would be clustered around large works sung in previous festivals. Many of these shorter compositions had rarely, if ever, been heard in America. Following the 1903 Festival, he told a reporter:

> When the third Bach Festival drew to its close the impression seemed to spread to a certain extent that the work of the Bach Choir was practically at an end. This, however, is not, and will not be, the case, for the field of the church cantatas of Bach is practically an unexplored one; the same is extremely true of the realm of orchestral works.[25]

The Elders discussed Wolle's newest request. According to the pastor, "the situation is a difficult one . . . the spirit of the musicians is everything that can be desired [while] the behavior of the audience from out of town is not by any means as reverent as is to be expected in God's House." The Elders did not "desire to obstruct in any degree the legitimate and worthy musical development of the choir[; however,] the loose arrangements in force at the last Festival could not be tolerated." What takes place in the sanctuary must further the mission of the church. After a "long discussion," the Elders "resolved to allow the use of the church on these occasions . . . Each seasonal celebration would last three days, with the 'Bach Cycle' extending through 1904 and 1905. The dates were 28, 29, 30 December 1904; 12, 13, 14, April 1905; 1, 2, 3, June 1905. There would be two sessions each day, one at four and another at eight."[26]

Wolle's ingenious plan combined the essence of the 1901 festival of major works with the design of the weeklong 1903 Festival. Adding vocal and instrumental pieces enhanced the messages of the *Christmas Oratorio*, the *Passion*, and the *Mass*. Here was musical richness, time for much needed rehearsal, and the reverence and church mission the Elders required. Equally important was the fact that Wolle had secured the continuity of the Bach Choir and the Bach Festivals.

NOTES

1. "Church Diary," March 1903, MABP.

2. Ibid., 11 April 1903.

3. *Sun (New York)*, 12 April 1903, Scrapbook #2, ABCB.

4. *New York Daily Tribune*, 9 April 1903.

5. *Bethlehem Times*, 27 April 1903, rpt., ABCB.

6. *North American (Philadelphia)*, 3 May 1903.

7. *Bethlehem Times*, 8 April 1903.

8. "Church Diary," 11 May 1903, MABP.

9. *Bethlehem Times*, 3 June 1903, rpt., ABCB.

10. Ibid.

11. Ibid.

12. Ibid.

13. "Official Diary," May 1905, MABP.

14. *New York Tribune*, 12 May 1903. All quotes in this section by Krehbiel are from this source.

15. *(New York) Sun*, 11 May 1903. All quotes by Henderson in the section are from this source.

16. "Official Diary," May 1903, 363, MABP. The source of all the pastor's comments in the section.

17. "Official Diary," May 1903, MABP.

18. *Bethlehem Times*, 16 May 1903.

19. "Critical of Hypercritical," n.d., unidentified newspaper clipping, ABCB.

20. *Bethlehem Times*, 16 May 1903.

21. Carl P. E. Bach, *Treatise* 3, n.d., volume in author's possession.

22. "Bach Festival Cantatas," 15 May 1903, unidentified news clipping, ABCB.

23. "Official Diary," May 1903, MABP.

24. *Musical Courier*, 21 December 1904.

25. Ibid.

26. "Official Diary," 5 October 1904, MABP. The source of the pastor's comments in this section.

Chapter 7

A Bach Cycle

1904–1905

PART ONE: CELEBRATING CHRISTMAS

Wolle designed the Bach Cycle's Christmas Festival so that every past local concern was addressed. This Festival was an expression of the church year, leaving no question of its sacred character. Because of the message and spirit of the season, he left the Moravian Christmas services uninterrupted. The Moravian Nativity scene, the Christmas *putz* traditionally occupying the entire front of the church, remained in place, nor did he request that pews be moved. There were no last minute arrangements made by The Choir's Executive Committee as there had been in the previous Festivals.

Wolle chose a number of the soloists from the Choir itself and emphasized the local makeup of the orchestra. This addressed the Moravian desire for local participation, and placed the Festival within the Moravian amateur music tradition. Five of the performances included chorales sung by the congregation, and visitors from out-of-town were asked to join in the singing, thereby participating in the service as the Moravians themselves did throughout.

The 1904 Christmas Festival was firmly a part of the mission of the church. Wolle included his boys' choir, and the boys' parents and families. The Moravian Trombone Choir not only announced each service; the group played in two of the cantatas.

Simultaneously, Wolle constructed a Festival that was unique and attractive to metropolitan music lovers. Following Bach's intention, he divided the *Christmas Oratorio* among the three days by singing two sections each evening. The afternoon programs included cantatas and instrumental pieces. Wolle offered two cantatas new to Americans, BWV 118 and BWV 79, and one that had been rarely heard, BWV 1. The Bach Choir was also presented in a new light, for it sang a Bach motet for unaccompanied double chorus.

The Christmas Festival was a great success, and the Church Elders were pleased. "The Festival partook of the character of true worship," the pastor wrote, and even though "many musical visitors were there from distant places [there was] little supercritical 'writing up,' with hostile feeling which marred somewhat the Festival of 1903."[1]

The pastor drew an important analogy between this Festival and the *Singstunde*. "It was truly viewed as a rendition of worshipful song, rather than a concert performance of difficult music." Thus he connected the Christmas Festival with a traditional worship service unique to Moravians. In fact, the *Singstunde* has remained a model for the Bethlehem Bach Festivals. Summarizing his feelings about the Festival, the pastor wrote, "The reverent spirit steadily deepened to the last chorale of the *Christmas Oratorio* on Friday evening." But, "[t]he church was not full," and with fewer attending, the pastor was afraid there might be a financial loss.

Though many music critics did not attend, Krehbiel was back in Bethlehem in spite of the busy New York music season. He reacted differently than he had the previous year:

> The attendance which was small the first day, seemed doubled at each succeeding session, and today, at both performances, the big, old church was crowded . . . This [the unaccompanied motet for double choir] was performed with great success. The Christmas Oratorio was given in splendid style.[2]

Wolle had addressed each of the performance issues, so that critics no longer had concerns with his interpretations.

CELEBRATING EASTER

It was Wolle's musical intention for the Bach Choir to study unknown cantatas and to sing them to the public.[3] Two of these cantatas comprised the program for Wednesday afternoon; in the evening there were three. Thursday was devoted to *The Passion According to Saint John*, a large work new to the Choir. Friday was again a day of cantatas and instrumental works.

Everything was arranged to lead the listeners to an expression of deepest mourning, concluding with a chorale, "Christ Had Risen from the Dead," preparing them for Easter and Ascension. Expressing the meaning of sacrifice, the singers wore black, and the pulpit recess was filled with palms and ferns, rather than chairs.

Again, praise was the critical response. One described the scene:

> The crowning glory of the afternoon session was the chorale, "World Farewell"
> sung by the choir in lightest possible pianissimo. The voice of every instrument
> was hushed and from the choir loft there floated down the soft strains that fell
> like a benediction. The effect was almost magical. Many people in the audience
> were unable to restrain their tears. Its rendition flung an aureole of glory over
> the afternoon's session.[4]

Wolle had used the sanctuary of Central Moravian Church with the elevated
choir loft in the back exactly as the Moravians had intended—the music of the
choir floating above the reverent listeners. The singers and instrumentalists
and Bach's music modestly conveyed the Christian Easter message.

The first evening the music evoked a quite different mood. "A Request"
was placed on every seat asking each person to approach the service in
reverence and quietness. One critic described the effect, "In the concluding
chorale, 'All my days have I extolled Thee,' the audience contributed to the
final outburst of harmony that for glorious volume of tone has never been
surpassed in the old church."[5]

Worshipers filled the church. Everyone was so moved that following the
close of the Festival "a large number of Dr. Wolle's friends and acquain-
tances walked up the street and called at *Bachheim,* where an impromptu
reception was held, while they extended their congratulations."[6]

The pastor's response expressed his satisfaction:

> An absence of self-sufficient musical critics from the great dailies of the cities
> was a marked relief, for while the music could stand criticism according to the
> highest standards, it could do more than merely seek a standard,—it could be
> regarded as worship.[7]

The *New York Times* carried a long review in which The Choir was praised
for an improved tonal quality and "thoroughness of preparation." However,
the orchestra still lacked the "technical ability to cope with the peculiar and
often very great difficulties of the score."[8]

CELEBRATING ASCENSION

The final offering of the Bach Cycle began jubilantly with the cantata, "The
Heavens Laugh, the Earth Itself Rejoice," BWV 31. On Friday afternoon
there were three works, two orchestral and one choral, with three cantatas in
the evening. The Bach Choir concluded the evening with "A Stronghold Sure

is Our God," BWV 80, based on Luther's Protestant Reformation text. As usual, the Festival ended with the *Mass*, and a critic recorded the response:

> A thrilling and inspiring ending. And as Dr. Wolle . . . released the last crashing chord with it came the joyous outburst of the choir, orchestra and soloists, who expressed their deep appreciation and admiration of Dr. Wolle by pelting him with showers of flowers.[9]

Dr. Wolle and the Bach Choir had triumphed over all obstacles. In a manner typical of his genius, he had offered more than anyone had proposed or required of him, and to the relief of the Moravian congregation, the Festival was not only a spiritual success but a financial one.

AFTER THE CYCLE: A STARTLING FAREWELL

When his summer church obligations were concluded, the Wolles left for the coast of northern Maine. There he received a letter from the president of the University of California, Berkeley, asking him to establish a music department and to organize a Bach Choir in the San Francisco Bay area. This offer promised Wolle that a professional orchestra made up of symphony players, whom he would select, would be at his disposal as well as the University's large Greek-style amphitheater on the hillside overlooking San Francisco Bay.

He accepted, provided that he could return to Bethlehem after a year if things did not go well. He sent a letter to the Church Elders requesting a leave of absence. The pastor recorded the reaction of the community to the news:

> Today our community was startled by the announcement from Bro. J. Fred. Wolle, our organist of the church, that he had accepted a call to the Chair of Music in the University of California, and would leave for the West within a month. Having declined several other flattering offers, this opening seems to be in direct line with the development of his work. The newspaper interview and the announcement have caused a great deal of discussion and regret among our people.[10]

The Wolles left Bethlehem. The Bach Choir was disbanded along with the Bethlehem Bach Festivals.

The achievement of the Bach Festivals was given the highest recognition in the *Bach-Jahrbuch*, in a summary of Bach performances worldwide from 1904 to 1907. There were many performances of the *Mass*. The Bach Choir of Bethlehem is among those listed. What is more significant is that in numbers of cantatas sung, Bethlehem's seven is exceeded only by the twenty-one of the Thomas Church in Leipzig, and thirteen of various groups in Berlin.[11]

NOTES

1. "Official Diary," 21–28 December 1904, MABP.

2. *New York Tribune*, 31 December 1904.

3. Using Wolle's titles, the cantatas were: "The Heavens Laugh, the Earth Itself Rejoices," "Bide with Us, for Eve is Drawing Onward," "Thou Guide of Israel," God Goeth Up With Shouting," "Oh Light Everlasting," "Now Hath Salvation and Strength," "Sleepers; Wake! for the Night is Flying." There were two instrumental works: "The Third Brandenburg Concerto" and "Suite in D."

4. "Large Audience Greets Singers," unidentified clipping, ABCB.

5. Ibid.

6. "The Closing Day of the Lenten Festival," unidentified clipping, ABCB.

7. "Official Diary," 14 May 1905, MABP.

8. *New York Times*, 16 April 1905.

9. *Globe*, 5 June 1905.

10. "Official Diary," 19 August 1905, MABP.

11. "Overview of the Performances of Bach's Works from the End of 1904 to the Beginning of 1907," [translation] *Bach-Jahrbuch* (1906): 114–29.

Chapter 8

The Wolles in California

1905–1911

The long train ride west from Bethlehem to San Francisco gave Wolle many hours to think about his acceptance of the unexpected invitation. Lehigh University had no academic music department, but Wolle loved working with students. At Berkeley, he would be a full-fledged music professor. Though he had no experience conducting symphonic music, he looked forward to working with a professional orchestra.

In Bethlehem, he had encountered many obstacles in his numerous attempts to develop a festival format that conformed to the conditions existing at Central Moravian Church. He had already designed four types of festivals, and each one had proved increasingly frustrating, even immobilizing him for a time. Bach festivals in California, however, would be a university offering to the community. There would be no church influence. In Berkeley he could begin anew, conducting Bach with a professional orchestra in a Greek theater. On his arrival in California, Wolle told a music critic, "I came to California because I expect to find a larger field for this exercise of my activities than I could find at home. I come here hoping to find large musical resources and therefore hope to achieve greater results."[1]

He could give organ recitals as well and maintain his place in America as a notable organ virtuoso. As he turned all these facts over in his mind, he surely felt that he was being asked to take the next step in bringing Bach to all of America. The president of the University of California had assured him of the support of the numerous communities in the San Francisco area. What the Wolles did not know—could not have known—was that most of what Wolle thought were facts were indeed not. Many were not even possibilities.

Being an Inter-view With Dr. J. Fred Wolle of Beth-lehem Who

Will Lead the Sym-pho-nies at Uni-versity of Cali-fornia

Artist sketch of J. Fred. Wolle

The Wolle family arrived in California in the fall of 1905. Professor Wolle was greeted as the musician from the East who could cultivate the Bay Area and make California a national music center. It seemed that everyone wanted to meet the couple. Receptions and parties all around town gave hundreds of San Franciscans an opportunity to meet this cultural hero, and the president of the University naturally made the introductions. Wolle was a musical star, and he and his wife and daughter immediately became part of the Bay Area social set.

In his inaugural speech Professor Wolle laid out his vision for a College of Music:

> If you would make real musicians of your people, let these perfect strains be branded on the brain—carved in the hearts. Go back to Bach—and then build forward through the classic, the romantic—to the ultra-modern. We will not stop at Bach, but let us begin with him.[2]

In his view, all music was summarized in the greatest masterpiece in Western music, Bach's *Mass in B Minor*; he rooted all of his plans in conducting it. He would immediately collect the forces required, and he assured everyone the performance would be an extraordinary one, worthy of California:

> I would say that I hope to have here a great performance of the Mass in B Minor. To this end I look forward to the late Easter temporary assembling of the vocal and orchestral forces of the city and vicinity, that, with your moral support and active co-operation will be enabled to show forth in all its beauty and power—a noble masterpiece.[3]

He articulated a grandiloquent plan that he broadened to cover the whole nation:

> a prophecy of coming achievements of this newly inaugurated [music] department that must grow to become a real and living force in the great singing life of this Western metropolis, a school that shall exert a dominant influence on the higher education of mankind through the length and breadth of this fair commonwealth—one of the mighty powers for good in musical America.[4]

He was prepared to devote himself entirely to the enterprise: "No labor shall be too arduous, no stone shall be left unturned, no challenge unexplored, by which I can assist, in the further development in the state of that art of which you and I are ardent devotees."[5] He assured his audience they had made the correct choice in selecting him to make California the future center of Bach performance in America:

> So I am here today, in response to your cordial invitation, to enlist your sympathy, to solicit your cooperation—and to promise, that, if you will stand by the chair of music for just twenty-five years—the latest graft of the music branch on the university plant will sprout, flourish, bud and blossom like the rod of Aaron.[6]

In Wolle's mind Bethlehem was a prelude for Berkeley, "Last June saw the completion of our nine-day Bach Cycle—and with it, the end of my work in Bethlehem—for the study of these works, doubtless it is, that have brought me here. Bach brings me from Bethlehem to Berkeley."[7]

In Berkeley, so many miles from Bethlehem, he finally expressed his reactions to the resistance he had overcome in founding the Bach Choir, the festivals, and the Bach cycle. He had never publicly done so in Bethlehem. Expressing his feelings there would have been too personal and non-Moravian. In Berkeley, however, he was able to tell how profoundly his personality and his musical activity in Bethlehem had been anchored in Bach's works:

So it came about that I went deeper and deeper into his music—until it so absorbed me, and fascinated me that I determined to concentrate all effort to the reproducing of his works, which should themselves proclaim their power. But I found that these works must be not merely produced—but must be produced in such a manner that they should appeal to the people. They must be popular. The people must learn to know, and knowing learn to admire and love them. That was not an easy task. The public shrugged its shoulders, and sneered and jeered. My best friends warned me of impending catastrophe if I persisted. The critics laughed heartily, before-hand, at the idea of a three day—to say nothing of a six-day, and a nine-day festival, consisting exclusively of the music of one composer—and that composer to be, of all men—Bach.[8]

Wolle's achievements in Bethlehem had come not because they'd taken place in Bethlehem, Pennsylvania, or were the musical legacy of the Moravian Church. To depend upon a specific locale negated one of his most strongly held beliefs, the universality of Bach's music. As Wolle emphasized,

It was said again and again by well-meaning persons who were supposed to know whereof they spoke, who should have known better, and who were otherwise sane, that to give the Mass in B minor, or, indeed, a nine-day Bach Cycle, was an easy task, because of the conditions, the environment, the atmosphere of our town. We were told, positively, that this work could not be accomplished in any other center. I have disputed this statement again and again. I have repeatedly denied the allocation. Now I am here for the purpose of disproving this foolish theory—am determined to show absolutely the falsity of this assumption.[9]

He enjoined his audience:

Let us now look forward to the day when it shall be sung in California—and let that rendition be such as has never been attempted or achieved. Your untold resources point to the symphony orchestra, the erection of a noble organ—all uniting in a great Bach festival, which, unless all things fail, shall arrest the attention of the musical nation.[10]

What constitutes a "superior" Bach performance is clearly set out in Wolle's own words:

What is the interpretation that will capture the brain and enchain the soul? Simply this. These works must be studied, note for note, measure for measure—phrase for phrase—until the technical material is overcome—until the mechanical element is mastered to a degree that must be letter perfect. Hand in hand with this drudgery must go the aesthetic study. The leader's definite, preconceived conception must be taken for granted. No grasping—no feeling about in the dark during rehearsal is possible. . . . The various parts must be assembled—section by section . . . so that the subject matter shall be stated in no uncertain manner—that the theme; counter themes shall be proclaimed always in a consistent—logical succession, that the resultant interpretation shall be appealing and convincing.[11]

His position on Bach interpretation was emphatic: "To take the greatest compositions the world has known, and reproduce them in so natural, so spontaneous a manner, that they will take hold of the masses."[12]

Within his aesthetic philosophy, he equated a bad Bach performance with what was accepted as tradition, a "tradition" he totally opposed:

> I have given some study to this question of traditions, that I may know what to avoid. I am told that the traditional method of playing Bach . . . is to "blast away" from beginning to the end of the composition . . . Furthermore, to play with metronomic stiffness . . . Bach lived two hundred years ago. You bring proof that he performed this toccata thus and so. I say that for Bach's day and generation—as Bach played it.[13]

Even if Bach himself had played that way, he added, that was no reason to do so now. Modern audiences demanded something different:

> But I hold, that in this day of ours, with its changed conditions—surrounded as we are—and situated in the modern—intense—high-strung—often sensuous music of a Wagner . . . we fail to hold the attention of the people with Bach's music if we are to give it a cut; dried—scholastic—imitation interpretation . . . his music must be rejuvenated—it must be . . . as modern in spirit as any composition of the present day, it must be given a modern setting. Finally, it must be individualized . . . I do not say that my interpretation is the right one . . . but it is my interpretation. It is something else, it is individual.[14]

Though professional critics had said more than once that his conception was too free, Wolle's presence at the University of California was proof that his conception had appeal. While he stood by the right to his own and others' personal interpretations of Bach, and he would devote his whole being to the task, he urged in return, "I earnestly direct your attention to the motto of my dear old Moravian Church, and sincerely trust that we may all observe her teaching . . . In essentials, unity; in non-essentials, liberty; in all things, charity."[15]

Not that the move to California had been without sacrifices. In an address to the university faculty and students, Wolle told his audience that his arrival in California

> closed the first chapter in my career. . . . I have left behind my family and church, and as my friends say, in coming here have murdered my only musical child, my Bach Choir, which has shown unparalleled devotion, and which has

given me all that I possess—I do so, because I believe I enter a larger field, promising greater and grander results.[16]

In the same address, Wolle shared the experience of his first evening at the University. That account shows him in a state of elation he had never expressed as a Moravian. A critic asked him about the American premiere of the *Mass in B Minor*:

"I said it was either the B Minor Mass or nothing."
"And."
"It was nothing." The professor went on. The chorus broke up. "I waited." For five years the professor "waited" and Bethlehem went unchorused until 1898. Then came to him a double quartet of women, asking him to lead them.
"But you forget," the professor told them, "that B minor mass."
"Oh," the women said (the professor recounts), "let us do it and get rid of the old thing."[17]

Now he stated openly what he had so desired when he lived in Bethlehem and what he envisioned for Berkeley:

I arrived in Berkeley on Monday evening, September the eighteenth about six o'clock. Several hours later, in company with a friend, I found my way to the Greek theater. Unaccustomed to your hills, and unacquainted with your campus, it was no easy climb amid the dark shadows of your spreading trees. But we groped our way to the topmost tier of seats. There my friend left me, to test the acoustics from the stage. Alone I sat, no roof but the canopy of heaven, no light but the shining stars, no companion but nature herself. It was an impression I shall not soon forget. For years, I had dreamed of just such a temple for my Bach Choir, to be reared on the summit of our Lehigh mountain, that mighty choral and orchestral works would be given a hearing amid worthy surroundings. But it was not to be; and here the very evening of my arrival, I found my temple. And sitting there, I dreamed dreams and saw visions. Upon the stage there appeared a chorus, five hundred strong; in front of the singers a superb orchestra, behind them, a noble organ. And there, in that wondrous environment of blended art and nature, in that natural God-given amphitheater, adorned with classic outline by the art of man, they lifted up their voices, and there went forth a shout of joy, a paean of victory, a jubilant song, and the great Bach Mass in B minor lived again—and one of the very greatest choral works of all time was re-incarnated.[18]

In addition to teaching courses in harmony and composition, Wolle quickly organized a student orchestra and a university chorus for a performance of Handel's *Messiah*. Simultaneously, he formed a symphony orchestra of Bay-area professional musicians and inaugurated a series of symphonic concerts in the Greek theater.

Wolle's musical activities were national news, and, according to an East Coast reporter, he had assembled an orchestra of "the best professional musicians in San Francisco" and scheduled the symphony series "to provide the community a fit rendering of music of the noblest sort."[19] He immersed himself fully in the literature of music for the symphony orchestra. Once he had mastered it, the same east coast critic wrote of his success:

> For the opening concert of the series, at the Greek Theater February 15, more people went from San Francisco to Berkeley than ever listened to a symphony concert in San Francisco. For the second symphony concert, on March 1, three times as many people gathered in the Greek Theater as had ever heard a symphony concert in California.[20]

The opportunity for Wolle to devote himself to conducting the general symphonic literature in a series of public concerts performed by a professional orchestra of his own choosing was not what had enticed him to Berkeley. He was not aware such opportunities existed, until he'd surveyed the possibilities. But, as a result, he was soon to become known not only as a choral conductor of Bach, but as a symphonic conductor of the full range of orchestral music.

Two months after he arrived in Berkeley, Wolle announced that the "world's greatest oratorios and symphonies will be rendered in the Greek Theater. The first series of concerts will consist of six symphonies, the last concert will be the occasion of the first appearance of the University chorus of 300 voices."[21] There was no mention of a Bach Festival or even of Bach. But, "should the series be successful the university will make the symphony concerts an annual feature of the university life."[22]

Wolle volunteered his time with the orchestra, but the university president was worried about paying the professional musicians. At that moment one seed was sown for the guarantor system of dependable monetary pledges and support above and beyond ticket sales that was and remains absolutely crucial to The Bach Choir of Bethlehem. "The financial safety of the concerts is already assured. Mr. F. M. Smith, the 'borax king,' . . . is backing the experiment. Mr. Smith has guaranteed the university against any possible financial loss that might accrue."[23]

After only a few months, Wolle had made the Greek Theater (built in 1903 by newspaper magnate William Randolph Hearst) the musical center of the area. Thousands of people attended his concerts, setting national records for concert attendance. Now that his programming no longer required liturgical justification, as it had in Bethlehem, a vast possibility of symphonic literature opened to him, and he dipped into it with great energy. The extent of the

repertoire he began conducting was astonishing even for a seasoned orchestral conductor. Except for pieces by Wagner, he had previously conducted
none of the orchestral works he programmed in Berkeley. In the six years he
lived there, he conducted most of the significant orchestral literature of his
time. The list included symphonies by Haydn, Mozart, Beethoven, Brahms,
Schubert, Schumann, Tchaikovsky, Mendelssohn, and Dvorak; and piano and
violin concertos by Chopin, Liszt, Beethoven, and Tchaikovsky. He scheduled a concert devoted entirely to Wagner. Other concerts featured descrip-
tive music by Richard Strauss, Wolf, Berlioz, Dvorak, Chabrier, Debussy,
Goldmark, MacDowell, and Rimsky-Korsakov. There were works by Bach,
Beethoven, Elgar, Glazounoff, Gluck, Grieg, Rameau, Rubenstein, Suk,
Weber, Saint-Seans, Massenet, and Nicoli. The only area he did not venture
into was opera. San Francisco already had an extremely active opera season.
He did, however, collaborate in dramatic performances in the Greek Theater
conducting incidental orchestral music for a number of plays.

Wolle proved he could do everything with immense success. He had his own
orchestra of nearly one hundred musicians playing for triple the number of
listeners who had come to the Bach Festivals in Bethlehem. The orchestra
musicians "come to its [the orchestra's] work with the enthusiasm and delight
in sharing in . . . this longed for opportunity to express in the highest degree
their hopes, their ambitions and their artistic ideals."[24] In a few months
Wolle had transformed himself from a church musician, a choral conductor
known for his Bach Festivals, and a concert organist of the first rank, into a
prominent American symphonic conductor. Praise for his work flowed from
newspapers across the country.

The second concert became international news: "Berkeley California is
now the sensation of the whole musical world. The first symphony audience
of four thousand and this second one of seven thousand looms larger in the
world's eye than Yosemite or the giant redwood."[25]

His classes were thronged. Over one hundred students were taking harmony
and over sixty, counterpoint! Four hundred students joined the chorus, and
twenty-five hundred were attending the symphony concerts.

Two tragedies struck the Wolle household in the early spring of 1906. Gretchen,
the Wolles only child, became deathly ill. At the end of the month, when doctors
had reported the youngster would survive, J. Fred.'s mother died. The concert he
conducted on 29 March included Tchaikovky's *Pathetic Symphony*.

The next concert was entirely music of Wagner. Earlier he had arranged
many Wagner selections for organ and had played them repeatedly in organ
recitals. People gathered outside the Greek Theater to hear the music. A
review of the concert included the following praises:

People were scattered all over the hills to the eastward of the amphitheater, finding shelter under the trees. They perhaps were the souls hungry for music, but who could not spare from their meager belongings even the small admission that is charged for the symphony orchestra . . . if there ever was an enterprise in art that belongs to the people, it is the symphony series.[26]

Wolle had proven not only that Bach was for everyone, but that the whole canon of Western symphonic music was as well.

The final concert of the season was to be *Messiah*, sung by the university chorus. The San Francisco earthquake struck before it could be performed, and the building housing the instrumental parts and many musical instruments burned. The symphony musicians were scattered. All musical activity in the area seemed lost in chaos.

Wolle's concert following the earthquake was one of the most moving performances he ever conducted. The fact that he could bring together singers and instrumentalists, reassemble his orchestra and begin rehearsals so soon after a natural disaster of this magnitude shows a force of character that was extraordinary. Despite the devastation, almost five thousand people gathered to hear the program.[27]

The concert was integrated like a Moravian *Singstunde*, beginning with Beethoven's "Ruins of Athens Overture" and concluding with his *Symphony No. 5*. Beethoven had called the opening motive "Fate knocking at the door." Wolle concluded with one of his strongest affirmations of life. The review includes the following moving paragraph:

There was a pathetic side to yesterday's concert, which, even with the gratitude in every heart that there was so much to be thankful for, could not be forgotten. As many of the musicians played in borrowed clothes of all sorts that had been saved in the fire, so they were also playing on borrowed instruments. The concert master, G. Minetti, lost all of his violins, and he had some very valuable ones. His story could have been duplicated at almost every stand in the orchestra. Help is at hand now however, as the proceeds of yesterday's concert will be devoted to the purchase of new instruments for the unfortunate ones. It would not have been possible to have prepared a more fitting programme than that of yesterday.[28]

Very soon afterward, plans to build a concert hall for a Bach choir were discussed among the members of the Berkeley Chamber of Commerce.

Three years passed before Wolle began organizing a Bach choir to sing the *Mass* in 1909 at a Bach festival in the Greek Theater. Much as he had done in Bethlehem, he created a choir with singers from Berkeley and Oakland church

choirs, supplemented with singers from the university. The conductors, however, felt that Dr. Wolle was usurping their singers for his own gain.

In addition, he had difficulty making arrangements with the university
for the festival. The editor of the *Pacific Coast Musical Review* reported,
"Dr. Wolle approached the musical committee of the University to manage
the event. Even though the director would have received not more than
two hundred and fifty dollars and the balance would have gone to the
University, the committee refused to have anything to do with it."[29] The
editor continued, "Then Dr. Wolle asked for the Greek Theater, and here
too all kinds of difficulties were put in his way in setting a date. Indeed,
not until the last minute could Dr. Wolle set a date, thus preventing him
from advertising the event sufficiently ahead of time to do much good."[30]
The editor concluded "the University . . . had no faith in the success of the
Bach Festival."[31]

Without the support of the University of California, the *Musical Review*
music editor reported that "Dr. Wolle was forced to find a guarantee of twelve
hundred dollars personally. He went to a few friends who were not in the
Bach Choir who guaranteed to pay half of the deficit in case there would be
one, and Dr. Wolle would pay the other half."[32] If not the producer himself,
Dr. Wolle worked diligently with others in California to devise a broader plan
to finance a single large event.

In 1909 the San Francisco Bach Choir sang the *B Minor Mass*. Trumpets in
the forest behind the Greek Theater played Moravian chorales to announce the
festival. As in Bethlehem, "The third [chorale] continued its note unbroken and
became the opening chord of the great chorus proper."[33] The festival generated
rave reviews: "The Bach choir . . . proved itself the greatest musical institution
that has ever appeared before this community."[34] The event was a financial
success as well; in fact, there was a profit. A second festival was planned for
the following year, and the Wolle family left for a summer in Bethlehem.

In organizing a Bach Choir with a festival in the Greek Theater, Dr. Wolle
had hoped to quell the jealousies encountered in planning the Bach festival.
However, exactly because he had produced a profitable Bach festival, jealousies flared. In addition, he encountered greed and deception that he had never
experienced in Bethlehem. During his absence, resentments boiled over.

The intrigue began with a series of newspaper reports that Wolle had
resigned his University of California position, had left to seek a position in
Bethlehem, and would not be returning to California, all of which he denied
in a letter to the editor. As final proof, he stated he had purchased round trip
tickets when he'd left for Bethlehem with his family. Believing in Wolle's

defection, a faction of "disgruntled [choir] members met during Dr. Wolle's absence, organized and slated rules and bylaws, and rushed the matter through without giving the great body of the choir an opportunity to have a say."[35] When Wolle returned, he was informed, "he had no more authority in the management of the choir . . . and that an executive committee was to manage all festivals in the future."[36] He would be allowed to rehearse the choir and receive a salary of three thousand dollars; if there were no profit he would receive nothing. He could be replaced at any time.

Despite these personal affronts, Wolle conducted a second festival in 1910. Responding to the Second California Bach Festival in the *Pacific Coast Musical Review*, Alfred Metzger wrote, "Dr. Wolle stands before us as the only possible figure in the musical area of California to bring a great annual California Music Festival to a successful conclusion."[37] But this "Triumphant Success" was not at all happy for J. Fred. Wolle.

Back in Bethlehem, important people were eager for Wolle to return and reinstate The Bethlehem Bach Choir, and they were taking steps they hoped would bring him east. Charles Schwab himself, president of Bethlehem Steel Company, made contact with Wolle. In his 1918 history of The Bach Choir, Raymond Walters, a Lehigh administrator and close friend of J. Fred. Wolle, described the encounter:

> The resumption of the Bach Festivals at Lehigh University was due to Mr. Charles M. Schwab. While on a business trip to San Francisco, the steel-master went to Berkeley for one of Dr. Wolle's choral productions in the Greek Theater of the University of California. He had a chat with Dr. Wolle in which he assured him of his hearty support if he should decide to go back to the East. Now Bach, transplanted, had not flourished as in the soil of a community with musical traditions and resources like those of Bethlehem. Mr. Schwab's offer of cooperation, therefore, was a vital factor in causing Dr. Wolle to return.[38]

Schwab's cultural vision for Bethlehem, however, was very specific. Schwab had a vision of a community of the Bethlehems as an ideal industrial city, with homes, parks, libraries, education, art, and musical facilities that would be exceptional.[39] On another occasion he had expressed his community goal more generally, "to further the cause of music and to enable as many as possible to enjoy its pleasure and benefits is a duty incumbent upon all good citizens."[40] However, Schwab first needed to create the conditions that would make Bethlehem an international cultural center.

If Dr. Wolle would return to Bethlehem, revive the Bach Choir, and re-institute the Bach Festivals, Schwab proposed that he would underwrite half of any deficit that might occur and would muster the support of the New York music critics, for he knew them well. Finally, he could foresee a Bach Temple, not a Greek theater, constructed in Bethlehem with Bethlehem Steel.

In his history, *The Bethlehem Bach Choir*, Walters devoted a complete chapter to Charles Schwab. Drinker received only one paragraph. Walters consistently praised Schwab, yet understated Drinker's influence in bringing about Wolle's return.

Walters was more balanced in assessing the importance of the Cleavers, "Mr. and Mrs. Cleaver were initiators and leaders in the revival of the Bach Festivals, and their work in season and out of season has been a factor in the Choir's success beyond computation."[41] Further, Walters stated, "Public and musical spirit at their best were represented by the group of citizens who, upon the initiative of Mr. and Mrs. Albert N. Cleaver, reorganized the Bach Choir in October, 1911."[42] A Philadelphia editor stressed the group nature of what probably happened:

> Bethlehem, Pa., is noted for two things—its Bach Choir and its steel works. They are here named in the order of their importance—and we are inclined to think Mr. Schwab would not take issue with us in this. For he is so conscious of the power of music as a factor in life that in 1911 he headed the group of citizens of that lovely city which successfully lured J. Fred Wolle, former leader of the choir, to return from his position . . . in the University of California to resume his directorship of this world-famed music organization.[43]

In any event, Wolle's return to Bethlehem was not a Moravian plan. Any vacuum created in the church in 1905 when Brother Wolle left Bethlehem for Berkeley had been quickly filled. Wolle had been away only a few months when the pastor of Central Moravian Church recorded the progress of the new organist, Albert J. Rau, with optimism:

> Many fears have also been entertained concerning the music, now that Bro. Wolle is no longer here. Under the direction of Br. Albert Rau, however, a fine large choir has been gathered, very few of the old singers were absent. With this was a strong orchestra which has volunteered for service.[44]

By Easter, the most demanding time for a Moravian Church organist, the pastor noted that Rau's acceptance by the congregation was complete. A year after Bro. Wolle's departure, the pastor described the healthy state of Moravian musical activity:

> In place of the former Bach Choir there are now a number of smaller amateur organizations which are studying music, and if these are rightly led they will perhaps accomplish as much in their way as was the more finished choir of singers which has gone to pieces since Bro. Wolle left for the University of California.[45]

Mrs. Linderman and J. Fred./Mr. and Mrs. Cleaver, bottom left

Later in the same year a "Bach Chorus" actually performed, "a delightful evening, using altogether the works of Bach." Rau probably conducted. Significantly, the performance was in the chapel of the Moravian Sunday School with no national pretensions.[46]

Rau, who was now in charge of music at Central Moravian Church, discovered the music of past Moravians. Rau's unexpected discovery was to have national significance when he became intensely interested in the hundreds of music manuscripts in the church attic. Here was evidence of a great American musical past associated directly with Bethlehem. He began conducting the music he found and became convinced the tradition must be revived. The revival began with a performance of Karl Henrich Graun's *The Passion*, only a few months before J. Fred. Wolle had arrived back in Bethlehem in 1911.

The program's resemblance to the first Bethlehem Bach Festival was striking. Rau had included the presence of the trombones, congregational singing, and an American premiere. That service, however, was free of the problems that had plagued Wolle's past Festivals; Rau had no worries about ticket sales, disrespectful listeners, critical disputes, rearranging the sanctuary, and professional singers and instrumentalists. The service, with a collection to cover the costs, received a spirited review in *The Moravian*. "The rendition was a success in every way; . . . every seat of the large auditorium was taken.[47]

It was not necessary to perform the music of Bach for Bethlehem to become a center of sacred music. Bethlehem would resume its rightful place in American music history by reviving Moravian music. Had J. Fred. Wolle not left Bethlehem, the focus would have remained the music of Bach, the Bach Choir, and the Bach Festivals. Rau had uncovered the rich music heritage of eighteenth-century Bethlehem. That music was quickly absorbed into the American Colonial revival. Today the two rivers of music run side by side in Bethlehem, each impacting American music in distinctive ways.

As Rau replaced Wolle in Central Moravian Church, so T. Edgar Shields took over Professor Wolle's positions as Lehigh University organist and choral professor. Shields also conducted the Oratorio Society, a choral group with no direct Moravian connections. It was supported by the residents who were the wealthy industrial, business, and professional elite associated with steel, cement, railroads, banking, and Lehigh University. Dr. Henry Drinker as president of the Oratorio Society made it possible for the group to perform in Lehigh's Packer Memorial Church. The connection between this choral group and Lehigh University through Drinker and Shields proved crucial when Wolle re-instituted the Bach Choir and its festivals.

Following Wolle's departure for California, Ruth Doster conducted a small study group, played solo recitals, and performed piano concertos with the Lehigh Valley Orchestra. After first winning a divorce from her wealthy attorney husband, Gen. Henry Doster, who had abused her, she married her stepson. But after a decade of prominence in Bethlehem, she left in disgrace. The couple moved to Manhattan. Her husband disappeared in Mexico and she committed suicide.[48]

Wolle was aware that these changes had occurred during his six-year absence. Only by returning to this changed community and planning to re-instate the Bach Choir and Bach Festivals could he find out if there was a future for him in Bethlehem. He must have been aware of the uncertainty. His nephew reported, "Yet at the end of six years, when his sabbatical came up, he and his family returned without hesitation to Bethlehem."[49] Had he not done so, it is doubtful there would have been a Bach Choir in Bethlehem again.

As the Wolles traveled back to Bethlehem from California, Dr. Wolle considered how little had gone as he'd hoped. The California Bach festivals had not materialized, he had begun his tenure conducting works of composers other than Bach, and he had conducted no Bach choral works for the first four years. The two Bach festivals he had struggled to organize had been unqualified successes, but he had had to deal with strife caused by other choral directors. Then, prospects for a festival hall were abandoned, and he was asked to resign from his church position in Berkeley because he'd replaced an entrenched vocal quartet with a volunteer choir. These events were reported as a "scandal" in Bethlehem newspapers.

In his 1972 memoir, *A Moravian Heritage*, Wolle's nephew Francis provided additional reasons for his uncle's decision to leave California:

> The academic atmosphere was alien to him and on the whole he did not care for it . . . "How do you lecture about music?" he would ask, "and for what are you supposed to give grades? . . . Working in and with music, singing or playing an instrument—in this way only does one get to the heart of what music is all about."
>
> His greatest irritation was "the pelicans," the ladies of the town, who came as auditors with no intention of doing even the slightest amount of class work . . . Yet "the pelicans" became his chief worshippers, because he could not turn off his dynamic charm.[50]

The nephew's account continues:

> To cap his initial disillusion his twelve-year old daughter Gretchen developed tubercular hip and was in bed and . . . at the height of her illness came the crashing San Francisco earthquake. It disrupted communication and caused great stress and anxiety . . . In the midst of this Fred's mother died . . . but because of his daughter's illness and because he was deep in the final rehearsals

for a choral concert, he could not make the long train trip across the country for her funeral. These shocks produced in the family a mind-set against San Francisco, so that they never accepted even the climate.[51]

A sabbatical enabled the Wolles to return to Bethlehem. As they traveled east, Wolle gave organ recitals in San Francisco, San Jose, and Chicago, then Winston-Salem and Washington, D.C.

Whether Wolle was deeply satisfied with his achievements is unknown; he never referred to them. At forty-eight years of age, he now had endless personal and social resources to draw on. That he did this so brilliantly is the continuation of this story. When Dr. Wolle was honored later at a banquet in Bethlehem, a Choir member revealed:

> many [in Bethlehem] were anxiously hoping that the day might come when he might return, and the festivals resumed. At the end of that period their wishes were gratified, and through the efforts of Mr. and Mrs. A. M. Cleaver, Mr. C. M. Schwab, and others in the old Bach Choir, a reorganization was effected.[52]

NOTES

1. "Wolle's Hopes High," *San Francisco Call*, 19 September 1905.
2. Wolle speeches, ABCB.
3. Ibid.
4. Ibid.
5. Ibid.
6. Ibid.
7. Ibid.
8. Ibid.
9. Ibid.
10. Ibid.
11. Ibid.
12. Ibid.
13. Ibid.
14. Ibid.
15. Ibid.
16. Ibid.
17. *San Francisco Call*, 24 September 1905.
18. "Berkeley Speech," Box 1, folder, ABCB. Wolle is inconsistent in his use of a capital letter or a small letter for the word minor. While I have remained true to the source, I use the present title as *Mass in B Minor.*
19. "Symphonies Out of Doors," *(Brooklyn, NY) Eagle*, 24 March 1906.
20. Ibid.

21. *San Francisco Chronicle*, 30 November 1905.

22. "Wolle Will Organize an Orchestra," *San Francisco Call*, 30 November 1905.

23. "Symphony Concerts at the University," *San Francisco Call*, 3 December 1905.

24. Ibid.

25. "7,000 in Hearst Theater," *San Francisco Examiner*, 2 March 1906.

26. "Wagner Program a Great Triumph," *San Francisco Call*, 13 April 1906.

27. "Thousands Hear Last Symphony," *San Francisco Chronicle*, 16 May 1906.

28. Ibid.

29. "Dr. Wolle and the Bach Choir," *Pacific Coast Musical Review*, 4 September 1909, 4.

30. Ibid.

31. Ibid.

32. Ibid.

33. *San Francisco Chronicle*, 23 April 1909.

34. Ibid.

35. "Dr. Wolle and the Bach Choir," *Pacific Coast Musical Review*, 4 September 1909.

36. Ibid.

37. "Triumphant Success of Second California Bach Festival," *California Music Review*, 28 May 1910.

38. Walters, *Bethlehem Bach Choir*, 90.

39. Ibid., 200.

40. Ibid., 229–30.

41. Ibid., 247.

42. Ibid., 91.

43. "The Boast of Bethlehem," *(Philadelphia) North American*, 3 January 1933.

44. "Official Diary," 3 December 1905, MABP.

45. Ibid., 2 April 1907.

46. Ibid., 23 November 1907.

47. *The Moravian*, 19 April 1911.

48. Doster Family papers from Dorothy Doster (granddaughter of Ruth Doster), now in possession of the author.

49. Wolle, *Moravian Heritage*, 44.

50. Ibid., 43.

51. Ibid., 43.

52. "The Bach Choir," Speech by Howard J. Weigner, Bethlehem, PA, 9 August 1932, Wolle Box 4, D 16, ABCB.

Chapter 9

Renewing the Bach Choir in Bethlehem

1912–1913

The Wolles moved into their Bethlehem house, now furnished with Oriental objects and art that Mrs. Wolle had bought in San Francisco. Aided by his supporters, Wolle began doing the five things he'd determined necessary to bring Bach back to Bethlehem: organizing a new choir; assembling an orchestra and selecting soloists; planning programs and schedules along the lines of the once-popular Bach Festivals; creating a governing board; and finding an organist position to support him, and his wife and daughter.

Given the many deep changes in Bethlehem during his absence, Wolle established The Second Bethlehem Bach Choir rather easily and graciously. That Bethlehem was basically free of the jealousies that had racked the California Bach Choir was extremely significant. Wolle did not have to rely on established area church choirs. Instead, The Oratorio Society of the Bethlehems, the chorus formed from the first Bach Choir when Wolle had left Bethlehem, agreed to reorganize as a Bach Choir with Wolle as its conductor.

The Oratorio Society was a secular, community chorus with singers drawn from a wide area. Its center was still in South Bethlehem, and the group rehearsed and performed in Lehigh University's Packer Church. The conductor was T. Edgar Shields. A Philadelphia reporter wrote of Shields' support, "With a spirit that deserves praise as all too rare, Mr. Shields' organization offered its services as a nucleus round which Dr. Wolle might build a reorganized and greater Bach Choir."[1] Wolle asked Shields to be the Festival organist, and he was pleased to accept that position and remained in it throughout Wolle's life. Shields also continued as chapel organist at Lehigh University.

The new Bach Choir began rehearsals in September 1911 in the Moravian Seminary for Women. The location was offered free of charge as the Moravian contribution to the Bach Choir enterprise.

Next, he set about to resume the Festivals. In early October he asked the Elders of Central Moravian Church for permission to hold a Bach Festival in the sanctuary. The church's Board of Elders' secretary reported, "After careful consideration [the Elders resolved] the church shall not be used for any concert or festival to which admission is charged."[2] The decision was impressively, indeed cleverly, stated. It struck at the essential point. The Moravian sanctuary could not be bought, by anyone, under any circumstances. While Wolle's request precipitated the decision, it was not directed at the Bach Festivals per se. Wolle, however, was stunned, feeling the Elders had "repudiated him and his work."[3] He was deeply hurt by their response.

While their public statement was objective, Wolle's nephew Francis recollected that the Moravians were not at all pleased with his return and had given him anything but a pleasant welcome. Albert Rau quite naturally did not want to surrender his church music position to a returning wanderer, no matter how famous he might be. Nor did the Elders want Rau to leave. Wolle was offered, and accepted, a position as organist at an Allentown church, assuring him an annual salary.

In the Moravian Elders' decision, the Bethlehem social and industrial elite saw an opportunity to realize their plan for a revival of a Bach Choir and a Bach Festival. In frequent professional and social contact, this group was used to working together and was experienced in making far-reaching decisions to create highly productive organizations. They knew exactly what had to be done so the Choir and Festivals could become self-governing and financially secure. Using their organizational skills and prior experience funding music organizations, they created the structure to make it possible. They envisioned the entire structure of the Choir organized on a business model, within which contributing guarantors would become a main sustaining element. This group had developed the guarantor system to finance the Lehigh Valley Symphony Orchestra founded in 1906, with Charles Schwab as one of the orchestra's guarantors, and Wolle had developed a similar system in California. Further, the orchestra was governed by a board with Schwab a member, within which was an Executive Committee. The guarantor system and the board organization were replicated exactly in the renewed Bach Choir.[4]

Only ten days after the Moravian Elders' meeting, these visionaries formed "an organization for the rendering of Bach music under the direction of Prof. J. Fred. Wolle."[5] Members of this governing board met in the "parlors of the Moravian Seminary,"[6] parlors that still exist in the building where J. Fred. was born.

Dr. Clewell, president of the Moravian Seminary for Women, and Dr. W. L. Estes, the prominent local surgeon of national reputation, moved that a "permanent Organization be formed."[7] Dr. Drinker was "unanimously elected President," and the name of the organization was "decided upon as The Bach Choir." The Board brilliantly formulated a concise purpose: "the rendering of Bach's Music under the direction of Prof. J. Fred. Wolle."[8] Convinced that the Bach Choir and Festival were cultural assets to Lehigh University, Dr. Drinker proposed that the University host the Festivals at no cost. Thus, the Bach Festival in Bethlehem was assured a permanent home in Packer Memorial Church on Lehigh's campus. Bach's music would not be secularized because it would be performed in a church.

The Board established four committees: Entertainment, Press; Publicity, Ticket, and Membership. A Program Committee was added at the next meeting. Cleaver and Dr. Estes were appointed to draw up a constitution and bylaws, and an Executive Committee was directed to plan a 1912 spring Bach Festival. Mr. Frank Hoch, cement company manager and publisher, agreed to be the secretary. This group of committed, innovative men and women proceeded to design and implement an ingenious financial process enlisting guarantors who would pledge to underwrite a festival. They had proceeded graciously and comprehensively. The typed minutes, only one-and-a-half pages, became the foundation for the Bach revival in Bethlehem and the first permanent and longest lasting Bach Choir in America.

In January, the Executive Committee agreed upon dates for a two-day Bach Festival. The numbering of the Festivals was continued from when they had ceased; the re-instituted Festival became the "Seventh Bach Festival." Wolle's salary was "fixed at $3000."[9] Again he had a Bach Choir, a Festival, an organization, a conductor's post, and a church position.

The press's reaction to Wolle's return to Bethlehem and his plan to re-instate the Bach Festivals was enthusiastic. The *Pacific Coast Musical Review* quoted the *Musical Courier*:

> Dr. J. Fred. Wolle has made an announcement which will be hailed with rejoicing among all educated musicians and music lovers. The Bach festivals at Bethlehem, Pa., which were abandoned when Dr. Wolle accepted the post of musical director at the University of California, are to be re-established in the charming Pennsylvania town. Dr. Wolle himself publishes this glad news to the music world. Nothing that has occurred musically in this country ever appealed more to the elevated taste of the musical fraternity than the Bach festivals formerly given under the direction of Dr. Wolle.[10]

A Buffalo paper reported, "One of the most welcome announcements of the present time is that Dr. Wolle has decided to return to Bethlehem, Pa., and will resume the Bach festivals that made Bethlehem one of the musical Meccas of the country as long as it lasted."[11] Fellow musicians praised his return as well. The assistant conductor of the Philharmonic Society of New York, W. H. Humiston, wrote:

> The musical world is to be congratulated on the return of Mr. Wolle to Bethlehem, from California, progressive as it is is not the place for an exclusive propaganda. Mr. Wolle's heart is in the Bach work and can exert a much wider influence in that way than in any other. And the Bethlehem Bach Festivals can be much more far-reaching in influence than any professorship in any university in the land.[12]

Charles Schwab's promise begged the question, "How was the other money to be raised?" Ticket sales would have to be the main source. In an announcement of the Festival, executive secretary Frank Hoch stated, "Taking into consideration the seating capacity of the auditorium and the number of sessions to be given, the prices of the tickets will be so gauged that if a reasonable number of seats be sold, the festival will bear its own expenses."[13] The Board moved to make the Festival as self-supporting as possible.

The Bach organization's system of guarantors completely encapsulated the philosophy of The Bach Choir and the Festivals. Wolle proposed the plan that he had devised to pay expenses not covered by ticket revenue when he had formed the California Bach Choir. Hoch explained how the plan would work in Bethlehem:

> The cost of this festival will be about five thousand dollars . . . it is deemed necessary to secure a Guarantee Fund of at least three thousand dollars. We must, therefore, find sufficient numbers of persons who will, in varying amounts, guarantee this fund, to be called for only in the case the receipts of the Society do not meet the expenses, and then only in the proportion that each guarantee bears to the whole amount.[14]

By February total pledges from guarantors amounted to more than expected. Thus, including his salary, the financial success of the re-established Bach Festival was assured even before tickets went on sale. The treasurer's report for the year 1911–1912 revealed, however, that "expenditures exceeded income."[15] The Festival was not self-supporting, so the guarantor system was implemented. The guarantors were assessed one-half of the deficit. Schwab paid the other half. He now joined with others as one of a number of guarantors making his original *carte blanche* offer no longer relevant and perfectly satisfying his personal desire for shared community responsibility.

The guarantor system spread the financial risk like stock investment, but it did more. In a brilliantly capitalistic way guarantors made the Bethlehem

Bach Festival an American festival. Unlike festivals in Europe sponsored by the state or royal patronage, the ordinary citizen was offered an opportunity to finance the Bach-for-every-American enterprise, the very reason for The Bach Choir and the Bach Festivals. The Board's financial plan also recognized the year-long efforts of the choir members, "who, working hard throughout the entire season preparing for the festival, should be relieved of any possible financial burden," though singers did purchase their own music which they proudly retained, often having it autographed by soloists, Dr. Wolle, and fellow choir members—in many cases passing it on to their children.

As Dr. Wolle rehearsed The Bach Choir preparing the singers for a special Bach Festival, a draft of the constitution and bylaws was discussed by the Board on 18 November 1911. The draft expanded the original constitution significantly, formalizing the division of power within the organization and proposing a broader mission for The Choir. Overall responsibility lay in the hands of a Board of Managers comprised of elected members. Appointing a musical director and fixing his compensation was handled by the Board of Managers. Within this Board was an Executive Committee of officers and committee chairs. While most decisions were placed in the hands of the Executive Committee, four times a year the committee reported to the Board of Managers and requested action from the members when necessary.

In addition to internal matters, there was a national mission: "To endeavor to establish in other cities and towns in the country, auxiliary Bach Choir Societies in order to disseminate knowledge of our Society and its purpose, and to obtain the good influence and support of all music lovers wherever they may be located."[16] The formation of these "auxiliary Bach Choir Societies" makes clear that from its inception, the influence of the society had been envisioned to include the nation. This was an American society for the promotion of Bach's choral and instrumental music, including the works of other composers, among all classes of people.[17] After an article-by-article discussion, the document was adopted, a document which served the society with only minor amendments throughout J. Fred. Wolle's life.

One great concern remained: the quality of the orchestra. The orchestra in prior Bach Festivals had always drawn negative criticism from the critics. Now that the Bach Festivals were no longer held in Central Moravian Church, it was possible to hire a professional orchestra. Wolle voiced his concern to Ruth Linderman, his extremely wealthy neighbor. One day, according to his nephew, she said to Wolle, "You mustn't worry so much about the orchestra. Engage the services of the Philadelphia Symphony, and I'll pay for the final rehearsals they will have in Bethlehem with the Choir."[18] With her annual gift of $1,500,

Mrs. Linderman assured the overall musical quality of the Festivals. Her support was the beginning of her involvement with The Bach Choir. She became its first woman president and was crucial in the Festival's survival following Wolle's death. Thanks to Mrs. Linderman the instrumentalists were recruited from members of the Philadelphia Orchestra, one of America's finest symphonies.

The Seventh Festival program continued traditions from prior Festivals. The *Mass* was the culmination. The Moravian Church Trombone Choir played chorales from Lehigh's Packer Church tower before each session and then "stationed near the organ played the simple melody of a hymn and the echoes had not died away when the choir, with a thrilling burst of sound, struck the first words of the noble invocation, 'Kyrie Eleison!'"[19] There was no applause. One of the cantatas, BWV 53 (no longer considered authentic), was repeated from a previous Festival. Three of the four soloists had sung before. The cantatas were sung in English, the *Mass* in Latin.

Prior innovations became traditions. The Festival spanned two days in May. The music on the first day varied with pieces selected and integrated by Wolle. Three of four cantatas, BWV 82, BWV 115, and BWV 180, were probably American premieres. A series of chorales was also sung.

Wolle left no written record of why he'd selected these four cantatas to re-instate the Bach Festivals. However, he left a coherent spiritual and historical message through his selection as in previous Festivals. The Bach Festivals were sacred Christian events taking place in a church, but no longer bound by a specific liturgy, exactly as Albert Schweitzer had proposed.

Two cantatas were sung in the afternoon on Friday, 31 May 1912, and two more in the evening. The spiritual and personal message was clear: rejoicing following adversity. The first cantata was "It is Enough," BWV 82 for chorus and solo. Schweitzer described this cantata as expressing, "The heavenly homesickness of the old man who is already detached from all the things of this world. Inexpressible joy wells up . . . ecstatic joy."[20] Bach so loved one of the arias, that he transcribed it for his wife, Anna Magdelena. This cantata expressed the joy felt by Wolle and his family, now safe and permanently home.

He wrote to Leipzig for copies from Bach's manuscript. "It is Enough" was sent on the RMS Titanic. "When the fate of the great vessel and the little package for Bethlehem became known to the Bach followers, they were in a quandary. Luckily a copy of this particular orchestral score was located in New York and copies of it were made in time for the Festival."[21]

The chorale, "World Farewell!" concluded this cantata. Breaking with tradition, it was sung unaccompanied, "with impressive effect, displaying what Dr. Wolle had been able to accomplish, particularly in shading."[22] The other cantata chosen for the first afternoon was "Christian Stand with Sword in Hand," BWV 115. Two independent chorales from other cantatas harmonized by Bach concluded the afternoon. The second chorale, "In dulce jubilo," ended in loud praise of God's grace.

Singing individual chorales as self-sufficient pieces of music is evidence of how creatively, forcefully, and indelibly Dr. Wolle superimposed the "individual interpretation" he had praised in Berkeley onto the new Bach Festivals. Bach had not intended the chorales to stand alone; they were part of larger choral works. Bach had selected existing melodies with texts that expressed the meaning of a cantata or a Passion. These melodies were familiar to members of Bach's Lutheran congregation. Further, Bach harmonized the melodies in the elaborate Baroque contrapuntal/harmonic style.

Chorales had always been the foundation of Moravian worship. So, for the Festival, it was natural that Wolle extract them from their Bach sources and group them to express a coherent meaning culminating with the Reformation hymn, "God's kingdom ours remaineth."

Further personalizing this innovation, Wolle had The Bach Choir sing "World Farewell!" *a cappella*. Bach always accompanied the chorales with instruments, but Wolle heard these compositions in a different way. For him they could become purely unaccompanied vocal music in the long tradition of European sacred choral music. He thus was tapping into deep vital roots of Christian sacred musical expression as his re-formed Choir was singing alone under his direction. In later Festivals, he repeated "World Farewell!" as a memorial to individuals who had died during the year, a practice that continues.

Listeners and even music critics praised his interpretation. "The effect was stupendous!" One listener wrote, "The tears came and I no longer held them back." A music critic reported, "Finally there were the chorales. In its share, the seated chorus, singing without accompaniment, electrified the audience with a chant of the most ethereal and delicate pianissimo, so exquisite and pure that, upon many requests, Dr. Wolle began the evening performance with the repetition of the verse."[23] In a review of the Festival, a reporter quoted a prominent Philadelphia musical critic who "stated in all his long experience he had never heard such excellent shading."[24]

For the opening evening Wolle selected a cantata that was an American premiere, "Soul, Array Thyself with Gladness," BWV 180. The second cantata, "Strike, Oh Strike, Long-looked-for Hour," BWV 53, was one of his favorites. He had conducted it in 1903 and in the Bach Cycle in 1905. As he conducted, "The entire chorus noted every movement of Dr. Wolle's hand."[25]

Again, he incorporated five independent Chorales to conclude the evening joyously and prepare the listeners for the *Mass* the following day. One critic noted significantly that grouping the chorales together echoed a Moravian

"Singstunde . . . sung with all the power and force of the choir and congregation. Dr. Wolle presided at the organ during the singing of the chorales and gave a delightful exhibition of his mastery of the instrument."[26] Finally, Wolle may well have shown his own mastery by improvising connections between the chorales.

The printed program featured a portrait of Bach. The Moravian Trombone Choir, playing in the belfry of Central Moravian Church, was on the back page of the cover. Along with the cantata-texts and chorale notation, the program listed the members of The Bach Choir, the names of the trombonists, the orchestra members, the officers, and the Festival committees. An innovation was to insert the titles of previous works and the performance dates. These are still included in Festival programs.

The Bach Choir and the Bach Festival were now fully organized. In eleven months' time everything required was successfully brought together, managed, performed, reviewed, and critiqued. Everyone involved in any way with the Bach Choir enterprise moved confidently forward planning for an Eighth Bach Festival in 1913. On the evening of 29 May 1912, The Choir elected ten of its members to a Board of Managers. Among them was Miss Agnes Wolle, J. Fred.'s cousin, who taught music at the Women's Seminary. Following the Festival the full Board of twenty-three Managers was elected including Charles Schwab and Ruth Linderman. A secretary was appointed to assist Frank Hoch, the executive committee secretary. Thus, the society employed its first staff member.

At the conclusion of the 1913 Bach Festival, the future of The Bach Choir and its Festival in Bethlehem seemed most secure when word came that Wolle had been offered an out-of-town position. A Boston church needed a top-ranking choirmaster, and in the wake of Wolle's triumphant Bach Festival, he had been asked to take the prestigious post. His initial reaction to the offer is not known, but it is clear that he did not refuse immediately. He let it be known that he had received an offer that was tempting.

Friends and leaders of The Bethlehem Choir reacted forcefully. Within only a few days, a plan to raise a $1 million endowment fund "for the purpose of placing the Bach Choir on a permanent basis"[27] was announced. The *Bethlehem Times* reported that "it was felt that Dr. Wolle should not be permitted to leave Bethlehem and accept the flattering offer at Boston, but that all efforts should be put forth to keep him here, thereby insuring the permanency of the Bach Choir."[28]

The Executive Committee took more time to react, but finally voted to raise Wolle's salary by $2,000. At a later meeting of the committee, Charles Schwab, president of The Bach Choir, appointed a committee to look into the matter of a suitable site for a Bach Choir Hall. Schwab's offer made national news. Had he gotten the idea from Andrew Carnegie who had built Carnegie Hall in New York City for the Oratorio Society of New York? *The Press (Philadelphia)* reported "if the people provided the site he would erect the building, so that his famous steel company band, The Bach Choir, and other organizations would have an ideal place to give concerts."[29] Though it was never built, Schwab remained committed to his idea for a local concert hall on a smaller scale. He had one constructed on land belonging to the Moravian Church that was used over fifty years for band and orchestra concerts but not for The Bach Choir. It was simply too small for The Bach Festivals.

Wolle did not accept the Boston offer, and the next twenty years became a time of unleashed creative energy, urgency, and fulfillment, immense success, and financial prosperity. While he remained the incandescent vortex, "Bach in Bethlehem" moved its focus from The Bach Choir to "Its Bach Festival." Working unflaggingly, The Bach Choir, Wolle, and his committed Board, focused on making Bethlehem the center of the Bach movement in America.

NOTES

1. "Bach Festival at Bethlehem Has an Impressive Revival," *Public Ledger (Philadelphia)*, 2 June 1912, Scrapbook #1, 88, ABCB.

2. "Minutes of the Board of Elders of the Congregation of Bethlehem, Pa. Volume opened 1877, October 9." Insert at p. 281, MABP.

3. Wolle, *Moravian Heritage,* 44.

4. "Lehigh Valley Symphony Orchestra," *Bethlehem Globe*, 8 December 1910.

5. "Minutes of the Executive Committee Meetings, 19 October 1911–May 1938," 19 October 1911, ABCB.

6. Ibid.

7. Ibid.

8. Ibid.

9. Ibid., 20 January 1912.

10. *Pacific Coast Musical Review*, July 1911.

11. "Buffalo," Wolle California Box, ABCB.

12. Walters, *Bach Choir of Bethlehem*, 102.

13. "Bach Choir scrapbook #1," n.p., ABCB.

14. Ibid.

15. "Minutes of the Executive Meetings," 17 September 1912, ABCB.

16. Ibid.

17. "Minutes of the Executive Boards," 18 November 1911, ABCB.

18. Wolle, *Moravian Heritage*, 44.

19. Ibid., 97–98.

20. Schweitzer, *Bach* 2:156.

21. Walters, *Bach Choir of Bethlehem*, 102.

22. "The Two Day Session of The Bach Choir," *Bethlehem Times*, 1 June 1912.

23. Walters, *Bach Choir of Bethlehem*, 97.

24. "The Two-day Session," *Bethlehem Times*, 1 June 1912.

25. Ibid.

26. Ibid.

27. "Bach Festival at Bethlehem Has An Impressive Revival," *Public Ledger (Philadelphia)*, 2 June 1912, Scrapbook #1, 88, ABCB.

28. "Minutes of the Board of Elders, PS. Volume opened 1877, October 9." Insert at p. 281, MABP.

29. Wolle, *Moravian Heritage*, 44.

Chapter 10

An American Center for Bach

1914

Renewal of The Bach Choir and its Festivals attracted hundreds of Bach lovers who traveled to Bethlehem. They were proof of Wolle's national reputation and of the drawing power of his innovative interpretations:

> There came in force pupils and teachers of the New England Conservatory of Music, at Boston; the Conservatory of Upsala, Michigan; Madame Bowman's School in Montreal; the Comstock Music School of New York; Miss Lankenau's School; Madame Froelich's Music School at Harrisburg, and forty-four other similar institutions and conservatories.[1]

For those attending the Festivals, then as today, the surroundings were an integral part of the experience. Critic after critic described the setting: the wooded campus of Lehigh University only a few blocks from the blast furnaces of Bethlehem Steel, seemingly a world apart. People stood in rapt attention at the sound of the trombones playing chorales from the tower of Packer Memorial Church, once considered the most beautiful church in Pennsylvania:

> And, now, as 4 o'clock on Friday afternoon draws near, the white long needles of sunlight pierce the canopying green of gently swaying and venerable trees, the pilgrims gather in reverent and expectant groups about the church . . . Presently from high up in the ivy-draped church tower is heard the trombone choir . . . as in the ancient voices float out on the springtime air in a sublime Bach chorale; a chorale perennial with grave and lofty beauty—"From highest heaven to earth I come."[2]

A Bach Choir historian described the experience:

Packer Memorial Church, Lehigh University

None of the splendid concert halls of Europe can vie with the Packer Memorial Church on the Pennsylvania hillside as a temple for the music of Bach. There, with the open windows framed in green and the breezes fresh from the mountains, we leave the dust and noises of the city far behind us and are transplanted into a slower-going and poetic world which seems more in accord with the age in which Bach lived.[3]

Those who had come for a weekend in the spring to hear Bach as interpreted by Dr. Wolle were deeply moved by his expression of Bach's spiritual message, and in the background was an expectant curiosity. What innovation was Dr. Wolle presenting this year? What delights await us in this Festival? He never disappointed his audience. The music of Bach spread from Wolle's subtle hands as if newly formed.

Wolle shaped Bach's music into a personal spiritual message. His musical artistry moved an admirer to write to Wolle, "The spirit of the performance (and that means your deep devotion to Bach and his religious ideal) was so overpowering, that I find it difficult to adjust myself to every day surroundings this morning. The church before the beginning, with the blessing of the chorale above our heads was most inspiring."[4]

Wolle gave Bach's text special emphasis through dynamic shading. If loudness made a word more expressive than softness, he selected loudness. When slowing the tempo increased the expressiveness and made Bach's emotional meaning more explicit, he slowed the tempo. An emotionally moved Festival patron expressed his feeling in a note to Wolle:

> I am on the train en route to New York following the wonderful yearly treat and inspiration that the Bach Festival always proves to be. There are really no words to describe the glories of this year's drink at the fountain-head and I wish I could find words to adequately thank you. It is a perfect miracle that you and your creation exist where some of us can experience it. I must record again my unbounded joy and satisfaction in your moderate tempi. It makes the music mean so much more, and no other conductor of Bach that I hear ever comes near to you in this respect.[5]

If singing to the accompaniment that Bach composed was not powerful enough, Wolle silenced the orchestra. To control every nuance of Bach's text and music, he had arias sung not by individuals as Bach had written them, but by an entire section of The Choir. Grouping cantatas according to their spiritual message for each Festival made them powerfully consistent. Even though Bach had written the cantatas for specific Sunday services, Wolle used the cantatas for another purpose. Rather than presenting them as one part of a specific sacred service, he made a number of cantatas into one complete expressive service. The effect was overpowering:

> What an experience to hear Ein' feste Burg for the first time—the wonder of the interpretation of that first chorus will not fade. And the grandeur; appealing beauty of the Magnificat! The "Before Thy Throne" was heavenly. It was a long time before I realized that the unusual beauty of the string tone was due to the fusion of the humming voices. I could go on describing my thrill—it was so often that I felt moved to tears.[6]

Another homeward bound Festival patron wrote how moved he had been:

> I will tell you anyhow of one of my impressions and it came very clearly—It was on Friday and it was the second thing that was sung—a choral[e] I guess you call it—which was sung in harmony and very softly and slowly and sustained so that there was no break; but one line just melted into the next—and the words were all about the joys that were awaiting us when we pass on to the Heavenly Kingdom. The whole effect was so exquisite that I had to take out my handkerchief which is a thing that is very rare with me I assure you because as we get along on life's road we cannot get the thrills that came quite often in our more tender years. This one thing alone was enough to repay me for going to Bethlehem.[7]

While Wolle's innovations disturbed some critics, other critics were enthralled:

Ah, those N.Y. "critics"! I only read one account, that of Downes in the N.Y. Times. I sat next to him during the concerts and we were together a good deal Friday evening. He is a nice fellow (and, I take it, a poor musician) but seems to think that unless you only say something derogatory of a performance you are no "critic" . . . One of the critics on my left, during one of the performances, literally "gave it up" (to follow the score). Leaning back, as if enchanted, he whispered, "My God—such virtuosity! It is too much, too overwhelming!"[8]

Amy Beach, one of the greatest nineteenth-century American composers, was exalted. She wrote telling him so:

Dear Dr. Wolle, After ten days of absence from Bethlehem I find myself still under the spell which you and your noble co-workers wove about us all at the Festival . . . Although my expectations had been raised to the highest power, I found what you gave us so far above their great technical perfection. As long as I may live, I shall never forget the "Sanctus," which, as you gave it, carried me into the Very Presence, among the angels and archangels bowing before Him.[9]

Wolle readily adapted the Bach Festivals to Lehigh University's Packer Memorial Church. Nearly every report lauded the new Festival venue as superior to the site of the original Bach Festivals. One person attending was particularly detailed and poetic in her praise:

Language seems futile and bromidic. You can only feel - - - - clear to the core of you. And all through the night. And the next day, the feeling stays and makes you want to be quiet and alone,—to remember. The tilted stained glass windows, showing in the sunlight green outside. The huge hushed audience, filling every space, even the transept steps and the open doorways, dark heads against the velvet lawn beyond. Vibrant stillness, almost palpable, into which, the music flows . . . And Dr. Wolle,—the amazing soul of it all! The choir is his own live instrument with which he lovingly recreates Bach's music,—organ, orchestra, chorus, all fused together by his long sensitive fingers, guiding the marvelous harmonies by his direct touch—no baton—nothing but himself,—and he is so small and unassuming, so uncommanding to the outward eye. A miracle! Tenderly he bends over his instrument and guides its wondrously co-ordinated vibrations. Such speaking powerful hands, expressing the whole gamut of human emotion . . . God bless Bach and Bethlehem and all that combines to reproduce this marvelous moment in May of every year.[10]

Wolle's entire life was devoted to making all of Bach's music accessible to everyone. Armed with this belief he performed Bach's organ works throughout America his whole life. He gave an entire Bach organ recital and the American premiere of Bach's *Goldberg Variations* at the St. Louis

World's Fair in 1904. People attending the fair enthusiastically applauded. When he conducted Bach's *Mass in B Minor* in California, seven thousand people attended. He transported his Bach message to Carnegie Hall, to the Academy of Music in Philadelphia, to the exhibition hall in Atlantic City, to soldiers in Allentown, to politicians in Washington D.C. Year after year thousands attended the Bethlehem Bach Festivals. Attendee Isabel Pennypacker expressed what the Festivals stood for beyond Bethlehem:

> The Bach Festival has taken rank as the most important event in the American musical world. If we measure greatness by high intelligence, by difficulties overcome, by skill and spirit, then the Festival becomes one of the nation's greatest products.[11]

The Ninth Festival (1914) demonstrated the extremes of Wolle's control of the choir. The Festival opened with the motet "Sing ye to the Lord a new-made song," BWV 225. He had premiered this motet for double chorus to American audiences in 1904. His philosophy of interpretation was now totally grounded in years of experience and he had already expressed the idea that if a choir knew the music well enough, the result would be an interpretation that went beyond the need for a conductor. That was achieved in this Festival. A Philadelphia critic described the effect in the opening session on Tuesday. "For a long time yesterday, in the midst of the motet, Dr. Wolle omitted all visible signs of direction, while the complex maneuvers of at least eight separate vocal parts held their perfect array and, moreover, rang out anon a fervent accent here, or moved through a long swell of increasing volume."[12]

The next day, he led The Bach Choir in his most daring innovation. He used no soloists in the Saturday singing of the *Mass*. All solo parts were sung by the members of each section. "Personally, I hope you'll always have the *Mass* done without soloists," wrote one admirer.[13] Thus, he had offered conclusive proof to the musical world of his total control of every detail of Bach's music, as well as the choir's complete responsiveness to the conductor on the one hand and the singers' absolutely thorough knowledge of Bach's *Mass* on the other.

NOTES

1. Walters, *Bach Choir of Bethlehem*, 104.
2. Ibid., 92–93.
3. Ibid., 92.

4. "Carla Spaeth, May 19, 1922," Wolle Papers, ABCB.

5. "Lynnwood Farman, May 12, 1928," Wolle Papers, ABCB.

6. Walters, *History of the Bach Choir*, 104.

7. "Edward B. Stalley, May 18, 1924," Wolle Papers, ABCB.

8. "F. J. Zeisberg, May 25, 1926," Wolle Papers, ABCB.

9. "Amy M. Beach, June 8, 1925," Wolle Papers, ABCB.

10. "Mary Ware Dennett," n.d., Wolle Papers, ABCB.

11. "Isabel Pennypacker, June 1, 1914," Wolle Papers, ABCB.

12. Walters, *History of the Bach Choir*, 112.

13. Wolle Letters and Papers, Box #1, A2, letter 5, ABCB.

Chapter 11

"My Bach Choir"

1915–1933

Bach Festival in Packer Memorial Church with Wolle at the piano

Recognizing that the 1915 Bach Festival would be unique, Charles Schwab brought his influence and power to bear to ensure that it would be reviewed by the most influential New York music critics. A Bethlehem *Globe Times* reporter wrote that just prior to the Tenth Festival in 1915, "Mr. Schwab in company with Raymond Walters, registrar of Lehigh University and chairman of the

Bach Publicity committee, this morning left for New York in Mr. Schwab's private [rail] car to bring to Bethlehem this afternoon as the guest of Mr. Schwab,
Mme. Sembrich, W. J. Henderson, for the *New York Sun*; Richard Albrich, of
the *New York Times*; and H. T. Frick of the *New York Evening Post*."[1]

Speaking at a pre-Festival banquet, Schwab prepared the chorus for the
presence of these notable critics. "Dr. Drinker and our friends have been
anxious to have Mr. Henderson, Mr. Frick, and other musical critics here, and
they are coming to this concert on Friday and therefore I think the choir ought
to feel very proud."[2] Schwab spoke of his own involvement in the success of
the Bach Choir, "I want to let you know . . . from my presence here, that I
am intensely interested in this choir, intensely interested in its work, intensely
interested in its success, and I take this opportunity to thank the ladies and
gentlemen personally."[3] Everyone in the invited party was treated lavishly on
board Schwab's private rail car and in Schwab's Bethlehem mansion.

Though Henderson was not a Wolle fan, writing in the *New York Sun*, he
was nonetheless impressed by the Bethlehem Choir's achievements:

> The Bethlehem Choir, which is now twice as large as it was in the beginning,
> contains good material and it has been well rehearsed. The members of this
> chorus love their duties and study all winter with enthusiasm. Some of their
> singing, as in the great opening chorus of the "St. John Passion," "Lord, our
> Redeemer," was superb in its splendor of tones, in the clarity of its treatment
> of the polyphony, in the variety of accent and color and the firmness of texture.
> Other choral numbers . . . were also admirably delivered. The "Mass" naturally
> went well. It is the battle-horse of the Bethlehem Chorus. The members of the
> Philadelphia Orchestra played excellently.[4]

While his review was somewhat cool, Henderson granted that The Bach
Choir, made up of volunteer singers, could be compared positively with any
professional choir. Henderson and his followers remained critical of Wolle's
personal interpretation in favor of one that was more "historically" based. Yet,
others felt, "the underlying sentiment of the text supplied ample warrant for
what he did along these lines, and the result was not at all incompatible with the
spirit of the music."[5] There was no such division of opinions among individuals
attending the Festivals. They were always deeply moved by what they heard.
"I never expect to listen to anything more satisfying and more soul stirring than
the *Mass* as it was given yesterday," wrote a listener in a letter to Wolle.[6] A
singer wrote, "I cannot express what a delight my engagement with the Bach
Choir was to me."[7]

Following the 1916 Festival, the singers gave Wolle a chair as a gift. In
return he wrote a poem that he had printed and gave a copy to each choir
member. He called the poem "To My Bach Choir" declaring unabashedly:

Ah! Dear Bach Choir, you are my child;
And though at times you drive me wild
Disdaining up-beats, bars and notes,
Your father fondly on you dotes.

He answered with total confidence in "His Choir":

As to requirements, there are none. With regard to age, our youngest member being fourteen and our oldest member being eighty-two. . . none with regard to sight singing ability, for judging from experience, I do not believe that one person in ten thousand can read music at sight; none with regard to vocal requirements, since up to the present time practically every applicant has been admitted.

Last night we had our first rehearsal of the season with an accession of about one hundred singers . . . There are no requirements as to music ability . . . We demand no dues; impose no fines and levy no assessments. The singers buy their own copies. We have no rules of any kind. Singers may attend rehearsals, or do as they please. We depend upon the esprit de corps, which as far as I know is unparalleled. The enthusiasm and devotion of the singers is without bounds.[8]

For a number of years the annual Bach Festivals were the primary activity of The Bach Choir. Following the 1916 Festival, however, the choir was invited to sing outside Bethlehem. The Philharmonic Society of New York celebrated its seventy-fifth anniversary in 1917. The orchestra would be performing Beethoven's *Fifth Symphony in C Minor*, the piece that opened the Society's first concert in 1842. To represent Bach, the other great composer of Western music, Wolle was asked to conduct The Bach Choir in sections from the *Mass* with orchestra and in selected chorales sung unaccompanied.

Wolle and the Bethlehem singers stepped onto the Carnegie Hall stage on 21 January 1917. His challenge was to ensure that the choral section of this secular concert celebration retained its sacred spirit. He had already brilliantly solved that problem in a number of festivals when he had reached deep into his Moravian heritage and conducted cantatas and distinct chorales as a Moravian *Singstunde*. The problem now lay in Carnegie Hall's secular concert space. Fortunately, because Moravians as a matter of practice held a *Singstunde* for any important occasion anywhere, it was naturally possible for Dr. Wolle and The Choir to move from Packer Church to Carnegie Hall with perfect integrity. The other innovation was to treat even sections of the *Mass* as part of the *Singstunde*. The whole *Mass* need not be sung.

The New York concert, entirely underwritten by Charles Schwab, was the first of a series of almost annual performances of The Choir in cities along the East Coast. These appearances culminated in a 1925 radio broadcast in

Washington, D.C., when The Choir and Wolle, at the invitation of President and Mrs. Coolidge, entered the new era of mass concert audiences.

The Carnegie Hall audience's response was extraordinary. Wolle received eight curtain calls. The audience rose, shouting "encore," and finally when there were no encores, gave a five-minute ovation.

Then, in the midst of great acclaim, the critical controversy over Dr. Wolle's interpretation erupted again. Krehbiel wrote a scathing review, "Never in the history of New York—we speak advisedly—has the genius of Bach been so outraged . . . in the employment of sickly, sentimental nuances and lamentable languishing ritardandos they [the chorales] were made to sound like sentimental love songs . . . After that it was difficult to sit out the performance."[9] However, another reviewer reported that the effect in New York was as it had been in Bethlehem, "Dr. Wolle's exaggerations and mannerisms are as patent in Carnegie Hall as in the Packer Memorial Chapel, but the sum total of results he obtains is equally transporting."[10]

The Bach Choir was engaged to return the next season. Wolle, his singers, and the audiences were in perfect agreement regarding how Bach should sound. The historical view articulated by conservative critics, whom Wolle had opposed his whole life, was simply not relevant to American Bach lovers.

In the 1917 Bach Festival, there were seven American premieres. The motet for double chorus, so effective in the 1914 Festival, was repeated. Wolle certainly had chosen "Sing to the Lord a New Song" to affirm the belief that Europe, in the midst of war, required a new song and that an American Bach Choir was singing that song. Since its inception, the singers accepted their conductor's personal philosophy of Bach for all Americans and Schwab's desire to have America become the focus of the Bach Movement, with Bethlehem as its center. World War I added a new dimension by deepening their feelings. Initially, Wolle had proposed that the Festivals be suspended because of their "German" association. However, he received total support for continuing them. In the view of Wolle's contemporaries Bach was a German "whom Prussia had not corrupted."[11] Furthermore, "The mind that conceived the *B minor mass* was powerless to conceive the Lusitania or the cruelty of her destruction."[12]

Thus, the Festivals in Bethlehem gained greater stature than before the war. The "loftiest ideals and aspirations of humanity" were being kept alive and expressed in America by The Bach Choir in Bethlehem, while they were being shattered in Europe. "It would, indeed, be a national calamity if war should be permitted to interrupt even one year of these noble and solemn festivals," wrote one critic.[13]

One of the profound ironies of the political circumstances was clearly articulated:

The most amazing contrast of all was that while the world was on fire, in the very city whose name is linked more closely to the war than that of any other in the land, we should have gathered to listen to the great Christian facts, set to the lofty music that only they can inspire, by the "master of masters," a German of another and a better German day.[14]

For George Nevin, a prominent church composer of the day, the dichotomies in the experience were so great that he asked, "Can it be that we are privileged to drop down in quaint Bethlehem where for a time the world seemed to be in harmony with the Infinite, or was it a dream?"[15] The *Musical Courier*'s Clarence Lucas took a futurist point of view. He reminded his readers just how difficult continuing The Bach Choir enterprise actually was for his contemporaries:

In imagination one can fancy the musical historian of the future writing about old Bethlehem and the remembered J. Fred. Wolle, who made his native city famous for the study of Bach's music in the uncouth age in which he lived, and who kept a glimmering lamp of art trimmed and burning during the dark and stormy days of the great World War.[16]

The Bach Festivals represented the way music-loving Americans wanted the world to be, a world of noble ideals and beauty, a world without war. That Bethlehem was both a massive manufacturer of war weaponry to defeat Germany and a place where the greatest composer of German musical culture was kept alive made the need for the Festivals greater.

Unexpectedly, the number of males in The Choir remained basically the same throughout the war. The Bach Choir was also unaffected by the flu epidemic in the later years of the war. Because of its necessary manufacture of war materials, Bethlehem was effectively cordoned off by the U.S. military so the male population could continue producing steel and avoid the raging pandemic.

In January 1918, The Choir returned to New York to sing again with the Philharmonic Society. That program was a high point for Wolle, for it combined Wagner's music, which he loved and admired along with Bach's. As in Bethlehem, the concert began with the trombone choir playing offstage. When it finished the Moravian chorale, "Son of God, to Thee I Cry," the "Kyrie Eleison" from the *Mass* burst forth. In fact the New York audience was greeted by a more daring innovation as Wolle had interspersed sections of the *Mass* with chorales. He made Bach's *Mass* itself a *Singstunde*. The spiritual message was expanded by individual sections interconnected by relevant chorales from cantatas selected and combined by Wolle. His religious nature exceeded his reverence for Bach, and his Moravian heritage emerged in this moment of deepest integrity. Unlike the first Carnegie Hall concert, the entire evening was now a sacred service. Wolle dared to perform Bach along with Wagner's sacred drama, "Parsifal." The reviewer for the *New York Sun* wrote that, "Each number given received the whole-hearted approval of the audience."[17] From then on the Choir performed nearly annually in New York, Philadelphia, Baltimore, and Washington, D.C.

On the afternoon of Sunday, 10 February 1918, Wolle and The Bach Choir gave their most explicitly patriotic performance of World War I. The United States Army Ambulance Service had a large training station in Camp Crane, Allentown. The invitation came from the commander of the camp, and Charles Schwab paid the expenses "incident to the present concert . . . in Honor of the U. S. A. A. S."[18]

The concert, attended by two thousand servicemen, began with everyone singing the "National Anthems of the Allies, The Star Spangled Banner, God Save the King, and The Marseillaise Hymn." A month earlier the Bach Choir had performed with the Philharmonic Society of New York in Carnegie Hall with the Moravian Trombone Choir. The Camp Crane concert included the same sections of the *Mass*, but a number of telling chorales were added. They were "The Crusaders' Hymn" and "Rock of Ages."

Walters gives the following moving account of the concert:

> The khaki-clad audience in Recreation Hall at the camp was made up of square-shouldered young Americans, most of them college men, from every state in the Union and every territory and island possession. Their reaction to the music of Bach was an interesting study. As the magnificent choruses of the "B Minor Mass" and the beautiful chorales were sung in the Choir, the multitude of upturned soldierly faces was a screen upon which were registered the great emotions, the spiritual content of this sublime music. And then, as each number was concluded, the light that never was on land or sea changed in these faces to a boyish glow and they clapped and cheered as they do when their crack "USAAC" basketball team wins a game.[19]

Wolle could have had no more fitting evidence of the universality of Bach and the ability to move people in the most trying of circumstances.

A second New York tour had been again completely underwritten by Schwab and included a reception at his mansion, Riverside, the largest mansion in the city and without doubt one of the most opulent. The visit of the Bethlehem singers was only one of many musical events Schwab arranged there. He employed a full-time organist who played frequently for Schwab and his guests. There were Sunday entertainments in which Enrico Caruso and other

Metropolitan Opera stars sang. Victor Herbert, Fritz Kreisler, and Ignace Paderewski performed for groups of select guests.[20]

In 1918, Raymond Walters, The Bach Choir's publicity chairman published *The Bethlehem Bach Choir: A History and Critical Compendium.* Walters saw The Bach Choir and Bach Festivals as a synthesis of the Moravian and the Lutheran music traditions. "[M]usical aptitude," he asserted "was a heritage of the Moravian congregation," and the hymnody of the Lutheran Church, a fundamental component of Bach's choral music, was part of that tradition.[21] Thus, Bethlehem was a fertile field for Bach to thrive in.

However, "these singers are not set apart by reason of talent or tradition or fortune."[22] Bach choirs and Bach festivals could come about anywhere in America. One of Walters' purposes was to spread "the tidings of Bach" through his history of the Bethlehem Bach Choir by telling how it came about in Bethlehem, and how it was sustained there. Walters was convinced, and rightly so, that The Bach Choir and the Bach Festival were not Moravian alone. They would not have begun without Wolle, and would not have persisted without the "imitation of others,—intelligent, devoted, and generous co-workers."[23] The success of Bach in Bethlehem "should be an encouragement to community choruses in other parts of the country because they have succeeded by qualities all may emulate—devotion and concentration."[24]

Walters explicitly reiterated Wolle's view of how to approach Bach. "It is Dr. Wolle's conviction that, although Bach's work was written and printed without expression marks, it should not therefore be given without expression."[25] Wolle, he writes, "believes in and practices modern interpretation of Bach."[26] This was Wolle's orientation even as a young man. The picture Walters gives of Charles Schwab is a flattering one. Schwab enjoyed Walters' book and gave copies to many friends and associates. His gift card inserted into the copies reads "With the Good Wishes of Charles M. Schwab."

Walters concludes with specific suggestions for choirs in communities that are "struggling with the problems of community music":

1. There should be obtained . . . an assured financial basis.
2. The conductor must be a musician with vision, persistence, and infectious enthusiasm.
3. Singers with trained voices are not necessary.
4. There is a danger in over-organizing a chorus.
5. Limitation to one composer is not . . . a policy to be advised.
6. There is . . . no insurmountable obstacle to other community choruses equaling what the Bach Choir has accomplished.[27]

For Walters, the Bethlehem-Bach enterprise was both art and religion. It was industry and business, melding wealthy and ordinary people, which could happen anywhere in the United States. A second edition was printed in 1923 as a part of the twenty-fifth anniversary of The Bethlehem Bach Choir and Wolle's sixtieth year. Choir members and the Board of Managers committee members were listed along with the titles of works performed from 1900 to 1922.

When Henry Drinker resigned as president of the Executive Committee in 1921, Charles Schwab had just resigned as president of the Oratorio Society of New York, to which office he had succeeded Andrew Carnegie at Carnegie's request. Schwab, who considered himself "retired from business," took Drinker's place. The committee's letter accepting Drinker's resignation expressed, "most earnest appreciation and thanks for services to the Bach cause which are beyond computing." The committee now viewed itself not only as supporting The Choir and its Festivals, but as part of a larger movement.

In his acceptance letter, Schwab reiterated the importance of music: "It has always been my conviction that music should be a part of every well-rounded human life."[28] He viewed The Choir as an exemplary national force. "I am happy to accept the presidency of a typically American organization that is upholding the best standards in choral music." Schwab was unable to make the meetings of the Choir Board, however, and his presidency became effectively honorary. The absence of consistent leadership was solved by the election of Ruth Linderman as vice president in 1924.[29] She began chairing the meetings in Schwab's absence. Ruth Linderman officially replaced Schwab when he "expressed a desire to be relieved of any active office in the Association." He was nominated "Honorary President."[30] Her first major decision was to cancel the 1924 Festival due to Wolle's ill health. When he recovered, he conducted the 1925 Festival.

The announcement that J. Fred. Wolle had recovered and that he would conduct a Festival in 1925 was received with relief by everyone associated with the Bach Festivals. Mrs. Theodore Roosevelt's response in a letter to him was typical:

Oyster Bay, Long Island, N.Y. Sagamore Hall, Sept. 30, 1924.
It is not easy to express my pleasure at hearing that Dr. Wolle has recovered from his illness.
The Bach Choir means to me that great spiritual exaltation that is given only by music, and music in its purest and highest expression—Lacking Dr. Wolle these notes are silent.

Faithfully yours,
Edith Kermit Roosevelt[31]

Of all the many, many critical reviews of Bach Festivals conducted by Wolle, one review written by H. L. Mencken recorded the unique atmosphere of the

Festival better than any other. He attended his first Bach Festival in 1923 and wrote an article for the *Baltimore Evening Sun* movingly describing his experience. Much of the review is given here because Mencken so sensitively sums up Wolle's achievement in creating sacred community Bach performances.

> What, indeed, is most astonishing about the whole festival is not that it is given in a Pennsylvania steel town, with the snorting of switching engines breaking in upon Bach's colossal 'Gloria,' but that it is still, after all these years, so thoroughly peasant-like and Moravian, so full of homeliness and rusticity. In all my life I have never attended a public show of any sort, in any country, of a more complete and charming simplicity. With strangers crowding into the little city from all directions, and two ticket takers for every seat, and long columns of gabble in the newspapers, the temptation to throw some hocus-pocus about it, to give it a certain florid gaudiness, to bedeck it with bombast and highfalutin must be very trying, even to Moravians. But I can only say that they resist the temptation utterly and absolutely. There is no affectation about it whatever, not even the affectation of solemn religious purpose. Bach is sung in that smoky valley because the people like to sing him, and for no other reason at all. The singers are business men and their stenographers, schoolmasters and housewives, men who work in the steel mills and girls waiting to be married. If not a soul came in from outside to hear the music, they would keep on making it just the same, and if the Packer Memorial Church began to disturb them with echoes from empty benches they would go back to their bare Moravian Church.
>
> I can imagine no great ceremonial with less fuss to it . . . If one has a ticket, one simply goes to one's pew, plainly numbered on a simple plan, and sits down. If one lacks a ticket, one is quite free to lie in the grass outside, and listen to the music through the open doors . . . The conductor slips into his place unnoticed, when a session is over he slips out the same way. It is indeed not a public performance at all, in the customary sense: it is simply the last of this year's rehearsals--and as soon as it is over next year's begin.[32]

Entranced by Bach in Bethlehem, Mencken was drawn to attend the Bach Festival each spring with Alfred A. Knopf until Wolle's death in 1933, when "we found the pleasant atmosphere vanished and stopped going."[33]

The year of Schwab's retirement saw another first for The Bach Choir during the "World Fellowship Through Music" concerts prompted as a peaceful gesture by Mrs. Calvin Coolidge. This three-day series was held in Washington, D.C., in mid-April 1925. The Bach Choir with many other groups was asked to participate. Everyone did so eagerly, and on 16 April, The Choir, accompanied by members of the Philadelphia Orchestra and the Moravian Trombone Choir, sang sections from *The Passion According to St. Matthew.*

The concert was broadcast by radio and was The Bach Choir's first on-air experiment. This was the only radio broadcast during Wolle's lifetime, though there were numerous "near" broadcasts of the Bach Festivals. He went so far as to write into the performers' contracts that there might be broadcasts, but for unknown reasons he never allowed them to take place. He never recorded with The Choir or allowed his organ recitals to be recorded, although the technology was available and other musicians were actively recording. For a person who so readily accepted the modernization of the organ and played on the two most advanced organs of his time at the St. Louis and Chicago World Fairs, his reluctance to embrace radio broadcasting and recording technology is difficult to understand. A report of the Washington broadcast noted that "Dr. J. Fred. Wolle . . . had been exceedingly reluctant to go on the air but yielded when the organization ventured from home." Even more puzzling is that "it . . . was said to be the first time the great Bach *Mass in B minor* had thus been heard." [34] It is a loss to the history of the Bach movement in America that J. Fred. Wolle left no audio example of his "Bach Choir" or his organ playing.

In 1928, Ruth Linderman announced the death of Albert Cleaver, the last founding member of the Board. The leadership of the Festivals now passed to a new generation. With typical idealism the Executive Committee described Cleaver as "a gentlemen of most gracious manners, and was intensely interested in the promotion and support of things which tend to elevate mankind."[35]

Wolle's own health had begun a slow decline and he resigned his church position in 1930. During the 1932 Festival he remained seated during the entire performance hidden from the audience by a mass of potted foliage. His minimal, but effective, conducting style became even more efficient. His hands shaped the musical phrases in endlessly varied ways. His fingers flexed and singers responded, his intense musical concentration radiated as always from his brow and eyes, and he smiled his pleasure when the music was exactly as he wished. One singer said, "He was too weak to stand and only moved his hands and fingers slightly, but we filled the church with vibrant sound."[36] It was Wolle's final Festival.

In December, Ruth Linderman wrote the guarantors, "the health of our devoted Conductor, Dr. J. Fred. Wolle, has become so seriously impaired that it has been impossible for him to resume rehearsals this Fall and a Festival in 1933 is out of the question . . . We all hope he will recover and resume his activities so that the festivals can be continued for many years."[37]

Wolle did not recover. On 12 January 1933, he died.

In Packer Church the Choir singers held a memorial service for their Dr. Wolle, separate from the service the Moravian Congregation held later for Brother Wolle. They took their assigned places in the front of the Church, and his friends took their seats in the nave. It was like the beginning of another Bach Festival. No music transformed the silence into spiritual joy. He had requested there be no music at the service. The presiding Bishop of the Episcopal Diocese of Bethlehem read the concluding prayers. The poem "He Leads Us On" from his youthful anthem was read. Bach's "World Farewell!", which the choir had sung for many deceased friends of the choir, was now only recited.

At the graveside, sixteen members of the Moravian Trombone Choir, who had introduced so many Bach festivals, played funeral chorales. The trombonists appropriately broke the silence, as they had so many times when they played from Packer Church tower. Now music might be possible:

> after the family had withdrawn, a small group of the Bach Choir, possibly fifteen or twenty, gathered at the grave and attempted to hum "World Farewell," but most understandably were overcome with emotion.[38]

Paul de Schweinitz, a boyhood friend, concluded the obituary he'd written for *The Moravian,* "Thus, one of the most notable figures in all Moravian musical history has been taken from us."[39]

Unfortunately J. Fred. Wolle did not live to experience the founding of two Bach Festivals directly resulting from the one in Bethlehem. They are the annual Bach Festival of Baldwin-Wallace College in Berea, Ohio, and The Bach Festival in Winter Park, Florida, home of Rollins College, also held annually. Both were patterned after the Bethlehem Bach Festival.

The Festival in Berea held its first performance in 1933 and recently celebrated its seventy-fifth anniversary. Albert Riemenschneider, the founder, was a close friend of Dr. Wolle. The Bach Choir of Bethlehem under its music director and conductor, Greg Funfgeld, traveled to Berea College to celebrate with them in a concert of the *B Minor Mass.* It is a flourishing musical event.

The Bach Festival Society in Winter Park presented its first performance in 1935. The Festival was patterned after the Bach Festival in Bethlehem as well. Like the Baldwin-Wallace College Festival, the one at Rollins College is flourishing and recently also celebrated its seventy-fifth anniversary.

Two days after Wolle died, The Choir's president, Ruth Linderman, called the members of the Executive Committee for a special session. Her son Robert, who was to become a crucial agent in the continuity of the Festivals, joined them. That group decided the president should appoint "a Committee of three to look into the question of the possibility of continuing the Bach Festivals in the future."[40] On 1 February, the Executive Committee reconvened and heard the special committee recommend that the Festival be continued, and a search began for a person "to come to Bethlehem and give his undivided attention to the Bach Choir."[41] Two conductors had already applied for the position, but the Committee, unprepared to make an immediate decision, devised an interim plan. The Bach Choir would sing the *Mass* in May in memory of Dr. Wolle, led by a conductor who would not necessarily become his successor. The manager of the Philadelphia Orchestra, whom Wolle had worked with for years, recommended Bruce Carey, head of the Music Department of Girard College in Philadelphia and conductor for the Mendelssohn Choir in that city, "as the only person . . . who was qualified and had the experience to give such a performance," and Robert Linderman went to interview him.[42]

Carey was "much interested in the possibility of putting on a performance of the *Mass* and felt that if the choir wanted to sing it and would give him their support and co-operation, that he could do it."[43] Carey had attended the Bach Festivals for years:

> he had "clocked" with his watch the tempos used by Dr. Wolle for the various numbers in the Mass and had made a graph on his score of the dynamic scheme used by the conductor . . . he had done that for the last five years. By the time he was through he had recorded as complete an account of the mechanics of Dr. Wolle's interpretation as can be put on paper.[44]

Linderman concluded his report noting, "It is understood that Mr. Carey would not be engaged as a new conductor . . . [but] simply as the best person available to give this special performance."[45]

This was a difficult moment for The Choir. Those who sang in "his Bach Choir" would never forget Dr. Wolle. Miss Staner and Miss Luckenbach, both over ninety when interviewed, had sung in the Bach Choir for sixty-two years. "What joyous years they were," said Staner. "Oh I wouldn't give those years up for anything. I always said that was the last thing I wanted to give up and it was." Luckenbach recollected Dr. Wolle's personal charisma. "He could organize anybody if he wanted to, that was willing to sing. He had that physical ability, and well, that spiritual ability really that he could just get people to do what he wanted." Both ladies fondly recalled the sense of community among the singers, and how it was fundamental to Wolle's Bach mission and success. "He would never put anybody out. Once you were in, you were in the family, and that was it. This was something. This endeared him to us," said Miss Luckenbach. "I don't see how anybody could have disliked him," added Miss Staner. She verified that Dr. Wolle had taught them new pieces by beginning at the end and moving forward. She also described his flexible fingers. "You couldn't miss anything . . . His little fingers at the end of the "Crucifixus" [in the *B Minor Mass*] . . . at the very end of the chorus it was and there were two notes and his little finger told you exactly when to change from one note to the other. Some say his little finger was for the altos, but it was for everyone." Staner ended: "In my opinion nobody could ever take his place. Nobody."[46]

Luckenbach also spoke of Charles Schwab. "He was very influential and a very good friend of Fred Wolle. He would stand up for him, and he did a lot of advertising. He would always speak up for the choir whenever he had an opportunity."

Most of the choir knew The *Mass* by heart and could have sung it without a conductor. Even so, it was difficult to imagine anyone taking Dr. Wolle's place. Though T. Edgar Shields' stepping up into Wolle's position might have seemed inevitable, Bruce Carey was the one whom the Executive Committee ultimately selected. Carey accepted their offer immediately.

Carey himself quipped, "After Dr. Wolle, if Bach himself came down from Heaven to conduct that choir, he would have had a hard time of it . . . However, feeling that someone must do it . . . I went ahead."[47] While he might have felt humbled, he was in no way intimidated. He felt that the tradition established by J. Fred. Wolle, "should be perpetuated," though he was not about to "slavishly imitate," and he hoped to be able to combine "difference in detail" with Wolle's broad outline; it was in a spirit of the best of will that everyone launched into preparing for the "Memorial Service by the Bach Choir of Bethlehem, Pa., In Memory of Dr. J. Fred Wolle Founder and Conductor 1898–1933."

The memorial program included a "resolution on the death of Dr. Wolle" by the Executive Committee and The Choir. One sentence stands out. "Out of materials no more exceptional than those at the command of any other interpreter, he had perfected an instrument in the Choir, responsive to his subtlest sense of every meaning in Bach, however exalted, or delicate, or difficult."[48]

According to a local newspaper report, interest was so high that there were One thousand two hundred in the audience for a public rehearsal two days before the memorial service. A reporter noted, "Mr. Carey has devoted more time than did his predecessor to the mechanics of the voice, placement of tone . . . the results are noticeably good."[49] In contrast to Wolle the organist, who "played upon his choir," The Choir was now being conducted by a person whose training was as a singer.

The memorial service attendance was as large as a Bach Festival. Many in the audience heard improvements in vocal quality. Also, "some of the choruses Mr. Carey carried along with greater speed but there were many who enjoyed the change," wrote one reporter.[50] Guarantors attending the memorial service were invited to maintain their support for a continuation of the festivals. At the meeting of The Choir's Board of Managers after the 1:30 p.m. session of the *Mass*, the Executive Committee was empowered to make the necessary plans and arrangements for the following year's Festival. "The sentiment expressed by representatives of the Choir favored the continuance of the Festivals and Mr. Bruce Carey as its Director."[51]

The following month Carey and his wife were invited to Bethlehem to discuss plans for the future. Carey told the Board's Executive Committee that he believed he could carry on the "the work of the Bach Choir in connection with his duties in Philadelphia. He was very much enthused with the spirit of the choir and spoke highly of everyone connected with the Festival." At that meeting Mr. Carey was formally engaged as "Director of the 1934 Bach Festival."[52]

NOTES

1. *Bethlehem Globe Times*, 28 May 1915.

2. Ibid., 20 May 1915.

3. Ibid.

4. Walters, *History of the Bach Choir*, 117–18.

5. Ibid., 131.

6. Wolle Letters and Papers, Box 1, A2, letter #7, ABCB.

7. Wolle Letters and Papers, Box 1, A2, letter #5, ABCB.

8. J. Fred. Wolle to P. W. Dykema, 19 September 1913, ABCB.

9. *New York Tribune*, 22 January 1917.

10. *Musical America*, 27 January 1917, scrapbook fragment, ABCB.

11. Walters, *History of the Bach Choir*, 134.

12. *Bethlehem Globe Times*, 12 May 1915.

13. Walters, *History of the Bach Choir*, 134.

14. Ibid.

15. Ibid., 145.

16. "Comments of a Critic on the Tenth Bach Festival," *Alumni Bulletin of Lehigh University*, July 1915.

17. Walters, *History of the Bach Choir*, 186.

18. All quotations are from the Program of the Bethlehem Bach Choir before the United States Army Ambulance Service, Allentown, PA, ABCB.

19. Walters, *History of the Bach Choir*, 169–70.

20. Robert Hessen, *Steel Titan: The Life of Charles M. Schwab* (New York: Oxford University Press, 1975), 286–87.

21. Walters, *History of the Bach Choir*, 37.

22. Ibid., v–vi.

23. Ibid., 38.

24. Ibid.

25. Ibid., 220.

26. Ibid., 221–22.

27. Ibid., 226–70.

28. "Minutes of the Executive Committee," 8 January 1921.

29. Ibid.

30. Ibid., 30 May 1921.

31. Scrapbook of the Bach Choir of Bethlehem, n.d., ABCB.

32. H. L. Mencken, *A Mencken Chrestomathy* (New York: Alfred A. Knopf, 1978), 543–44.

33. H. L. Mencken, *Thirty-five Years of Newspaper Work* (Baltimore, MD: Johns Hopkins University Press, 1994), 124.

34. That the performance was of the *Mass in B Minor* is an error. According to the program of the festival, the performance was of Bach's *St. Matthew Passion.*

35. "Minutes of the Executive Board," 27 December 1928, ABCB.

36. Told to the author, November 1999.

37. "Minutes of the Executive Board," Letter drafted 5 December 1932, ABCB.

38. Ibid.

39. *The Moravian*, 18 January 1933.

40. "Minutes of the Executive Board," 14 January 1933, ABCB.

41. Ibid., 1 February 1933.

42. Ibid., 11 February 1933.

43. Ibid.

44. *Public Ledger (Philadelphia)*, 12 March 1933.

45. Ibid.

46. Audio interviews in the ABCB.

47. Ibid.

48. "Minutes of the Executive Board," 13 May 1933, ABCB.

49. "Rehearsal of the Bach Choir," unknown source, scrapbook, ABCB.

50. "Bach Choir Officers Decide to Continue Festival Next Year," unidentified source, scrapbook, ABCB.

51. "Minutes of the Executive Board," 13 May 1933, ABCB.

52. Ibid., 2 June 1933.

Chapter 12

Years of Transition

1934–1938

Though the Board of Managers continued to elect Charles Schwab honorary president of The Bach Choir, his presence diminished rapidly and his financial influence had ceased by the time of Wolle's death. His fortune had been all but lost in the Crash of 1929, and with his resources depleted, he was forced to close his New York residence and offer it for sale. He took a small apartment in the city. While he remained a member of the Board of Bethlehem Steel Corp., in 1935 he was told by a group of stockholders that he had "outlived his usefulness." They repeated the charge in 1936:[1]

> By the mid-1930's, his body was ravaged by illness [diabetes] and his spirit increasingly broken by the accusations leveled against him. He told B. C. Forbes, "It hurts me—it hurts me very much—to be branded as nothing but a greedy, selfish, self-seeking. mercenary, merciless, fellow callous toward workmen and toward everybody else."[2]

Early in the century he had been recognized as one of the twenty-five most powerful men in America and among the wealthiest. Schwab's powerful connection with Manhattan critics and conductors was broken by his death, and it was many years before the Bach Choir sang again in New York.

The Bethlehem Bach enterprise itself remained untouched by the Crash of 1929 and the Great Depression that followed. Its financial resources actually increased. The financial contributions by the board grew greatly, the number of guarantors doubled by 1933, and the Festivals were selling out.

Feeling that her job was done, Ruth Linderman resigned from the Executive Committee. She was succeeded by Henry S. Snyder who in 1908 had been appointed by Charles Schwab as vice president in charge of all financial, legal, real estate, and transportation matters at Bethlehem Steel. By the time Snyder had joined the direct governance of The Bach Choir, he had retired as a wealthy and socially influential man. He and his wife had built a country estate that they made the social center of Bethlehem's many wealthy beneficiaries of the rail, cement, and steel industries. Snyder soon made supporting The Bach Choir a social obligation. Supporting "Bach" became a required investment in cultural capital.

With support for The Bach Choir and its Festival assured, the Executive Committee engaged Bruce Carey for the individual Festivals in 1934 and 1935, and both years The Choir strongly endorsed him. After the 1934 festival, Carey wrote a letter advising the choir of the Committee's persistent requests that he continue as conductor but "drop all activities other than my school work and devote this year [1935]—the anniversary of Bach's birth—to the 1935 festival."[3] For a one-year contract this stipulation seemed unreasonable.

With the passing of Wolle, the Executive Committee decided to record performances, something Wolle had been reluctant to do. The Committee contacted Columbia Records with a proposal to have The Choir record Bach's *Passion According to Saint Matthew*. The manager of the Masterworks Division, "advised all negotiations fruitless if Philadelphia Orchestra was engaged, also that [Rose] Bampton is exclusive Victor,"[4] meaning that Bampton, a featured soloist, could not sing on a Columbia recording. Broadcasting the Festivals was also discussed, "and referred to the officers for further investigation." Thus, two efforts to move The Choir into the ever-expanding Bach Movement in America using commercial media had failed, and would continue to fail until the future conductor Ifor Jones recognized the importance of recording and radio.

The audience was pleased with Carey's conducting: "After each session Mr. Carey was highly complimented for the success he is making in his cultural training."[5] Raymond Walters described how he was continuing Wolle's Bach interpretative legacy: "Mr. Carey's methods of instructing and conducting are his own. His interpretation is frankly and avowedly that of Dr. Wolle. Maintenance of the Bethlehem tradition in the interpretation of Bach is assured."[6]

Immediately following the Festival the Careys left for Germany to do further research. Carey returned for the 1936 Festival with the scores of four cantatas new to Bethlehem and to the United States. In addition, as the first indication that a shift of power had occurred, "Director Carey was instructed to include in the 4 P.M. Friday session a Chorale Group."[7] This instruction is significant, for the Executive Committee would now have a voice in the musical content and organization of the Festival.

Bruce Carey

The support of all who attended the Festival was overwhelming, and the Executive Committee offered Bruce Carey a three-year contract, which he accepted. However, he insisted on continuing his full-time employment at Girard College in Philadelphia. Though he did not live in Bethlehem, Carey was fulfilling his contract beyond what was expected. He added two cantatas to the next Festivals, which were probably American premieres, and he received praise from every corner.

Board president Snyder also fulfilled his role by introducing a high social profile to the Festival. The Bach Festivals would no longer be exclusively sacred services focused on the spiritual messages expressed by Bach. At the conclusion of the *Mass*, the Snyders held a supper party for 250 guests at their country estate. That supper party became an annual "outstanding social event," and receiving or not receiving an invitation defined Bethlehem's social hierarchy. Numerous teas were given during the Festival as well.

Following the 1938 Festival, the Executive Committee held a special meeting, "to consider the re-appointment of Dr. Carey [he had received an honorary doctorate from Moravian Female Seminary in 1936]."[8] That the committee needed to consider extending Carey's three-year contract was natural. Surprising to everyone else was that there was discussion of appointing anyone else to the position. Members of the Executive Committee, led by Robert Linderman, "had for some time past been quietly exploring the possibilities of a conductor . . . meeting our requirements."[9] If Carey were to continue, he must be full time, for the same salary, and he must reside in Bethlehem. Carey chose not to meet these conditions. The Executive Committee agreed Carey should not be asked to return despite "literally hundreds of complimentary comments on the Festivals."[10]

Dr. Carey's termination by letter and conversation "left the severance of our official relations on a very satisfactory and amicable basis."[11] Henry Snyder communicated the decision to the representatives of The Choir before a public announcement in the press, to "counteract the criticism of the Choir members who were devoted to Dr. Carey."[12] The Executive Committee was acting unilaterally without consulting The Choir, the guarantors, or the Board of Managers. Further, the president met with a prospective replacement, Prof. Ifor Jones, and directly "engaged him as Director of the Choir." Jones was young and nationally recognized, and he consented to move to Bethlehem and to devote his entire time to The Choir and the Festivals.[13]

The yearly contribution of the soloists to the reputation of The Bach Choir was inestimable. There were more than seventy-five. Nearly all had national and international reputations.

The first professionals included in the Bach Festival were the vocal soloists. Though using professionals was a strong point of difference between Wolle and the Moravian Elders, Wolle persisted and drew singers in New York, Boston, and Philadelphia who could sing Bach's recitatives and arias at a time when Baroque singers were rare. Yet, Wolle found them and the critics consistently praised their performances. Wolle had conducted the *Mass* four times—1914, 1927, 1928, 1929—with the solos, duets, and recitatives sung by the appropriate sections of the choir.

Three were local; two sopranos, Lucy A. Brickenstein—"had little to do, but did it most successfully" (1903); Bertha Mae Starner; and Howard Weigner, bass, also secretary of The Bach Choir. The two sopranos sang in nearly every Wolle performance.

Most had notable careers. Some of these outstanding performers were Mary Hissen De Moss—"gave a most satisfactory rendition" (1903); Gertrude Stein—"a genuine pleasure at all times to listen to her" (1901); Rose Bampton—"the ideal voice which Bach had in mind when he wrote the beautiful solos for that register [contralto]." Bampton was a star at the Metropolitan Opera in New York and other international opera houses. She was the only singer to continue as a soloist following Wolle's death. She continued with Carey, who added Louise Lerch and the highly praised recitalist Lilian Knowles. The Philadelphia tenor performing at almost every festival, Nicholas Douty—"sang the tenor arias very artfully" (1917); tenor Edward Johnson and bass Herbert Witherspoon each later became managers of the Metropolitan. Other returning basses were Julian Walker—"eminently successful" (1903); Charles Trowbridge Tittman—"customary meritorious performance in his recitatives" (1932); and Julius Hutchons, bass—"the finest singer of that register the festival has had for many years" (1943).

The years of transition were over. A new era was beginning.

NOTES

1. Hessen, *Steel Titan*, 296.
2. Ibid., 298–99.
3. Bruce Carey to the Bach Choir, 20 June 1934, ABCB.
4. "Minutes of the Executive Board," 5 October 1934, ABCB.
5. "Bach Choir Sings Passion," *Bethlehem Globe*, 18 May 1935.
6. Walters, "Bach at Bethlehem," *The Musical Quarterly* 21, no. 2 (April 1935): 188.
7. "Minutes of the Executive Board," 16 January 1936, ABCB.
8. Ibid., 3 June 1938.
9. Ibid.
10. Ibid.
11. Ibid., 8 July 1938.
12. Ibid., 3 June 1938.
13. Ibid., 8 July 1938.

Chapter 13

A More Comprehensive Scope

The Third Conductor

Ifor Jones

Robert Linderman had concentrated his search on Ifor Jones as the conductor to replace Bruce Carey. Linderman had followed Jones's work for five years with great interest, and reported to the Executive Committee that "[h]is work was outstanding and that he was highly recommended by other musicians."[1] Jones was a choral conductor and organist at Rutgers University where he had performed Bach's complete organ works, and he founded the Handel Choir in Westfield, New Jersey. In the ten years he had resided in America he had become known nationally as a virtuoso organist, a fine choral conductor, and an expert in the performance of Baroque music. After attending a performance by the Handel Choir, members of the music committee were "much impressed with his work" as well as with the musical reputation Jones had established in this country.[2]

Jones was born in Wales in 1900, the son of a miner. His parents were highly musical and sang in local choirs. They took young William (who was called Ifor only later) with them to rehearsals. During one rehearsal he left the pew, with that dramatic assertiveness he never lost, ran up the aisle, pulled on the conductor's coattails and shouted, "You're doing it wrong, you're doing it wrong!"[3] He became the church organist at age eight and was soon playing recitals as well as conducting choirs. During World War 1, he played organ concerts for the benefit of "war-aiding agencies."

The prodigy entered the Royal Academy of Music in London at nineteen and began winning prizes in composition and organ. He studied conducting and became organist and choirmaster at a London Welsh church and an assistant professor at the Academy upon graduation, and then took the position of coach, accompanist, and assistant conductor of the Royal Covent Garden Opera House. These positions solidified a highly dramatic approach to music making.

Jones came to the United States in 1927 and had since given two hundred recitals coast-to-coast. These performances brought him to the attention of music professors at Rutgers, and he was hired as Professor of Harmony and Composition. He chose to leave the United Kingdom and settle permanently in the United States. He organized a student Bach Cantata Club, and in founding the Handel Chorus he began highly successful work with amateur community singers. His personality was a sharp contrast to the style of his much older, restrained, and undemonstrative predecessor, Bruce Carey. He later quipped with a chuckle that if he had followed Wolle directly, "It would not have done; it just would not have done at all."[4] Mrs. George Halliwell, a choir member since its inception in 1898, remarked, "Good heavens, I didn't expect such a child!" when she first met Jones.[5] Jones was thirty-nine.

The music committee had decided that the Friday program of the 1939 Festival would consist of four cantatas, "Praise Thou the Lord, O My Spirit," "God is My King," "Thou Guide of Israel," and "It is Enough" motet; "Come,

Jesu, Come"; and the *Magnificat*. Typical of the times, all titles were in English without catalog numbers. As a gesture of welcome, Gretchen Wolle, J. Fred.'s daughter, contributed "fifty portfolios containing the orchestral scores of the Bach cantatas given by the Bach Choir from 1912 to 1932, inclusive, as used by her father."[6] The scores went to Lehigh University and the orchestral parts to The Bach Choir. The gifts have been "a generous aid in sustaining the tradition of the Choir" and are still used.

Jones began rehearsing early in October 1938 in the Moravian Seminary and College for Women. President Snyder introduced Jones to the singers, stressing his "appreciation of the importance [of The Choir] in the world." Following the first rehearsal, Snyder told the Executive Committee things had "passed off splendidly. The new director was received with great enthusiasm . . . Mr. Jones is pleased with the results so far achieved."[7] That first rehearsal was also an important local event. A reporter wrote that Jones had begun the rehearsal with the Credo [of the *Mass*], "to which special attention was given."[8]

In a meeting preceding the 1939 Festival, Jones introduced The Choir officers to new technology, the public address system. He demonstrated how the Festival could be transmitted to a loudspeaker in the auditorium of a nearby university building. Purchase of the equipment was authorized, and it was first used in the 1940 Festival. This forward-looking request highlighted the desire of the officers to respond favorably to their new conductor. Fundamentally, it heralded the beginning of the major role broadcast and recording technology would play, and continues to play, in expanding The Choir's audience.

Jones's first Festival was not only sold out, the *Bethlehem Globe Times* reported, but "virtually as many persons were holding advantageous places on the campus, on chairs, rugs, and blankets, as occupied seats within the chapel."[9] Local headlines asserted, "Ifor Jones Proves Himself a Master," "Great Throng Thrilled by Fine Choral Work Under New Director." Music critics from Philadelphia and New York agreed Jones sustained the high standards expected of The Choir. One found the performance "at times electrifying and dynamically overwhelming."[10] Gretchen Wolle's response was both direct and surprising. "Mr. Jones directs more as my father did than any other conductor I have seen . . . All hail the new regime."[11] The first wife of Leopold Stokowski thought it was "perfectly splendid. Your new conductor is very fine."[12] Mrs. Theodore Roosevelt "held court under a big shade tree. She occupies that same seat in the church she has held for years."[13] Shortly after the Festival Jones wrote a letter "TO THE MEMBERS OF THE CHOIR. To know that we all . . . had a thrilling time, is satisfying . . . What more could a conductor ask? . . . I am very humbly grateful to you."[14]

In mid-September, following the 1939 Festival, Jones announced a major change in The Choir routine. Rehearsals would not be in The Moravian

Seminary for Women. They would move to a nearby Episcopal church. Since the Moravian Seminary hall had been a contribution of the Moravian Church to the welfare of The Choir, that decision meant that the only direct involvement with Moravians now remaining was the Moravian Trombone Choir. It still played at the Festivals and announced the *Mass*. Jones's letter to the singers announced the move and included a personal note, "It is apparent that a number of you experience the same impatience that I do, to get going . . . The month of September seems endless, and I am longing to hear the Credo again!"[15]

The Choir's rehearsals were being revitalized under the new conductor; its past closed with the death of Charles Schwab. The Executive Committee entered the following memorial into its record on 13 December 1939:

> In the death of Charles M. Schwab the Bach Choir loses one of its enthusiastic spirits and its most liberal supporters. A lover of music and an organist of no mean ability he was naturally drawn to the work of the Bach Choir, and co-incident with his affiliation with Bethlehem undertook a direct interest in its affairs and assumed a large portion of its financial obligations. A great admirer of the late Dr. Wolle, he gave every encouragement and support to his work. Elected a member of the Board of Managers and Executive Committee in 1912, he served as President of the Society from 1921 to 1925. Upon his retirement as President he was elected Honorary President, which position he occupied at the time of his death. We record our deep sorrow at his passing and our sense of loss in his wise counsel and liberal support.[16]

In 1940 the Thirty-third Bach Festival was dedicated to the memory of Charles M. Schwab.

Ten years later Jones delivered to the Executive Committee an unusually long report in which he emphasized the condition of The Choir in great detail. It was his summary of what he had achieved in his ten years as conductor. Everyone was more dedicated, more vibrant, and ready for an expanded schedule. The Choir was no longer the same group he had taken over from Carey:

> The whole psychology has changed. They [the singers] do not consider themselves as amateurs or volunteers. The emphasis now is on learning notes, singing properly, loyalty, and the hope that, God willing they will still be singing in the Bach Choir twenty years from now . . . The singers have confidence in their work and their combined abilities . . . the time is ripe—almost over ripe—for a broadening of our policy where the Festival is concerned. The Choir is quite capable of more work than it has been doing during the last twenty years . . . each succeeding year we are slowly but surely building eager audiences for our concerts. . . . Saturday morning sessions have also established themselves in the framework of the Festival . . . a Festival that has become more comprehensive

in its scope, and this is inevitably so, unless it is our desire to remain in our little bailiwick—and someday be "passed by." The Choir, always the focal point, has earned its place in the center of things, and fully deserves a new outlook on the whole idea of the Bach Festival in Bethlehem.[17]

Jones's report was no exaggeration. The Bethlehem Bach Choir entered publishing by supporting a series of editions of cantatas with English texts published by Schirmer and Company, an American firm. These landmark editions are discussed in detail in the following chapter. The Choir entered the era of recorded music with cantata "No. 78 Jesus, Thou my wearied spirit" in 1948. In one year thirteen thousand copies were sold.[18] A new plan was discussed to record all of Bach's choral works. The director of RCA wrote, "I take profound pleasure in having a small part in furthering, in developing and in bringing to the experience of our whole country something which you have made at Bethlehem that is uniquely beautiful and worthy."[19] For unknown reasons the project was never continued. However, Bach's *Mass* and *The Passion According to Saint Matthew* were recorded for "Voice of America" and "The [Choir] President stated that the U.S. State Department was in the process of making a film of the Bach Choir and had hired the Pathescope Production Corporation of New York to do the filming."[20] The first New York City appearance conducted by Jones was in 1946 in Carnegie Hall. Final plans for The Choir's appearance at the Cathedral of St. John the Divine in New York City were discussed at a special meeting of the Executive Committee on 3 April 1947. The name of The Choir was changed. "On motion it was resolved that the Choir be known as the "BACH CHOIR OF BETHLEHEM."[21] The purpose of the group was expanded as well:

> The Bach Choir of Bethlehem is formed for the purpose of encouraging a greater general interest in, appreciation of, and aesthetic and spiritual benefit from the choir and instrumental works, both sacred and secular, of Johann Sebastian Bach, through the education of the members of the Choir and the public in the works of Bach; and through the performance of the works of Bach, under competent musical direction, to the end that the highest standards of performance may be achieved and the perfection of creative art may be obtained.[22]

In view of the expanded audience, and the capability of the Bach Choir to study more Bach works, in 1950 a Second Bach Festival weekend was proposed in recognition of the anniversary of Bach's death in 1750. Saturday morning performances were added and became part of the Bethlehem Bach Festival tradition. The following account of the eager attendance and the critical praise these additions annually received in the press is typical:

More than five hundred people filled the Cathedral Church of the Nativity for Mr. [E. Power] Biggs recital. They were treated to superbly conceived playing of a brilliantly-chosen program . . . Mr. [Ralph] Kirkpatrick's masterly playing of the complex and monumental Goldberg Variations is justly celebrated. An overflow audience went directly from Mr. Biggs recital to the Parish House, filling every available seat to enjoy this musical experience.[23]

Jones brought a dramatic approach to his interpretation of Bach's music, one deeply rooted in his background in coaching opera. That drama had immediate appeal, and by Jones's fourth Bach Festival, the Choir could print phrases of adulation in its promotional brochure: "Never have I heard that Bach *Mass* sound throughout so well or make throughout such clear sense, musical and spiritual"—*New York Herald Tribune.* "Unfailing high standard of performance. Ifor Jones is a gifted and dynamic director"—*Philadelphia Bulletin.* "Ifor Jones conducted with fervor and highly keyed sense of the drama of the music"—*Baltimore Sun.*

In the *Herald Tribune,* Virgil Thomson not only praised The Bach Choir's "tradition and continuity," he went further and granted that "they may not embody always the latest in Bach scholarship, though at present they show considerable awareness in that regard."[24] The *New Yorker* found the *Mass* "perhaps more romantic in some details than the one we usually encounter around town, but it had a logic of its own."[25] Years later Ifor Jones was emphatic in his relationship to Bach research promoted by "purists" and "traditionalists." Jones is his own man, calling Bach affectionately "the old boy," "old fellow," and The Choir as "my bunch." "The work we do here," he told a reporter, "is that which I feel in my bones . . . I draw my conclusions from studying the works themselves."[26]

World War II affected the Festivals but did not deter them; the spirit of carrying on prevailed. For some, extended working hours at the steel mill made it difficult to attend rehearsals regularly; gas shortages curtailed travel to Bethlehem but did not make it impossible; and social activities, always such a prominent part of the Bach Festivals, were less extravagant because of food rationing.

Locally The Bach Choir and the Festivals became memories of order and beauty for soldiers. The first issue of the *Bach Choir Bulletin* contained a report beginning with the question:

How does it make you feel when you hear that the "boys" in the service think a great deal and often about the Bach Choir? We have received letters from a few and hear about others who take time out to let us know that the rehearsals and the Festival mean a great deal to them. We used to wonder whether, after the war, they would again find any pleasure in singing with us . . . It seems we were wrong. It means that their return must find us as strong an organization and as vigorous in our enthusiasm as when they sat with us. [27]

In a later *Bulletin*, the reference to those in military service was more personal and more expansive:

It was good to see John Shields and George Kreska at the rehearsals a few weeks ago. We would like to hear about the other "boys" in the service. When they return to visit us they insist that the conductor not mention their presence. Perhaps it is because they just want to drink in all they hear, so that they can take back as much as possible to keep them company until they come back again. There are about sixteen boys in the forces and we are looking forward to seeing them again and hear them yell their heads off in the Credo and Cum Sancto![28]

Postwar the Bach Festival remained the most important event in the local social calendar. Because of steel, railroads, coal, cement, and zinc, Bethlehem continued generating vast wealth with the inevitable resulting emphasis on social prestige. Local newspapers began printing a social column beside the reports of the musical Festival events. What follows is a random selection of items from "In Social Circles," May 1946:

Among the nearly 80 guests who will gather at the lovely home of Mrs. James V. Honeycutt on the Bath Pike this evening for their sixth "after Bach" supper party are many interesting persons. . . . Dr. Ifor Jones, director of the choir and his wife Lillian Knowles . . . will be among them and the Honeycutt's house guests, Dr. and Mrs. Francis Adler. . . .

* * *

Mr. and Mrs. Walter S. Trower of New York and Connecticut, here for the Festival are the house guests of Mr. and Mrs. Robert Young, 827 Beverly Ave., who entertained informally last evening after the second session . . . Mr. Trower is president of the American and Iron And Steel Institute and is well known here.

* * *

Mr and Mrs John Arthur Frick will have a family dinner at their home, Salisbury House, Allentown Rt. 10, this evening . . . many members of their family are here for the Festival.

* * *

Mr. Stone directs the famous Handel and Haydn Society of Boston, which has just completed its 131st season . . . that musical group is to Boston what the Bach Choir is to Bethlehem.[29]

For many outside Bethlehem the Festival became and remained a significant yearly event. Locally the Festival is known affectionately simply as "Bach," as Bethlehem Steel is called "the Steel." Even today a conversation-starter among strangers between sessions might begin, "And how many times have you come to Bach?"

In a decade when war had caused scarcity, turmoil, and suffering, Jones and the Board of Managers had expanded the Bach Festivals and promoted broadcasting, recording, and filming of its performances. The Choir Board and Jones had correctly assessed the broadened scope of the Bach Choir of Bethlehem in American musical life.

NOTES

1. "Executive Committee Minutes," 3 June 1938, ABCB.

2. Ibid.

3. "Welshman, Who Directs Bach Choir, Began Career at Age 7," *Bethlehem Globe Times*, 13 May 1946.

4. Alfred Mann, "A Tribute for Ifor Jones," *American Choral Review* 12, no. 2 (April 1970): 1–2.

5. Ibid.

6. "Executive Committee Minutes," 1 November 1938, ABCB.

7. Ibid.

8. "Bach Choir Rehearsal Proves a Rare Treat," n.d., ABCB.

9. "Bach Choir—Leader Jones Scores," *Bethlehem Globe*, 20 May 1939.

10. "Comments of Metropolitan Newspaper Critics on Bach Festival Here," No source, n.d., ABCB.

11. "Bach Choir—Leader Jones Scores," *Bethlehem Globe*, 20 May 1939, ABCB.

12. Ibid.

13. "Comment of Metropolitan Newspaper Critics on Bach Festival Here," No source., n.d. ABCB.

14. Ifor Jones to Bach Choir, 14 June 1939, ABCB.

15. Ifor Jones to Bach Choir, "To the Members of The Choir," 15 September 1939, ABCB.

16. "Minutes of the Executive Committee," 13 December 1939, ABCB.

17. Probably 13 June 1950, ABCB.

18. "Minutes of the Board of Managers," 25 October 1949, ABCB.

19. "Bach Choir, Director For Perfection in Recording," unidentified news article, 1944, ABCB.

20. "Executive Committee Minutes," 13 June 1950, ABCB.

21. "Minutes of the Board of Managers," 24 April 1945, ABCB.

22. Ibid.

23. Unidentified newspaper clipping, 21 May 1949, ABCB.

24. "Music," *Herald Tribune*, 20 May 1944.

25. "Musical Events," *The New Yorker*, 2 May 1946.

26. "Bach Director Dislikes Traditions," unidentified newspaper clipping, ca. 1948, ABCB.

27. *Bach Choir Bulletin*, 10 January 1945, ABCB.

28. *Bach Choir New*, 19 February 1945, ABCB.

29. *Bethlehem Globe*, 1946, ABCB.

Chapter 14

A Distinguished Career

1951–1969

There was every reason to assume that Dr. Ifor Jones's repeated successes would continue, indeed, that they would expand. The number of guarantors had increased from 402 in 1950 to 423 in 1951. The performances of orchestra, soloists, The Bach Choir, and Jones's conducting were continually praised by both local and national music critics. A *New York Times* reviewer characterized the social spirit of the Festival as "a cross between a garden party and a Sunday service." Musically, "in the *Mass*, the choir came fully into its own . . . Its tone rang out with new purity and clarity."[1] For post–World War II audiences, the U.S. State Department had spent a year and a half making a film, "Voice of a Choir," which was now on view as part of Voice of America.[2]

As a Bach scholar, Jones had prepared sixteen cantata editions during his first decade as conductor. Seven were performed and published in 1941, four in 1942, one in 1943, three in 1947, and one in 1948. The *Missa Brevis in G* was performed in 1960 and published in 1961. English versions of the cantatas included the original German as well.

In every way, these editions are superior to those printed in Germany or in England. Each opens with an introduction in which the purpose, source, and general meaning of the cantata is expertly described. Comments from Bach scholars such as C. S. Terry and Albert Schweitzer amplify the textual notes, as does the detailed instrumentation that Jones believed Bach had expressed. Jones's description of the second movement of Cantata No. 146 is typical. "Three elements unite to form this remarkable chorus: a ground bass, a freely moving solo part, and an independent chorus superimposed. This unique device produces a work of consummate artistry and craftsmanship."[3] About

Cantata No. 23, Jones writes, "The final Amen brings to a close one of Bach's most deeply moving choral works."[4]

Many editions with English translations had been published by both German and English presses; however, while these translations were always literary, they seldom matched Bach's settings word-for-word. Bach had taken great care in expressing every specific word musically; Jones's editions consistently matched music and text as closely as possible. One example from Cantata 78:

Bach: "Ach! ich bin ein Kind der Sunden, ach! ich irre weit und breit."
Diack: "Ah! a child of sin am I, ah! afar I go astray."
Stein/Jones: Ah! I am a child of evil: ah! I wander far and near."

Because Jones included expressive markings, words, and musical tempos to the vocal parts, "This accompaniment, which the Editor has arranged from the original instrumentation, may be played on a keyboard instrument and may also be used as a conductor's guide."[5] The complete Bach works that Jones had used had belonged to J. Fred. Wolle.

Every cantata edition was directly related to a Bethlehem Bach Festival performance. Therefore, Jones's editions are a significant part of the legacy of Bethlehem to the Bach movement in America. Jones's editions remain superb documents of musical scholarship and interpretation as it existed before late twentieth century Bach scholarship changed performance style and taste, and are lasting evidence of Dr. Jones's formidable understanding of Bach's music. There is no evidence Jones ever used or was influenced by the translations of Henry Drinker (the son of Dr. Drinker, president of Lehigh University), except the English text used in a performance of the Coffee Cantata in the 1956 Festival.

Despite the growing brilliance of his performances, the Board's slowly rising disaffection with Jones surfaced early in 1954. Jones felt that The Choir was his to do with as he pleased. The Board felt that Jones was under contract and that he should follow that contract. This dissatisfaction came to a head for the first time over Jones's rehearsing sections of *A German Requiem* by Johannes Brahms "by way of diversion."[6] The Executive Committee said this "should not be undertaken."[7] At a "Special meeting with Dr. Jones," the secretary-treasurer, Elmer Mack, recorded in the Minutes that, "Jones specifically and categorically stated that he did not need to be bound by the terms of the existing contract with the Choir."[8] Board members held that studying music composed by someone other than Bach was "certainly in violation of the tradition of the Choir."[9] There was no question that the conductor was subject to the contract, and Jones agreed to remove Brahms from the rehearsals. "All a misunderstanding," he said. Rehearsals from then on were devoted entirely to Bach.

Yet, more conflicts arose. Jones's contract stipulated that he was full-time conductor of The Bach Choir. He was told that any conducting or teaching outside The Bach Choir was possible only after it had been agreed upon by the Executive Committee. However, as his reputation in the American musical scene increased, he received invitations to conduct elsewhere, attend conferences, and offer classes. He began arranging these engagements without the consent of the Board. Directed to curtail his teaching, he complied. The question of outside employment, however, came up a number of times during the ensuing years, though in the end Jones consulted the Committee and followed its dictates. The Board also found it necessary to reprimand Jones for not attending its meetings. His attendance was part of the contract; he began to attend.

In addition the music committee wanted more say in the Festival program and the selection of soloists. The Executive Committee ruled that Festival planning, programs, and decisions on the selection of artists were to be submitted to the music committee a year in advance. Recommendations of the music committee would then be reported to the Executive Committee. Elmer Mack was chair of the music committee as well as secretary-treasurer of the Board. Committee members held oversight with a "proper share of responsibility."[10] The committee requested, probably at Mack's suggestion, "an outline in writing of procedures" from Jones.

Jones clearly felt this was a personal issue "between two adult men" and wrote a response directly to Mack, probably on the recommendation of the Board president:

> Sitting here in this office, with all this wonderful musical history around, scores and parts in the cabinets, many of which I myself copied and revised over the years, and the business of the organization in the duties, it seemed ridiculous that there should be a "you do this" and "I do that" arrangement between adult men. It makes for an unnatural and unhealthy "division", whereas the relatively small amount of "business" between us in the course of any given season, can the more easily become a matter of mutual understanding and discussion during the cup of coffee in the office in the morning, or a phone call or what have you. All this, of course is what we wish to make of it, you as Secretary-Treasurer and I as Musical Director. I have always been for the closest relationship with the business "element" of the Bach Choir as a whole. The Musical Director *is* a part of the whole, a part of that business in which he bears a significant responsibility, and no less significant than that of any other "office" or group concentrating on and toward the same ends . . . I do think, however, that as I told Dr. Estes a few weeks ago, this office here can only fulfill its various functions if there be a friendly, co-operative relationship. I am sure this can be achieved.[11]

By the end of 1956, open conflict between Jones and Mack had boiled over. "An exchange of opposing viewpoints ensued between the Director and Mack whereupon the Director was excused from the meeting, and Mack orally presented his resignation to the Committee. It was declined."[12] Mack retained his position on the music committee and Jones submitted a three-year plan to the music committee. The conductor accepted that the ultimate Board responsibility for the Festivals was musical as well as financial. The struggle between "opposing viewpoints" had apparently been resolved.

The Fiftieth Bach Festival was celebrated in 1958 amid a time of fiscal growth and musical change. Tickets sales were excellent, and the number of guarantors increased to 496. Dr. Estes, now Board president, expressed that "very grateful thanks and appreciation of the Ex. Comm. be extended to Mr. Elmer L. Mack, Secretary-Treasurer for his continuing efforts in behalf of the Choir beyond the call of duty."[13] Most importantly, the committee made a decision of lasting significance for The Choir to sing more cantatas in German.

The music committee examined Jones's three-year program very carefully and challenged the authenticity of Cantata BWV 189, which Jones proposed to perform in the 1958 Festival. The discussion revealed that the strain between Jones and Mack had not been resolved. Routinely, secretary Mack submitted the minutes of meetings to Dr. Estes for his corrections. When it was apparent that Jones intended to perform the disputed cantata, Estes, as president of the Board, could not sanction this and in April 1958 wrote to Mack:

> I believe it should be a matter of record somewhere that at one of the meetings which Ifor attended we certainly brought up the question of the fact that the authorship of Bach of said Cantata had been definitely questioned and with rather definite finality by a well-known Bach authority.[14]

Mack responded to Dr. Estes's letter:

> I am quite sure we made no reference at the meeting of April 15th to the authenticity of Cantata 189. I remember quite distinctly that I wanted to avoid any embarrassment to Dr. Jones in open meeting. After all, as he says, I have "limited musical knowledge" and I am sure he would have been furious had I opened it up. For that reason I handled it entirely through the Music Committee, and just talked with Jones by telephone . . . I think it was Saturday, April 5th.[15]

Mack noted the "opinion[s]" of four scholars that "No. 189 is spurious." Jones programmed the cantata anyway.

In 1959 Jones accurately "forecast a marvelous Festival next May."[16] Favorable reviews notwithstanding, Dr. Estes himself appointed an advisory committee "to assist in a reappraisal of Choir objectives."[17]

Elmer L. Mack was elected president of the Board of Managers in 1960, a post he held for five years. It soon became apparent that Jones's appraisal of Mack as a person of "limited musical knowledge" had been inaccurate. Mack had been the youngest first bass in the 1904 Festival and had sung in The Bach Choir for a "total of 60 years of service . . . in one capacity or another."[18] Mack's influence in the management of The Choir had become pervasive. He followed the business and industrial model in which he had functioned with great civic success. Mack had been a bank director, an insurance company director, the president of a Bethlehem hotel corporation, president of the Rotary Club, the Boy Scout Council, and the public library. He was a college, church, and archives trustee and a member of the boards of the Moravian Music Foundation and the Philadelphia Lyric Opera Co. Employed by one of the area's main anthracite coal mines, he was a person of vast experience with business, civic, and cultural influence.

For Mack, The Bach Choir was no different from the other organizations and businesses he'd been connected with; he saw all organizations as clearly hierarchical with the president as head. In his view the Board of Managers, specifically the Executive Committee, employed the conductor. The various committees had oversight of the organization's activities. The Board leadership shared Mack's view. This was not Jones's choir.

Mack was intensely interested in the history of The Bach Choir. When its office was moved into the Brethren's House, a part of Historic Bethlehem dating to 1748, he had a room set aside and dedicated to Wolle. A "Memoir" Mack wrote commemorating the one-hundredth birthday anniversary (1963) of J. Fred. Wolle revealed his full awareness of the details and context of the history of the enterprise:

> At that period [1898] Bach's work was hardly known in the new world, and his polyphonic style, so different from the plain hymns of Protestant America, could not have grown uncultivated in the American soil. It needed an apostle, and it needed singers who could find their way along its many contrapuntal paths.
>
> Luckily, since almost every institution is the lengthened shadow of a single man, the apostle was then growing up in Bethlehem, J. Fred. Wolle.[19]

Mack held the spiritual mission of The Bach Choir foremost in his mind. He told the singers, "We want our Festival to fill a gap spiritually and musically in a world that today is beset with trouble. If we fail in that I shall no longer be interested."[20] When Mack retired as president of The Choir in 1964, the Board of Managers said, "that Mr. Mack has been so completely devoted to The Choir, that he should be known as "Mr. Bach Choir" as long as he lives."[21] He was designated "Honorary President . . . for life."

Much of the early struggle between Mack and Jones was not only a conflict of personalities, but a struggle for the ultimate responsibility for musical as well as financial and promotional activities of The Choir. Jones's view was that his genius "entitled him to the Choir." It was "his" Choir.[22] He could dictate the music it would perform. He could act however he wanted during rehearsals. When Jones "kindly" stepped in to rehearse a church choir in which future Bach Choir president Thomas Church sang, Church wrote, "He treated us very gently and not at all as he treated the Bach Choir. With the Bach Choir he could be cruel at times, correcting an individual sharply before the whole group."[23]

Musically Dr. Jones was able to report continued success. An additional recording of both choral and instrumental music was produced and successfully marketed:

> 1961: "If the success of this Festival is measured by the increasing number of guarantors and ticket sales, then we are indeed enjoying unique success."[24]
> 1962: "Chapel seats for both week-ends have been sold out and we are endeavoring to direct traffic to Packer Auditorium for the sound transmission."[25]
> 1963: "Upwards of 8000 albums sold" of the Book-of-the-Month Club recording of the *B Minor Mass*.[26]

C. H. H. Weikel replaced Mack as the chairman of the music committee. A former steel mill laborer, Weikel had risen from a lowly job in the steel mill to become vice president and assistant to the president of Bethlehem Steel in charge of research. He "became one of the top commercial research professionals in the steel industry."[27] Music committee minutes make clear that under Weikel's leadership members took seriously their duties of spiritual and musical oversight. A person with great managerial and intellectual gifts, he took over a board-centered organization that had been structurally stabilized by Mack. Jones now regularly submitted programs several years in advance. Every cantata was discussed before approval by the Board.

When Mack resigned in 1965, Weikel replaced him; as the new president, Weikel delivered "A Brief History of The Bach Choir" before a meeting of the guarantors in 1965:

> Actually, our organization is closely akin to that of a major corporation having share-holders, officers, departments, etc. The organization is actually a simple one . . . What we have in this organization are guarantors, somewhat like stockholders. A Board of Managers of 25 persons who are elected for a term of four years from the guarantors and from the choir. The Board of Managers then elects an Executive Committee and also the active officers of the choir consisting of a president, three vice-presidents, secretary, assistant secretary, treasurer assistant treasurer . . . executive secretary. There are a number of committees such as the Music Committee, Publications, Press and Publicity Committee; and a Nominating

Committee. These committees are all active and the President is an ex-officio member of all committees. There is also a committee of representatives of the choir which is elected by the choir members. This committee is free to discuss any matter at all relating to the choir.[28]

Interestingly, Weikel never mentions the conductor as part of the corporate group.

Two problems now were more often discussed: the quality of the soloists and the personnel of the orchestra. In 1963 Ifor Jones wrote to Elmer Mack: "Soloists have been a constant problem." In 1965, the Executive Committee "discussed the criticism raised relative to the poor quality of the soloists."[29] The following year the Board of Managers and the Executive Committee faced the "increasingly difficult problem in obtaining soloists due to the increasing demand of the Metropolitan Opera and the substantial increase in fees."[30] Soloists were ultimately selected by the music committee from a list of four in each voice group given to the members by the Director. Jones wanted to develop a group of singers whom he had trained and who would sing in a number of successive Festivals. Unfortunately, for whatever reason, that never came about.

There was a similar crisis with the orchestra when the Philadelphia Orchestra, which for many years had been a part of the Festivals, began to tour in May. An orchestra manager now had to be hired to engage musicians for individual Festivals. Neither the soloists nor orchestra problems were solved while Ifor Jones remained conductor.

The Festivals, however, were always sold out. Adding a third weekend was seriously discussed, as was the possibility of building a concert hall large enough to accommodate the increasing audience. In response to this anticipated demand, a Thursday evening public "rehearsal" for local people was added to the Festival calendar. The number of guarantors grew, and The Choir was invited to sing at major musical events on the East Coast. At a concert in Baltimore, their performance of the *B Minor Mass* was described as "the most musically inspiring orchestral evening of this or any recent season."[31]

Audience growth, notable musical achievements notwithstanding, and solidification of Board power finally culminated for Jones in 1968 when the Board demanded his resignation. Members had finally reached their limit of constant clashes and disagreements with him.

The first discussion to seek his removal had taken place during an Executive Committee special meeting on 18 July 1968. Weikel had resigned as president due to poor health. Kenneth Houck, vice president of the Board, presided. An assistant vice president for industrial and public relations at

Bethlehem Steel Corporation, he had become an officer of The Choir in 1960. Both he and his wife had been singers since 1941. Elmer Mack was also present. The minutes of the meeting are very brief:

> The general welfare of the Choir was considered and discussed at some length. The continued service of the Director was considered, whereupon it was agreed that secret ballots be taken whether or not his service be terminated and, if so when. On the question: "Shall the Director, Ifor Jones, be given notice of the termination of his service?" the vote was: Yes—8, No—1.[32]

Three members voted for Ifor Jones's immediate dismissal. Six voted that he remain to conduct the Festival the following year. At a meeting on 1 August, Weikel's resignation was received, a new president was elected, and "the recommendations of the Executive Committee"[33] were considered. Of the twenty four voting members present, twenty one voted in favor of resignation. With Weikel's resignation accepted, Judge Carleton T. Woodring was unanimously elected president. An attorney, former judge, and past three-term member of the Pennsylvania Legislature, Woodring would lead the Board in the most difficult personnel decision the members had faced.

There must have been previous meetings and many behind-the-scenes conversations that do not survive in the Minutes. In fact there are no minutes at all for the first half of the 1968. But when the officers met on 1 October, a new Board president reported that he had met a number of times with Jones. As the conductor had refused to resign, the Board of Managers would have to require a resignation.

At the same meeting Kenneth Houck diplomatically announced his resignation "in order to avoid, so far as possible, any personal issue in the current controversy between The Bach Choir and its Musical Director."[34] A few weeks later Jones's refusal to resign led the Board and the Executive Committee to reinstate the singers to whom Jones had given "involuntary leaves of absence."

Jones's musical genius, powerful conducting, and profound knowledge of Bach had sustained him for nearly thirty years. But his verbal and physical abuse of singers had so deeply offended a sufficient number of singers and the Board, who were ultimately responsible for the "general welfare of the Choir," as to make his resignation necessary.

Dr. Jones submitted his final Festival program while the planning committee began screening a "wide range of applicants" to replace him. At a dinner with the Board and the singers following the Festival, Jones was publicly honored for his contribution to The Bach Choir. Temperamental until the end, he stormed out of the banquet and severed further relations with anyone associated with The Bach Choir of Bethlehem.

Woodring had been president for less than two years in 1972 when he was succeeded by Houck, who had rejoined the Board after Jones's departure. Houck became one of the longest serving presidents in the history of The Bach Choir.

Ten years later Houck dispassionately summarized Jones's contributions in his booklet BACH IN BETHLEHEM A MUSICAL TRADITION [*sic*]:

> During the following years, Ifor Jones encouraged the interest of the younger generation in the choral music of Bach, and took many talented young people into the ranks of the Choir. He was responsible for many important features; among them the addition of Saturday morning programs at festival time, consisting of instrumental works or recitals of eminent singers and players; and the inauguration of a repeated performance for a second weekend, which had made it possible for a greater number to attend the Festival. Those innovations have become a standard and continue in present-day Festivals.[35]

In his history, Houck made no mention of Ifor Jones's performance editions of Bach cantatas. However, these editions had placed Jones among the major Bach scholars of his time. Since Jones had undertaken the editions with the full backing and support of the Board, they remain a contribution of The Choir to general Bach scholarship. Perhaps of greater significance is the fact that Jones's editions supplied American singers and choral conductors with unsurpassed performance scores during and immediately following World War II, when they were scarce or even unavailable.

In 1970 a lengthy "Tribute to Ifor Jones" appeared in the *American Choral Review*, a musical periodical edited by Jones's successor, Dr. Alfred Mann. Many accomplishments are described including the one hundred and forty-five Bach cantatas he directed with The Bach Choir of Bethlehem. Thirty-three were new to the Festivals and thirty were United States premieres. But the reviewer's tribute concluded that the

> honor most befitting his distinguished career was the applause; unprecedented for a choral performance in sixty-two seasons, that ended last year's Bethlehem Bach festival—a unique occasion in which audience and choir joined in admiration and gratitude.[36]

NOTES

1. "Critic Finds Deeper Meaning Implied in Bach's *B Minor Mass*," source unknown, 19 May 1952, ABCB.

2. "Minutes of the Executive Committee," 16 October 1951, ABCB.

3. Ifor Jones, ed., "We must through great tribulation," No. 146 (New York: G. Schirmer, 1942).

4. Ifor Jones, ed., "Cantata No. 23" (New York: G. Schirmer, 1947).

5. Ifor Jones, ed., "Cantata No. 78" (New York: G. Schirmer, 1941), 3.

6. "Minutes of the Executive Committee," 26 January 1954, ABCB.

7. Ibid.

8. "Minutes of the Executive Committee," 1 February 1954, ABCB.

9. Ibid.

10. "Minutes of the Executive Committee," 24 January 1956, ABCB.

11. Ifor Jones to Elmer L. Mack, 11 November 1955, ABCB.

12. "Minutes of Special Meeting," 3 November 1956, ABCB.

13. "Minutes of the Executive Committee," 17 June 1958, ABCB.

14. W. L. Estes Jr. to Elmer L. Mack, 29 April 1958, ABCB.

15. Elmer L. Mack to W. L. Estes, 1 May 1958, ABCB.

16. "Minutes of the Executive Committee," 31 March 1959, ABCB.

17. "Minutes of the Executive Committee," 21 January 1958, ABCB.

18. C. H. H. Weikel, "A Brief History of The Bach Choir." Unpaginated TS, 14 May 1965, ABCB.

19. "Memoir Adopted by Bach Choir of Bethlehem At Executive Committee Meeting, March 26, 1963 On the Occasion of 100th Birthday Anniversary of Dr. J. Fred. Wolle—April 4, 1963. Elmer Mack, President," ABCB.

20. "Minutes of the Annual Meeting," 11 May 1962, ABCB.

21. Special Meeting of Board of Managers, 15 September 1964, ABCB.

22. Taped interview with Mary Meilinger, ca. Spring 2003, ABCB.

23. Thomas Church to the author, n.d., in the author's possession.

24. "Minutes of the Executive Committee," 22 June 1961, ABCB.

25. "Minutes of the Executive Committee," 27 March 1962, ABCB.

26. "Minutes of the Executive Committee," 21 June 1962, ABCB.

27. Edmund F. Martin with David J. Morrison, *Bethlehem Steelmaker* (Bethlehem, PA: BMS Press, 1992), 98.

28. Weikel, "A Brief History," unpaginated typescript.

29. "Minutes of Executive Committee," 22 June 1965, ABCB.

30. "Minutes Board of Managers and Executive Committee," 25 October 1966, ABCB.

31. "Minutes of the Annual Meeting," 12 May 1967, ABCB.

32. "Minutes of the Executive Committee," 18 July 1968, ABCB.

33. Ibid.

34. Kenneth L. Houck to Carleton T. Woodring, 1 October 1968, ABCB. "It would be typical of Bethlehem Steel Corporation to insist that Houck resign in order to prevent damage to Bethlehem Steel Corporation's reputation." John Jordan in a conversation with the author.

35. Kenneth L. Houck, *Bach in Bethlehem a musical tradition* (Oak Printing Co., Bethlehem PA: 1979), unpaginated.

36. Ruth Hutchison, "A Tribute to Ifor Jones," *American Choral Review* 12, no. 2 (April 1970): 46.

Chapter 15

Connecting with Bach

1969–1976

Alfred Mann

When the Executive Committee demanded Ifor Jones's resignation, they did so because of interpersonal problems between the conductor and the singers that were becoming insurmountable, problems in no way obvious to the public. Listeners at annual Festivals still overflowed onto the lawn around Packer Church. Notable musicians, fashionable couples, politicians, and Bach lovers continued their annual "Pilgrimage to Bethlehem." Jones's musical style was not in question. His grand, dramatic interpretations of Bach sung in English still moved Festival goers. Granted, some music critics did feel his interpretation was dated, and Bach research was changing ideas about the performance of Bach's music.

Committee members were convinced that a more personal, less temperamental, more mild-mannered conductor was needed to end the difficulties and preserve the integrity of the Choir. As a replacement for Ifor Jones, they found Dr. Alfred Mann, a professor at Rutgers University. Kenneth Houck, chair of the music committee, became Mann's champion, making a detailed summary of Mann's qualifications for the committee:

> Dr. Alfred Mann is an internationally renowned authority on Baroque music who was trained under one of Bach's latter-day successors at St. Thomas's in Leipzig. Dr. Mann has combined his career as a most distinguished choral conductor with that of scholar and author, who has explored in depth the teaching of the classical masters. He studied at the State Academy of Music, Berlin, and the Royal Conservatory in Milan. In the United States he continued his studies at the Curtis Institute of Music and Columbia University. He is Professor of Music at Rutgers University. He is also editor of *The American Choral Review*, one indication of the growth of musical scholarship associated with Bethlehem Bach.[1]

An expert bass player, Mann also performed on the recorder so well that as a student at the Curtis Institute of Music, he had been asked to instruct flute students interested in playing recorder.

Mann's father was a painter who remained in Germany when his wife, Edith, and son Alfred immigrated to the United States. Alfred's association with Baroque music began by studying with his mother. Edith Mann was a well-known harpsichordist who concertized and made recordings of the music of seventeenth-century keyboard masters. She played the complete cycle of Bach's harpsichord concertos in the United States. In a tribute to his mother, Mann wrote, "She left, both as performer and writer, a legacy characteristic of a pioneering generation to whom the rediscovery of the past had been an unfailing incentive for clarifying the ever growing demands of the present."[2]

Dr. Mann was also known as well for his scholarly performance editions of works by Handel. He had been a professor at Rutgers University for twenty years and conducted the Rutgers Collegium Musicum, and the Cantata Singers of New York, was a guest conductor of the American Concert Choir, and had performed in Carnegie Hall.

Mann seemed ideally suited for The Bach Choir. Not only was he one of the most recognized music scholars in both America and Europe, but he was mild mannered, self-effacing, modest, socially adept, not temperamental—a welcome antidote to Jones. While he would not live in Bethlehem, or resign his position at Rutgers, he would commute to Bethlehem staying overnight in the Choir's offices.

The music committee was now more than willing to overlook the residency requirement. They offered him the position, and he accepted immediately. Before appearing in Bethlehem, however, he spent six weeks on a European tour sponsored by the American Philosophical Society. He attended performances of works by Handel in both West and East Germany, was elected to the editorial board of the International Handel Society, and would assist in their preparation of a complete edition of Handel's works. While in East Germany, he visited Bach's church in Leipzig and spoke with his former teacher, Kurt Thomas, the thirteenth successor of Bach. In the fall of 1969, Dr. Alfred Mann took his place on the podium as the fourth conductor of The Bach Choir.

Mann's plans were to align The Choir as directly as possible with what was known about Bach and his music. Locally, Mann would also connect The Bach Choir to its Moravian roots and to the Bethlehem community. The Bethlehem Bach Festivals would be sacred concerts, but they would also be, through Mann's extensive program notes, opportunities for the audience to understand each piece within the frame of Bach's work—the first time programs had been used in this way. The Bach Choir would become an active participant in Bach research, and would travel to Leipzig to sing in Bach's church.

Finally, Mann would seek solutions to what he called, "One of the foremost—and most vexing—concepts that arose in the twentieth-century musical practice . . . authenticity in the presentation of early music."[3] In one of his first interviews with the local press, Mann stated that his concern

> will be in exploring how the conclusions of modern Bach scholarship may be absorbed into the work of an organization that in its devotion to the cultivation of Bach's works is without parallel in this country.[4]

In another interview Mann was more emphatic:

> We must constantly search to bring out something new of Bach . . . To stand still, or rest on past honors would be fatal. Dr. Jones is aware of this and I intend

to be. It will be my obligation to bring a fresh approach to each festival and never to allow it to grow stale. I realize that this is a large assignment, but it is a fascinating one.[5]

Mann's guide for "a fresh approach to each festival" would be Kurt Thomas. A number of years before Mann arrived in Bethlehem, he and his colleague William Reese, soon to become the assistant conductor of The Bach Choir, had worked on an English adaptation of Kurt Thomas's *Lehrbuch der Chorleitung*, published in English in 1971 in New York by Associated Music Publishers. In the "Forward," Mann and Reese wrote, "The translators have assumed this task on the basis of close acquaintance with the author's work both as students in his conducting classes in Berlin and as hosts to various courses given under his direction in the United States."[6] In so doing, Mann and Reese both established a personal connection with Bach.

In the final chapter, "General Observations on Choral Literature and Program Planning," Kurt Thomas expresses the ideas that became central to Mann's view of the Festival and The Bach Choir of Bethlehem, that "a musical composition and its individual quality claim placement in a certain framework or function."[7] Later, "The works selected should preferably have a common theme of subject. I think the most plausible and intelligible programs are those built around such a subject or theme."[8] "What are the unifying elements for a compelling program?" Thomas asks. "One point of departure is an historical orientation."[9] Thomas expands this view and roots it in Baroque practice:

Recent trends to place sacred music once again within the framework of a church service or *vespers* [author's italics]—as has been the practice for centuries in the motet concerts of the Thomanerchor, Leipzig, or the vespers in the Kreuzchor, Dresden—and to encourage the participation of the congregation, as well as the increasing number in "open sings," show an awareness of the proper setting and function of choral music.[10]

That is the foundation on which Mann and Reese built the next thirteen years with The Bach Choir.

The first Bach Festival Mann conducted was thoroughly influenced by its tradition, by Thomas's principle of choral programming, and by new scholarship in Bach performance. The Festival included all of Bach's motets and naturally concluded with the traditional singing of the *Mass*.

An exhaustive examination of the motets had appeared in *American Choral Review* in 1965. Mann edited the journal and came to The Bach Choir with a deep understanding of these works. Unlike the cantatas, the motets had direct performance links to Bach:

Not tied to the liturgy, however, the motets kept their place within the mainstream of living music. . . . They are the only works that have been performed continuously without interruption until our own time. . . . They did not have to be rediscovered like the cantatas and Passions.[11]

The connection of Moravian music to the Festivals had become more subtle, but no less significant. In Bach's practice, the *Kantorei* tradition, a motet was a sacred choral piece with "an autonomous freedom of instrumentation that can be varied according to the instrumental resources available and the musical structure of the compositions concerned."[12] That described the spirit traditionally practiced by the Bethlehem Collegium Musicum in Bethlehem's Central Moravian Church. Along with the *Singstunde*, instrumental accompaniment had made it possible for J. Fred. Wolle to associate Bach's music with the church. Thus, Mann connected the Bach Choir with Bach's musical legacy and Moravian music traditions.

Mann had translated an article by Wilhelm Ehmann for the *American Choral Review*, which gave eight specific suggestions for performing the motets:

1. Reduce the choral forces.
2. Use a strong keyboard.
3. Add instruments to the bass.
4. Double the voices with strings.
5. Use a brass ensemble for chorales.
6. Add a small choir.
7. Follow the original dynamic markings.
8. Use woodwinds if available.[13]

According to a local press review, "Dr. Mann Rediscovers Bach," the rediscovery involved singing the motets in German, with accompaniment and soloists.[14] When the evening open rehearsal was over:

Applause broke out spontaneously, still unusual at the festivals, and one felt it was only right. . . . This is going to be a landmark festival. Dr. Mann has proven conclusively that he is the legitimate successor of Wolle, Carey, and Jones, a distinguished company.[15]

A new conductor for The Bethlehem Bach Festivals was national news, and Mann's first performance was covered by music critics from New York and Philadelphia. Comparisons between Mann and Jones were inevitable. The critics commented positively on the "increased clarity"[16] and the faster tempi. "The *Mass* is some 20 minutes shorter under the new director's aegis."[17] While one critic saw Mann's "deficiency in the rudiments of the craft of conducting . . . it would be well for him to do something about it as soon as possible,"[18] another found "his beat easy to follow."[19] A third reporter described Mann's conducting in detail:

> He is a man who seemingly dances when he conducts, but his feet never leave the ground. He seems to infuse the score with a bright, baroque light, and to pass his enthusiasm straight on to his vocal and instrumental forces.[20]

One singer commented, "Dr. Mann always conducted a lighter *Mass*."[21]

President Woodring reported, "The transition from the former conductor to our present one has proceeded with little or no trauma."[22] Mann "reviewed the pleasures and difficulties of his first festival" at a meeting of the Executive Committee. He "stressed the importance of maintaining a strong base in the Bethlehem community but of retaining national standing through the quality of the programs of the Choir."[23] Thus, he laid out his vision of a broad plan for community development and national standing.

To that end, and guided by new Bach research, the next Festival would reenact a Leipzig Christmas program presented by Bach in 1723. The participation of the Moravian College Choir to sing authentic antiphonal sections of the *Magnificat* would include the broader community. The Festival program would also include a Bethlehem Bach premiere of the "Sanctus in D Major," BWV 243. Plans for a "very special event" in 1973, the hundredth singing of the *Mass*, included the possibility of singing it at St. Thomas Church in Leipzig, thereby increasing the national status of the Choir. But the travel proposal was rejected as premature.

Mann had been with The Bach Choir for only two years before two major celebrations in its history: the hundredth rendition of the *Mass* in 1972 and The Choir's seventy-fifth anniversary in 1973. Mann discussed the plans for the 1972 anniversary with a local reporter, who

> asked him if he had a definite idea of what the Bach Choir should be . . . Crossing his legs, he began to answer the question, saying each word as though it were a separate unit. "In order to keep abreast, the strongest contribution one can make is in the type of program that is presented. 'In other words, the entire program for a Bach Festival must be selected keeping in mind an historical as well as musical unity. Dr. Mann said with a flourish. "I like to present the entire vista of Bach's work."[24]

As the two anniversary years began, there was a slight complication in scheduling the celebration of the one hundredth *Mass*. Should it take place in 1972 or wait until 1973, which would be the 75th anniversary of The Choir? The ultimate decision was to separate the anniversary of the *Mass* from the Festival and present it as a separate offering that would be a gift to the community requiring no tickets. The local public television station filmed the event and distributed it nationally. The film was run by two hundred educational television stations on Christmas Eve.

The event was reviewed by national music critics. A critic for the *(Washington, D.C.) Evening Star* echoed the sentiments of others:

> Promptly at 7:30 p.m. the brass choir, a longstanding tradition that goes back to the 18th century, played a chorale, and without waiting for the echoes to die down, the conductor Mann launched his singers and players into the heart wrenching opening chord of the Kyrie.
>
> It was, by and large, a very moving performance, especially for those conscious of the history of the choir who were performing it. Mann prefers leisurely tempos . . . There is no sense of haste in his reading—one feels instead a sense of inevitable and organic growth.[25]

Before the 1972 Festival, Mann told the Board of Managers that "the 1972 program is most unique and that nowhere else in the world could the six masses which Bach wrote be heard in one program."[26] The Bach Choir had performed all of Bach's motets, masses, and oratorios under Mann's direction, presenting a vista of Bach's works. The Bach Choir gained international influence in yet another way that year. It became the headquarters of an American chapter of *Neue Bach-Gesellschaft*, an international organization newly formed for the propagation of Bach's works. That honor stemmed from Mann's connections as an international music scholar of the first rank. He had been elected to the board advising the group on publications of Bach and named secretary of the American chapter. One of the period's most significant contributions to Bach scholarship, the authentication of "Bach's Calov Bible" and an in-depth study of its contents, was the result of Mann's connection with the American chapter. For the first time, he was participating directly in all aspects of Bach scholarship: performance, programming, and publication.

This Bible became known to scholars in 1969 through an article, "Bach's Bible," by Christoph Trautmann published in *American Choral Review*.[27] This Bible was owned by Concordia Seminary in St. Louis, Missouri. Mann suggested that Dr. Howard Cox, a professor of theology at Moravian Seminary and a singer in The Bach Choir, make sense of the many underlinings and annotations in its three volumes. Dr. Ellis Finger, professor of German at Lafayette College and also a Bach Choir member, would translate from the German. This intersection of talent from The Choir proved to be one of the most important contributions to Bach scholarship made in the last part of the twentieth century. It was verified through chemical analysis that the various notations in the Bible were in fact Bach's, research that took ten years. *The Calov Bible of Bach* was published in 1985 over the bylines of Howard Cox, editor, and Ellis Finger, translator.[28] Cox described how Mann figured prominently in every phase of this project:

> Finally, there is one major contributor to this project whose interest, efforts, and expertise have been involved from beginning to end, Alfred Mann, professor of musicology at the Eastman School of Music. Professor Mann first made known to me the existence of Bach's Bible. Subsequently, he procured the microfilms and offered much valuable advice and assistance. In the final stage of this project he was assigned by the editor to do the final review and revisions of the translation. His contributions to this project over the ten-year period of research were largely behind the scenes, but they are substantial.[29]

In a journal article detailing his research, Cox reported, "Three subjects seem to have captured Bach's interest . . . (1) God's providential order; (2) Bach's [own] divinely appointed vocation; and (3) the origin of church music."[30] Bach wrote, "With devotional music God is always present with His grace."[31]

Two prominent musicians joined The Bach Choir in 1972: Dr. William Reese and William Whitehead. Reese became associate conductor, a newly created post. Reese was professor of music at Haverford College, conductor of the Philadelphia Chamber Chorus, and artistic director of several musical festivals, and he and Mann were very close colleagues. Initially, his role was modest, conducting a small group of singers in the Saturday morning performance of Bach's organ *Mass*. Fully committed to Mann's innovations, Reese supported them directly in rehearsals and the Festival concerts he conducted.

The second musician was William Whitehead, organist of First Presbyterian Church of Bethlehem and, for a number of years, organist for The Bach Choir. Among his notable contributions was the production of a long-play recording reenacting the organ recital in which Felix Mendelssohn "initiated in fact, the rediscovery of Bach's organ music."[32] This historic Whitehead recital and the recording were made in Bethlehem on The First Presbyterian Church organ. Alfred Mann wrote the record jacket notes.

Greater musical activity required increased administrative support and board governance. The new position of executive secretary had been created when Joyce Lukehart replaced Margaret Freefield who was retiring after thirty years as secretary. The office moved to Heckerwelder Place in Bethlehem. As staff demands became greater, so did the obligations of the Board. Kenneth L. Houck was elected the new Board president in 1972. Known for strong leadership, he immediately ordered that "a review of expenses over the past ten years will be made."[33] Houck was the first president to launch an era of accountability that would facilitate the forward movement of The Bach Choir.

Mann had masterfully made Bach, Felix Mendelssohn, The Bach Choir, Bach, and Bethlehem an actual musical unit. Houck provided the genius to create a staff and Board that could sustain this expanding unit.

In 1973 what the press called "Bach At 75" marked the anniversary of The Choir's founding in 1898. As always, Mann kept the history of The Choir foremost in mind by choosing the *Christmas Oratorio*, the major work that Wolle had given its American premier as part of Second Bach Festival. Wolle's intention had been to present the main events of the Christian church year in the 1901 Festival; Mann mirrored Wolle's intention by adding the "Easter" and "Ascension" oratorios to the 1973 celebration. He had created an opportunity for listeners to hear all three of Bach oratorios.

Associate conductor Reese led a smaller ensemble and the Festival soloists in Saturday morning performances of the two oratorios. The headline in the *Bethlehem Globe-Times* read, "Dr. Reese's Conducting Draws High Praise."[34]

Following the 1973 Festival, a plan was proposed to the Executive Committee to make the performance of the *Christmas Oratorio* an annual event. The performance was for the townspeople, Mann said.[35] When the time came, The Bach Choir completed its two years of celebration by performing the *Christmas Oratorio* for the Bethlehem community, as Bach had for his Leipzig congregation, making it possible for people who did not normally attend the Festival to experience Bach's music. The Christmas performance was underwritten by a local sponsor as a community event and took place in the Bethlehem high school auditorium before more than eleven hundred people who, as was customary, joined in singing the chorales. The last part of Mann's grand plan had been realized.

Minutes record that Mann closed the year by informing the Board explicitly of the programming principles he had derived from Kurt Thomas, choirmaster of St. Thomas Church, Leipzig, and Bach's successor:

Two anniversary years have produced great gains for the Choir. [Mann] feels that the St. Matthew Passion is a good follow up to the last two Festivals. The Festivals for 1975 and 1976 will consist of cantatas chosen from the 95 which have never been performed in Bethlehem. Dr. Mann stated that he felt three things are necessary in a Festival: (1) one great classic work on every program; (2) one strong, name soloist; and (3) a point of view expressed in the program. He is considering for the 1975 Festival some of the 75 cantatas which Bach wrote with Psalm settings.[36]

The year 1974 saw increased musical innovation and expansion of Choir
activities beyond Bethlehem. Eugene Ormandy, conductor of the Philadelphia
Orchestra, invited The Bach Choir to sing the *Mass* with the orchestra the
following year in Philadelphia and in Carnegie Hall. Ormandy's invitation
was seen as affirmation of The Choir's national image. Members of the
Executive Committee accepted unanimously. However, those performances
would once again raise unanticipated and harsh questions about The Choir's
size, changes in the nature of performance of Bach's choral works, and The
Choir's obligation to the community and to its singers.

Mann's next innovation was to have The Choir sing *The Passion According
to Saint Matthew* in German. Previous performances had been sung in
English, but singing Bach in German was consistent with the current Bach
scholarship. Furthermore, Mann was convinced he could increase the
musical understanding of the singers by studying the music with them in the
original language. Singers confirmed that singing in German did deepen their
understanding of the music, and some noted that it changed the tone quality
and increased The Chorus's expressiveness. The "continued use of German
cannot help but focus the bland singing of the chorus. Their dedication to
Bach must be acknowledged, but their lack of lively tone is also a fact, and
German will help bring it into line."[37] Another reviewer commented, "The
phrasing was smoother in the original tongue."[38]
     One critic supported singing in the original language as a means to focus
on the text and music rather than the conductor. "Mann's conducting is
carefully devoid of personality whims, for he places himself entirely at the
disposal of the composer. The razzle-dazzle finales of previous seasons are a
thing of the past, and he lets Bach speak for himself."[39]
     A balanced comparison of Mann and Jones by a Philadelphia critic said
"Mann's conception of the *Mass* is a beautiful one. His chorus sounds
particularly luminous, though not as weighty as it seemed years ago.
But, if that is so, weightiness has been sacrificed to welcome clarity and
refinement."[40] As always, Mann was mindful of presenting "vistas of Bach's
works." He described "the St. Matthew Passion as the highpoint in Bach's
career in Leipzig and the *B Minor Mass* marks the summit of Bach's career as
a composer."[41] Like all of Mann's innovations, singing in German effortlessly
became part of The Choir's "tradition."

Reese's Saturday morning performances also received rave reviews from
both critics and audiences. A reviewer described the *Double Violin Concerto
in D minor*, BWV 1043, in which "[b]oth [violinists] sustained the highly
lyrical writing, notable during the soaring Largo. Reese exerted supple

direction, never interfering with the limpid flow or losing the necessary pulse. Everything changed for the final Allegro. Reese unleashed a fiery climax, bringing the audience to their feet with salvos of applause."[42]

Bach's *Christmas Oratorio* was sung again for the Bethlehem public as a part of the celebration that was now assuming national overtones as Bethlehem designated itself "The Christmas City." Members of the audience the previous year had expressed disappointment that they were not hearing The Choir often enough, and Mann agreed to add choruses from parts IV, V, or VI. He told the press, "This year's performance was based on the tremendous response of last year."[43]

The new year, 1975, brought new opportunities for The Bach Choir to broaden its audience and prestige. International in scope, the main event was a centennial concert tribute to Dr. Albert Schweitzer, one of the foremost interpreters of Bach's organ music and a Bach scholar renowned for his two-volume *Bach*. This concert in Carnegie Hall was The Choir's fourth invitation to the great concert venue. They sang two choruses from the "St. Matthew Passion" and the "Kyrie" and "Gloria" from the *B Minor Mass*. The music critic for the *Bethlehem Globe Times* wrote, "The New York audience heard the Bach Choir at its best." The Choir sang with the American Symphony Orchestra conducted by Richard Westerberg, director of music at the Cathedral of St. John the Divine and a close friend of Mann. An estimated audience of twenty-seven hundred heard the concert.

A Boston critic's review of the 1975 Bach Festival again brought attention to two aspects of The Choir: its size and the Moravian chorale played before the opening of the *Mass*. Controversy rose from the critique written by Michael Steinberg, music critic of the *Boston Globe*. He wrote:

> What, in the end, is not to be escaped concerning the Bach Festival is that there are too many bodies on that stage. I found much to enjoy in the two programs . . . and I would have enjoyed everything still more had there been one third as many singers.[44]

A defense of the group's size that articulated the essential nature of The Choir appeared as a letter to the editor of the *Bethlehem Globe Times* from a Choir member:

> I have come to understand that the uniqueness of the Bethlehem Bach Choir is that despite its large membership it has always been able to make beautiful sounds with incomparable music of our revered and beloved Bach.
> Mr. Steinberg, coming as he does from a greater metropolitan background, has entirely missed the point of community. We are a choir composed mostly of small

town people who together are able to do something very special and wonderful. Throw out 100 of us, retain only the youngest, finest voices, and you will destroy the singular marvel that is the Bethlehem Bach Choir. The Choir would then be no different from any other group singers of Bach . . . I fervently hope that neither the Board of Directors nor Dr. Mann will take too seriously Mr. Steinberg's remarks.[45]

Mann explained simply, "Each year many young people come to the September auditions. It is our policy to take every single one who is qualified . . . Instead of reducing the number of auditions for next year, I plan to expand it."[46] As for the chorale's preceding the *Mass*, he justified it as "tradition" dating from the first performance of the *Mass* in 1900. Yet a Philadelphia critic of the same Festival felt the size of The Choir no disadvantage: "Among the wonders of springtime, is the wonder of this amateur chorus, now at about 150 members; a bit smaller than formerly, and how it copes with the long, florid or sustained phrases of Bach's music."[47]

Quite generally there was only high praise, and Mann and The Bach Choir were elevated to positions as secure national musical standards:

Mann is in the front rank as a conductor of Bach. His inclination and temperament is centrist, and his readings convey a rare and wonderful coming together
of thoughtfulness and spontaneity.[48]

That praise was sustained in Philadelphia at two sold-out performances at The Academy of Music, one on a Friday afternoon and one the following evening. The Bethlehem reporter wrote, "The audience seemed to be amazed . . . Comments of 'fabulous' and 'unbelievable' rang out" at the end of the concert."[49] He noted, however, that there were times when the 170 voices did overpower the orchestra. *The Philadelphia Inquirer*'s music critic was more direct in criticizing the size of The Choir, using the term "authentic" performance. But he laid the blame for this outdated interpretation on Ormandy:

Eugene Ormandy, aware of the difficulty of authentic performance with the
forces at hand, appeared to be trying to go in two directions at once. The 180-
voice choir required substantial instrumental forces to balance it. That is the
essence of the 19th-century interpretation of Bach. But Ormandy dipped to
intimate instrumental support when the soloists were singing and the divergence
of approach set up that way removed whatever unity might have emerged in the
performance . . . This is not to say the piece did not have its moments.[50]

As Ormandy left the stage, he was overheard telling The Choir, "Bravo. Terrific."

In New York the same differences of experience between the audience and music critics was repeated. Describing the audience reaction, Houck said, "The tremendous ovation of the audience was the most gratifying experience."[51] The *New York Times* music critic began his rather brief review, "The 19th-century tradition of performing Bach's choral works with too many singers and too many instrumentalists dies hard . . . On the whole not a very satisfying *B Minor Mass*, for all its weighty assemblage of talent."[52]

In the New York audience was a former choir member, who, as a student at Lehigh University, had sung performances of the *Mass* with the Philadelphia Orchestra in 1921 and 1922 with Dr. Wolle conducting. In a letter to the editor of the *Bethlehem Times*, he compared these performances of the *Mass* with the one he had just heard in Carnegie Hall. "It seemed to me that he [Ormandy] did not communicate with the singers in anything like the degree that Dr. Wolle always did . . . He fixed his gaze on us . . . That opening moment [of the *Mass*] was one of the greatest thrills of my entire life, which I remember to this day."[53]

The Bach Choir climaxed 1975, a year of anniversaries, with a Moravian concert in Central Moravian Church singing the annual Advent candle light service, a Bethlehem tradition for over two hundred years. Working with the church Elders, Mann, choir director Richard Schantz, and organist Monica Schantz reunited the music of Bach and the Bethlehem Moravian hymn tradition seventy-five years after the Bach Choir had left in 1905. This was Mann's ultimate affirmation of the histories of the Bach Choir and of Bethlehem, the Christmas City. The Choir sang the traditional Moravian service that had so decisively shaped the design of the Bach Festivals. Mann had fully realized Kurt Thomas's principle of presenting sacred choral music as part of a sacred service. In so doing, Mann had made Bethlehem like Bach's Leipzig.

NOTES

1. Houck, *Bach in Bethlehem*, unpaginated, ABCB.

2. Alfred Mann, "Dawn of a Choral Era," *American Choral Review* 15, no. 3 (April 1978): 5.

3. Alfred Mann, "Introduction Dawn of a Choral Era," *American Choral Review* 20, no. 2 (April 1978): 8.

4. *Morning Call*, 3 May 1969.

5. *Bethlehem Globe-Times*, 19 May 1969.

6. Alfred Mann and Gustav Reese, "Introduction," *American Choral Review* 13, no. 2 (1971), iv.

7. Ibid., 82.

8. Ibid., 84.

9. Ibid., 83.

10. Ibid., 83.

11. Wilhelm Ehmann, trans. by Alfred Mann, "The Romantic A Cappella Tradition," *American Choral Review* 15, no. 2 (April 1973): 7–8.

12. Ibid., 10.

13. Ibid., 23.

14. *Bethlehem Globe-Times*, 8 May 1970.

15. Ibid.

16. *New York Times*, 11 May 1970.

17. *Evening Bulletin*, 11 May 1970.

18. *New York Times*, 11 May 1970.

19. *Evening Bulletin*, 11 May 1970.

20. "Mann's Debut with Choir Shows Hidden Faces of Bach," May 1970. Unknown newspaper source, ABCB.

21. Singer in casual conversation with the author.

22. "Board of Managers Meeting," 17 October 1970, ABCB.

23. "Minutes of the Executive Committee," 16 June 1970, ABCB.

24. *Globe-Times*, 18 December 1971.

25. *(Washington, DC) Evening Star*, 23 May 1972.

26. Board of Managers Meeting, 11 October 1971, ABCB.

27. Christoph Trautmann, "Bach's Bible," *American Choral Review* 14, no. 4 (October 1972): 3–11.

28. Howard Cox, ed., and Ellis Finger, trans., *The Calov Bible of Bach* (Ann Arbor: UMI Press, 1985).

29. Ibid., x.

30. Howard Cox, "The Scholarly Detective: Investigating Bach's Personal Bible," *The Bach Journal of the Riemenschneider Bach Institute* 27 (1994): 15.

31. Ibid., 39–40.

32. "Mendelssohn's Bach Recital," record jacket, n.d., ABCB.

33. "Minutes of the Executive Committee," 18 June 1972, ABCB.

34. "Minutes of the Executive Committee," 14 May 1973, ABCB.

35. "Dr. Mann Praises Audience," 24 December 1973, source unknown, ABCB.

36. "Minutes of the Board of Managers," 31 October 1973, ABCB.

37. Ibid.

38. *(Easton, PA) Express*, 11 May 1974.

39. *Bethlehem Globe-Times*, 11 May 1974.

40. *Evening Bulletin*, 13 May 1974.

41. Ibid.

42. *Bethlehem Globe-Times*, 13 May 1974.

43. *Bethlehem Globe-Times*, 11 November 1974.

44. *Bethlehem Globe-Time*, 5 May 1975.

45. *Bethlehem Globe-Times*, 13 May 1975.

46. Ibid.

47. *Philadelphia Inquirer*, 12 May 1975.

48. *Bethlehem Globe-Times*, 11 May 1975.
49. *Bethlehem Globe-Times*, 5 December 1975.
50. *Philadelphia Inquirer*, 6 December 1975.
51. *Bethlehem Globe-Times*, 9 December 1975.
52. *New York Times*, 10 December 1975.
53. Letter to the Editor, *Bethlehem Globe-Time*s, 12 December 1975.

Chapter 16

Mann's Last Years with the Choir

1976–1980

For the 1976 Festival, Mann chose cantatas that Bach had composed for ceremonial occasions. Reese conducted the "Wedding Cantata," BWV 202, which was its first performance by The Bach Choir and Reese's first appearance as a choral conductor in Bethlehem.

William Parberry, conductor of the University of Pennsylvania Choir and the University Choral Society, reviewed the Festival for the *Bethlehem Globe-Times*. In a detailed analysis of the performance of the *Mass*, he repeatedly raised issues of authentic performance practice, questions now becoming standard for critics but unusual then. Twice referring to rhythm, Parberry concluded, "Mann's decision went along with a sort of nineteenth century performance tradition . . . Concerning Dr. Mann's approach to matters of performance practice, one can say that he is, at best, inconsistent."[1] Nevertheless, in programming Mann remained totally consistent and historically accurate.

Following the May 1976 Bach Festival, the American Chapter of the *Neue Bach-Gesellschaft* (The International Bach Society), which Alfred Mann was instrumental in founding and locating in Bethlehem, held its first meeting at Moravian College Theological Seminary, hosting scholars from across the country. Two unique features marked the conference, an exhibition of Bach original manuscripts from American public and private collections (among them a harpsichord Fantasia, BWV 919, owned by The Bach Choir), and a discussion by Professor Howard Cox of Bach's Bible; Cox's study is discussed in Chapter 14. The Society's session provided an ideal melding of performance and scholarship under Mann's direction, and the desire of The Bach Choir's board members to promote its international status.

An invitation for The Choir to sing internationally was reported by president Houck at the Annual Corporate Meeting on 14 May 1976. "The Choir has been greatly honored by being invited to sing the *Mass* . . . as a part of the International Bach Society week-long festival."[2] The Executive Committee had already considered the risks and complications of such a trip to Germany and joyously accepted the invitation. The Bach Choir would sing in West Berlin in August 1976 and then travel to Leipzig in East Germany to sing a service at the St. Thomas Church, the tomb of Bach. The diplomatic permissions were arranged by the U.S. State Department and the German Bach Society. A German tour company made the hotel arrangements in Berlin. When the necessary travel plans were completed and the date for departure was nearing, a Choir representative assured the Board, "The choir members are very enthusiastic about the upcoming trip."[3]

More than 250 singers, soloists, orchestra musicians, and spouses departed from New York on 21 August 1976. Mann was delayed at home by unexpected surgery; he would join them later. Once everyone had settled into his hotel, Reese began rehearsing the *Mass in B Minor* in the Kaiser Wilhelm Memorial Church. Adjusting to the acoustics of the large hall proved difficult, but when The Choir moved to the concert hall, rehearsals "went flawlessly." The pressure was intense. Said one singer, "From the point of view of the choir we were very worried the first time we had a rehearsal in *Philharmonie* Hall . . . We thought, 'Oh my God, we're out of our league' . . . Most of us were really discouraged, but then we began to get the range of things."[4] The Bach Choir rehearsed frequently over the next few days, but members were also able to relax a bit during brief tours of both West and East Berlin.

The arts editor of the *Bethlehem Globe Times* traveled with the group, and his daily phone calls gave Lehigh Valley readers detailed reports on the extraordinary success of the trip. The West Berlin audience of more than 2,500 gave the performers an "unprecedented two curtain calls prior to the intermission and four similar long ovations including a standing ovation for the choir plus a standing ovation for Dr. Mann."[5]

The West German music critics' responses were reported by the Allentown *Call-Chronicle*. As in the United States, critics objected to the romantic interpretation and the large size of The Bach Choir. However,

> one major German critic granted that it was a "performance about which opinions differed. Bach purists wrinkled their brows on good grounds; the majority of the audience, however, was delighted by the conductor's conception, totally thrilling, heightened for the final effect and often almost operatic.[6]

The arrival in Leipzig was delayed at the East German checkpoint as guards processed the buses, and the audience sat for hours in Bach's church waiting for the American musicians. A bass singer in charge of the tour recalled sitting for hours in a stalled bus. "We were quite late at the church, and those people stayed and waited until we got there, young and old. The church was full. And they were appreciative of our being there."[7]

The late arrival left no time for rehearsal. Too large for the choir loft, The Bach Choir was placed in the side balcony of the church. They sang two motets as part of the "Evensong Service," and William Whitehead, The Bach Choir organist who had also played in Berlin, performed organ solos. After the service, president Houck placed a wreath on Bach's grave saying, "We lay this wreath with reverent esteem and respect for Bach, his church and his successors at St. Thomas in Leipzig."[8]

The depth of the experience was best described by a soprano:

The most memorable experience was singing at the Evensong at the Thomas Kircke in Leipzig. And knowing that people had walked for hours to be there. And also knowing that just before we got there a Protestant minister had immolated himself in protest against the Communist regime who would not allow his children to be involved in church activities; a week or so prior.

And before we went to Leipzig there were some men caught at checkpoint Charlie. Some of The Bach Choir has been over to East Germany and were coming back and some men tried to come across the check point with them to escape. And they were brutally beaten by the guards in front of The Choir members.

To go into a service knowing these things was incredible. I cried the entire service. Could not see my music. Luckily I had it memorized. And when we left the church, people pressed up against us to give regards to this person and that person who had escaped to the West.

For a person raised in freedom, it was an overwhelming experience. And to think that a number of people who walked there had never been in a service like that. There was a part of the service when there was The Lord's Prayer, and most of the people did not say anything. They didn't know it!

That made a difference in my concept of personal freedom. It was a learning experience that I shall never forget.[9]

Returning to Bethlehem, the singers, orchestra members, and "tag-a-longs" were all greeted with cheers and embraces. One man, who had been waiting for his wife outside his truck, was especially eager to return home with her. He told an inquiring reporter, "I'll give you two minutes to talk to my wife. I've got a bottle of champagne in the back of my truck."[10]

Both The Bach Choir and the City of Bethlehem were honored in 1976 by the National Federation of Music Clubs, when the Federation placed a bronze plaque on Central Moravian Church in recognition of the importance of The Bach Choir in the history of American music. The plaque reads:

> In this Church the Annual Festival of the Bach
> Choir of Bethlehem was initiated on March 27
> 1900 by the first American performance of the
> *Mass in B Minor* of Johann Sebastian Bach.

An extremely eventful year closed with The Bach Choir's participation in the Central Moravian Church's Christmas Vigils, singing the two motets it had sung in Leipzig. Desire for the free tickets was so high that "Due to the great demand church officials suggested that those who attended last year allow others to participate this year."[11] Mann told the local arts editor, "The Leipzig performance was an incredibly moving experience for us. . . . We were able to bring this performance from Bach's Church in Leipzig back to the choir's home community of Bethlehem."[12]

Consistent with Mann's guiding principle to provide each festival with a "signature," the next two Festivals were both musicological and celebratory events. The 1977 Bach Festival included four sacred cantatas based on chorales and "The Birthday Cantata," BWV 249a. This was the first time these cantatas had been sung in Bethlehem. One reviewer noted, "Nothing could be more appropriate. For the use of these chorales underscores the musicality of Bethlehem's early settlers, and the Moravian auspices of the Bach Festival's founding."[13] People were reminded that it was J. Fred. Wolle's childhood discovery that Bach's works contained chorales that had initially attracted him to Bach. The 1978 Bach Festival had other Wolle associations. The Bach Choir sang *The Passion According to Saint John* that had been Wolle's first American Bach premiere.

The meeting of the American Chapter of the New Bach Society in Bethlehem in 1979 served as an arena for American Bach scholars to share their research. The conference was again held at Moravian College. The focus of the conference was *Bach in Bethlehem Today*. Two conference publications were printed that year: *Bethlehem Pilgrimage* by Paul A. Willistein Jr., a journalist and choir guarantor; and *Bach In Bethlehem Today: A Conference Report* edited by Alfred Mann.

Mann recognized that times were changing. Seventy-five years after the founding of The Bach Choir, numerous Bach performances were taking place in the Bethlehem area, and national and international performances of Bach's music were taking place frequently. The Bach Choir was no longer unique, and The Bethlehem Bach Festival was no longer the only place to hear Bach's music. "No modern Bach ensemble, whatever its effort and qualifications, can expect simple or self-evident justification for its style of performance," Mann explained in true scholarly fashion:

> What the community needed to study through the opportunities afforded by a Bethlehem Bach Conference of unprecedented scope were the challenges of its tradition, the challenges of the established program and its new aspects year by year, of the Choir's unique exclusive devotion to Bach performance, and of the unique dedication of an entire community to the music of Bach.[14]

In his ten years as conductor, Dr. Mann had confronted directly the myriad issues of performance practice. For the conference, he had assembled an impressive group to examine two basic questions: "Was a community chorus of amateurs rising out of the romantic performance tradition continuing to sing Bach's choral works still viable?" and "Could the Bach Choir still lay claim to national and international leadership in Bach performance?"[15]

Robert Freeman, head of the Eastman School of Music, spoke to variability. After discussing the ever-increasing cost of concert performance and increasing distance between the composer and the concert audience, Freeman concluded:

> In Bethlehem, through continuing involvement and repeated exposure, the music of Bach has become once more part of the community. In closing, I would like to offer a tribute. We might say that Bach, visiting a performance of his music at Lincoln Center would have been surprised by the setting, by the style of presentation, and by the ways in which more of the city's population remains uninvolved with the music. In Bethlehem, where this music has become an integral part of the community, a community in which people from all walks of life experience his music directly and with obvious enthusiasm, he would have felt, I think, more at home.[16]

In the afternoon workshop "Bach Audience," a participant expanded beyond The Bach Festivals:

> One of the most useful things the Bach Choir of Bethlehem has accomplished in recent years is a conscious move back into the community. By offering Bach's music in a community service in Bethlehem's Central Church at Christmas, the singers and the Festival Orchestra have given the home community a new awareness of its special cultural achievement and have paid homage to the finest renditions both of the city and the Choir. Everyone is invited; tickets are free . . . to cope with the great disparity of supply and demand, the possibility of opening the afternoon rehearsal for the service to members of the community is being considered. These are ideal ways of offering an antithesis to exclusiveness.[17]

The answer to Mann's "community chorus" question was rousingly affirmative.

There was no direct answer to the question of The Choir's leadership in interpretation. However, performance and interpretation were viewed as a facet of editing. "The editing of performance material for the *B Minor Mass* continues in Bethlehem from year to year . . . and it serves as a constant reminder that despite the performers' wish to be faithful . . . the work can never be frozen into a rendition that represents an ultimate "correct" edition."[18] Granting the inevitability that performances will differ, a member of the audience affirmed that "Interpretation may be considered willful or faithful, but in order to be strong it is bound to be individual."[19] When asked, "Are not critics taking a great deal upon themselves when they question an interpretation of a particular piece of Bach's Music?" the response was that, "The critic must share with the performer and editor a sense of humility before the work of the composer, and this humility is embodied in the spirit of research."[20] The second question was answered in the affirmative. As one of the leading performers of Bach's choral music, The Bach Choir could lay claim to national and international leadership.

Whatever the research issues of performing Bach's music, a loyal audience continued to come to Bethlehem each spring. At the 1977 Bach Festival, a reporter asked people outside Packer Memorial Church why they had come to Bethlehem. Because their responses are so telling his entire short article is given:

The crowd waiting around the door of Packer Chapel at Lehigh University gradually increased in number as the time for the opening concert of The Bach Festival second weekend drew near.

What brought these people to this spot for this particular occasion? They are seldom polled, but yesterday was going to be different. And when they responded, they did so in metaphysical terms, in simple words that perhaps indicated a human difficulty in coming to terms with the ineffable.

[New Jersey] We love the *B Minor Mass*. My husband went to Lehigh. He has come here for the past 20 years.

[Philadelphia] I like Bach. I've been coming here since I was eleven years old and I think it's one of the nicest things I do all year.

[Oxford, England] I came because my friend here had a ticket.

[Maryland] is a 15 year festival veteran. As a choral director himself. he has something of a professional interest in the event. Of Bach, he says, "His faith shines through his music. He accepted life with all its problems."

[Pennsylvania] a recent graduate of the New England Conservatory of Music, is an oboist in the festival orchestra. She has been coming to the rehearsals since the age of five and to festivals since junior high school age. "I fell in love with

Bach as a child," she explained. "It's been the dream of my life to have an association with the Bach Festival."

And so they continue to come, year after year those who find their attraction easy to explain, and those who can find no words that are adequate.[21]

The "lawn activity" outside Packer Memorial Church was colorfully described by a woman who had been an usher for thirty-six Bach Festivals:

> Dr. Ifor started the second weekend because so many young people wanted to take part and could not get tickets with only one weekend . . . I can remember just after World War ll, hundreds of young people crowding onto the lawn, bringing their musical [*sic*] scores, and singing along with the chorales. It was quite a sight . . . There were elaborate picnics on the lawn. Some of the ticker-holders would go outside, and their uniformed chauffeurs would bring their picnic baskets to them, and it was not unusual to see people unwrap gold knives, forks and spoons for their picnics.

Elaborate Festival social events also took place throughout town. She recalled:

> There were very elaborate dinner parties all over the town . . . and many of the visitors wouldn't bother to go to the Friday 4 p.m. program, but would appear at the evening performance after their social activities . . . Some of the ticket holders would drive up to the chapel area, get out of their cars and look around for someone who appeared as though he was eager to get into the afternoon program . . . Many of the young people, in turn, tried to look interested, in hopes of getting one of these precious tickets.

Among her most lasting memories, she said, were "people buzzing as a famous personality entered the chapel . . . nods as the widow of President Theodore Roosevelt would arrive.[22]

A third publication, *Bach in Bethlehem A Musical Tradition,* appeared in 1979. A chronological historical account written by Houck referred to Wolle as "beloved leader" and praised Ifor Jones as "a worthy successor to J. Fred. Wolle . . . who took many talented young people into the choir . . . [added] the Saturday morning programs" and a second weekend to the Festival. About Alfred Mann, Houck wrote:

> After a tenure of thirty years, Dr. Jones was succeeded in 1979 by Dr. Alfred Mann, internationally renowned authority on Baroque music who was trained under one of Bach's later-day successors at St. Thomas in Leipzig. Dr. Mann has combined his career as a most distinguished choral conductor with that of scholar and author.

Houck wrote in closing, "Today more than 700 guarantors contribute up to an amount specified . . . as their share of the inevitable annual deficit."[23]

Then a major contingency forced Mann and the Board of Managers to confront a profound decision. In late 1979 Mann was offered a position as senior musicologist at the prestigious Eastman School of Music. At a special Board of Managers meeting, the secretary recorded, "Dr. Mann consulted with his family and Mr. Houck and the decision was made to accept the offer."[24]

To smooth the transition, Mann decided not to leave The Bach Choir immediately. He agreed to remain and conduct the 1980 Bach Festival. Mann told the singers, "It may take an appreciable amount of time to work out a solution for us, but I am assured that it will be a good solution: in the meantime, let me rely on your patience and trust."[25]

The year closed with the Moravian Christmas Vigils:

Last night's service, which annually combines those durable, largely eighteenth-century Moravian hymns with the music of Bach, was a water-mark event—it was probably the last appearance of Dr. Alfred Mann, Bach Choir artistic director, as choir conductor for the Vigils. . . . Dr. Mann said he is confident that the tradition of Bach in Bethlehem at Christmas, begun during his tenure with the choir, will continue.[26]

Alfred Mann conducted one more Bach Festival, May 1980. Rather than selecting from Bach's large works for his final performance, Mann's unifying theme was the contemplation of the Cross and man's quest for salvation. That quest reaches profound resolution in the conclusion of the *Mass* with *Dona nobis pacem* (Grant us peace). "At the conclusion of the *Mass*, a wave of applause began at the back of Packer Chapel and quickly swept over the audience, bringing everyone to his feet. Dr. Mann turned, smiling, and with his arms out, acknowledged this well-deserved ovation." According to the *Bethlehem Globe Times*, "There wasn't a dry eye in the house."[27]

NOTES

1. *Bethlehem Globe-Times*, 17 May 1976.
2. "Minutes of the Executive Committee," 16 May 1976, ABCB.
3. "Minutes of the Executive Committee," 21 June 1976, ABCB.
4. *Bethlehem Globe-Times*, 1 September 1976.
5. *Bethlehem Globe-Times*, 27 August 1976.
6. *Call-Chronicle*, 5 September 1976.
7. Anonymous Choir Member #1 in audiotape interview with author, ABCB.

8. *Morning Call*, 1 September 1976.

9. Anonymous Choir Member #2 in audiotape interview with author, ABCB.

10. *Bethlehem Globe-Times*, 1 September 1976.

11. *Bethlehem Globe-Times*, 29 November 1976.

12. *Bethlehem Globe-Times*, 20 December 1976.

13. *Bethlehem Globe-Times*, 21 May 1977.

14. Alfred Mann, *Bach in Bethlehem Today* (Bethlehem, PA: Moravian Book Shop, 1979), 11.

15. Paul A. Willistein Jr., *Bethlehem Pilgrimage* (Bethlehem, PA: Moravian Book Shop, 1979), 19.

16. Mann, *Bach In Bethlehem*, 21.

17. Ibid., 44.

18. Ibid., 54–55.

19. Ibid., 56.

20. Ibid., 56.

21. "Simple Words Tell Why They Come," unknown source, 20 May 1977, ABCB.

22. *Bethlehem Globe-Times*, 21 May 1977.

23. Houck, *Bach in Bethlehem*, unpaginated, ABCB.

24. "Minutes of the Board of Managers," 24 October 1979, ABCB.

25. "New Appointments," *Bethlehem Bach Choir News* 11 (Winter 1979): ABCB.

26. *Morning Call*, 17 December 1979.

27. *Bethlehem Globe-Times*, 19 June 1980.

Chapter 17

In Mann's Footsteps

1981–1983

William Reese

The Board felt Dr. William Reese was the logical person to replace Dr. Mann. Reese had been highly successful as the assistant conductor of The Bach Choir for ten years, and he shared Mann's view of the purpose and programming for The Choir.

A graduate of Amherst College, Reese had earned a master's degree in music from Columbia University, a doctorate in music from Berlin University, and a degree in conducting from *Die Musik Hochshule* in Berlin. Like Mann, he was an academic, holding a professorship at Haverford College. Like Mann, he had founded and was conducting a singing group, the Philadelphia Chamber Chorus. Reese had worked vocally with The Bach Choir, and the singers liked him.

The planning committee had considered other candidates, but it can be assumed that the decision to offer Reese the position came fairly easily. It can also be assumed the committee knew that Reese would accept. The Executive Committee met shortly after Mann's final Bach Festival. "Dr. Reese told the Committee that he is delighted to have the honor of being named Music Director and Conductor of The Bach Choir . . . He [also] commended the Board of the Choir for its foresight in creating the position of Associate Conductor."[1]

Members of the Board chose Greg Funfgeld, music director of First Presbyterian Church of Bethlehem, to be Associate Conductor. He lived in Bethlehem and had observed many rehearsals of The Bach Choir. Immediately upon his appointment: "Mr. Funfgeld told the Committee that he is very honored to have been named Associate Conductor of the Choir. He will conduct the Saturday morning program which will include The Peasant Cantata which has never been performed in Bethlehem."[2]

In September, Reese and Funfgeld began preparations for the 1981 Festival. Following Mann's thematic musicological focus, Reese selected cantatas and motets that expressed Bach's profession of faith in the events of baptism, communion, marriage and life after death. He assured the public that he had only one goal for The Choir: "To keep tradition."[3]

Musically, the *Mass* was central to that tradition. Even during Wolle's early Bach Festival experiments, the *Mass* had always been the culmination of the festival program, as it continued to be under the direction of Carey, Jones, and Mann.

Mann had written, "It became apparent how deeply rooted the *Mass* is in all of Bach's writing."[4] Reese continued Mann's design of linking everything to the *Mass*. The intricate and multiple interconnections Mann saw between the *Mass* and Bach's other choral works became a part of every performance Reese conducted.

Reese not only accepted Mann as his guide for the Festivals, he took his place before a community of singers that had been psychologically and musically reshaped by Mann. When an interviewer asked what Mann's rehearsals had been like, one singer contrasted Mann with Ifor Jones. "Ifor was forceful and did not mind making an example of somebody. When Mann came, it was totally different, and it was difficult for The Choir to settle down because they were used to being ridden and told what to do."[5] This singer continued, "One of the things he [Mann] did so well [was to] set the scene spiritually and emotionally in a way I never experienced with Ifor, with Reese or anyone else."[6] But, another singer commented, "Ifor was more dramatic. He was very colorful. And would make interesting comments. With Mann one might feel a little bored because he worked with a section for a long time and the rest of us were just sitting there . . . . We were well trained when we sang."[7] It was the Board's intent to have the new conductor step effortlessly into Mann's shoes.

With the arrival of a new conductor, the local press set out to examine the heart of The Bach Choir community. They interviewed singers from across the history of The Choir, from a first-year singer to an alto who had sung for sixty-three seasons. Speaking of Reese, the young soprano said she'd been nervous in the audition, but "Dr. Reese is very down to earth and very pleasant to work with . . . Those two hours every Monday go by quickly." As the oldest member she had sung for Wolle, Carey, Jones, Mann and Reese. "The last three years I've been singing the *Mass* from memory. I used to hold a book, just for show, but I don't even do that anymore." She let nothing "interfere with her commitment to Bach Choir. I simply set Monday aside for Bach . . . I can depend on Bach to keep me in trim." A tenor, an engineer, compared Mann with Reese. "Over the past seven years, first with Dr. Mann and now with Dr. Reese, I've learned a lot about Bach. Dr. Mann emphasized the meaning and symbolism in the music. Dr. Reese has taught us how to find the notes for entrances, and drills note-for-note perfection." All the singers interviewed clearly placed the music of Bach and the singing of that music in the community of The Bach Choir well ahead of the conductor. A math teacher mused "Bach amazes me. I can't believe what his mind must have been like—the perfection of the fugue alone. I don't think there's anyone to rival him." A bank teller enthused, "I really enjoy Bach. There's so much to find in his music." A geologist confessed, "I love Bach—although occasionally I get a terrific craving to go out and do Brahms!" A librarian and her engineer husband agreed, "The more we sing it the more we appreciate the kind of genius he was. And there's still so much we haven't heard." An 82-year-old lady concluded, "After so many years you can't help but have it in your being. It becomes a very great part of you."[8]

No sooner had Mann announced his departure than Board President Kenneth Houck announced his own resignation after having served for ten years. He died soon after. Recalling Houck, a singer said, "He was a product of Bethlehem Steel. When he needed to behave, he behaved beautifully. He was tough. If he felt the board needed him to be a certain way he could be that way."[9] A Board member recalled how well Houck had functioned as president. "We all worked at Beth Steel, so Ken could call a quick meeting in his office. He ran a good meeting. He had a very dry sense of humor. He had the respect of the Board and certainly had The Bach Choir at heart, seeing that our investments were well taken care of. He reorganized a lot of that." And always Houck's philosophy was to spread the word about Bach. Commenting on this outreach, one Board member said, "It was at that time we began to get people on the board who were residents of Allentown."[10]

Throughout the long history of The Bach Choir, a variety of issues and events had threatened its equanimity. Every performance organization has a backstage subject to turmoil, where what takes place can threaten the performance, perhaps the entire enterprise, of which the public sitting out front remains completely unaware. Each crisis facing The Choir had been averted by strong board leadership, by the dedication of the singers, and, occasionally by replacing the conductor.

However, Reese's situation rapidly deteriorated. Profound differences between Reese and Mann as conductors now emerged. An ability to handle personal relations with singers and orchestra members stood out as the defining difference between them. One singer characterized Mann as a person of "great intelligence and great calm, a very, very spiritual person. People loved him. He took great pains to cultivate other people. He was an extremely humble man. He would never say I know better than you."[11] Another longtime Choir member confirmed this characterization. "Alfred was a very gentle, loving man. He liked people. He was soft spoken. Very delicate and The Choir responded to him as I recall very well."[12]

On the other hand, one singer recalled, "Most people didn't like putting up with Reese. He was abrasive. I never felt emotionally comfortable singing under Reese. He was very stand-offish."[13] When a past president of The Choir asked someone who sang under Reese to describe him, he responded, "Reese was very poor on interpersonal relationships and had succeeded in alienating essentially all of his constituencies, e.g., choir members, staff, soloists, orchestra members, the board of managers. Things got so bad that the decision was finally made that he had to go."[14]

The turning point came when members of the orchestra signed a petition demanding Reese's resignation. They threatened to stop playing in The Bach Festival if Reese were in charge. Such a warning obviously endangered the organization. President Thomas Church responded calmly. "I just kept in mind that Reese had agreed to remain with The Choir three years." Church did not have to remind Reese of this. He resigned of his own volition, writing to Church:

In the spring of 1980 when the position of music director of The Bach Choir of Bethlehem was open and the choice of an outside candidate seemed difficult, I took it upon myself, as associate conductor with firsthand experience with the Bach Choir, to volunteer to take over for a limited term, until such time as a suitable musician of high caliber who had the time and dedication necessary to fit the post satisfactorily could be found."[15]

Church read the letter to The Bach Choir members at rehearsals for the 1983 Festival, which would be Reese's last. He recommended Greg Funfgeld, the associate conductor, as his successor. Reese described Funfgeld as a "suitable musician of high caliber who had the time and dedication necessary, who could assume the post satisfactorily."[16]

Reese remained active elsewhere as a church organist and choir director. He died in March 2006, age ninety-five. His obituary mentioned that he "conducted the Bethlehem Bach Choir in Bethlehem, PA for a number of years." Dr. Mann died six months later. His obituary, "Alfred Mann, 89, Musicologist And Historian of the Baroque," contains Mann's notable accomplishments as a professor, translator, author, editor, instrumentalist and includes this sentence, "He was also a choral conductor and directed the Cantata Singers in New York and the Bach Choir of Bethlehem, in Pennsylvania."[17]

In May 1998 during The Choir's two-year-long anniversary celebration of its founding and its American premiere of the *Mass*, Alfred Mann, William Reese, and Greg Funfgeld sat together at a Bach community banquet.

Reese, Funfgeld, Mann

Their lasting respect and collegiality for each other were expressed in a letter Reese wrote to Funfgeld following the 1998 Bach Festival:

> What a joy and what an honor it was to be with you and the Bach Choir last Friday. You certainly have created a virtuoso choir. I was delighted with the sound and was able to hear each voice line clearly. I am happy that all aspects of your undertaking are progressing so well. Sincerely, Bill[18]

NOTES

1. "Minutes of the Executive Committee," 24 June 1980, ABCB.

2. Ibid.

3. *Morning Call*, 22 December 1980.

4. Alfred Mann, "Bach Studies Approaches to the *B Minor Mass*," *American Choral Review* 27, no. 1 (January 1985): 1.

5.Anonymous Bach Choir Member #2 in audiotape interview with author, ABCB.

6. Ibid.

7. Anonymous Bach Choir Member #1 in audiotape interview with author, ABCB.

8. *Bethlehem Globe-Times*, 8 May 1981.

9. Anonymous Bach Choir Member #2 in audiotape interview with author, ABCB.

10. Anonymous Bach Choir Member #1 in audiotape interview with author, ABCB.

11. Anonymous Bach Choir Member #2 in audiotape interview with author, ABCB.

12. Anonymous Bach Choir Member #1 in audiotape interview with author, ABCB.

13. Anonymous Bach Choir Member #2 in audiotape interview with author, ABCB.

14. Anonymous e-mail correspondence in the author's possession.

15. *Bethlehem Globe-Times*, 21 September 1982.

16. Ibid.

17. *New York Times*, 27 September 2006.

18. William Reese to Greg Funfgeld, 11 May 1998, ABCB.

Chapter 18

A Renewed Choir

1982–1990

The analytical skills of the new president, Thomas Church, were deep, subtle, and brilliant; and he set out to make the detailed choices he felt necessary to renew The Choir. Church faced problems involving every aspect of The Choir: The annual Festivals, the conductor, the Board of Managers, the function of the officers, regional misconceptions about The Choir and its audience, the selection of soloists, lowered performance standards, and deteriorating finances.

His first major consideration as Board president was the hiring of a new conductor. Reese's resignation was accepted on 1 September 1982, and his recommendation that Greg Funfgeld, "be named to succeed him" was taken seriously.[1] Funfgeld had already made a mark in Bethlehem as organist and choir director of the First Presbyterian Church, which many Bethlehem Steel managers and executives attended. The congregation recognized his outstanding musical talent and was charmed by his young, vibrant personality. He'd already filled in when Reese was unavailable and had conducted the Christmas Vespers in Central Moravian Church, and The Bach Choir reacted well to him. Church attended rehearsals and was so impressed that he hired him.

Plans for the 1983 Festival were made at a later meeting. A smooth transfer of batons was agreed to so that Reese would conduct the *Passion According to Saint Matthew* and Funfgeld would rehearse and conduct the *Mass*. After the Festival, Funfgeld would become the full-time conductor and music director.

Church described working with Greg as like "riding a bucking bronco." He was young, energetic, and overflowing with ideas and talent. Tom Church and Greg Funfgeld proved to be a remarkably compatible duo, and they had the total backing of the Board. One member articulated precisely the spirit of renewal, "The Bach Choir of Bethlehem is in competition with many Bach Choirs in the world and now is the time to build the spirit in the Choir to be the best in the world."[2] Being best became a driving force. With the Church-Funfgeld collaboration formally in place, things began to move rapidly in that direction.

In an Executive Committee meeting, "Mr. Funfgeld said that the orchestra is one of the first problems he will undertake in the fall [of 1983]."[3] Church agreed "the orchestra had to change." The orchestra, made up mainly of retired Philadelphia Orchestra musicians, had grown old. "Mr. Church told the Board that the Festival Orchestra has not been up to par the last few years . . . [Funfgeld] asked for the support of the Board in making necessary changes in the orchestra personnel."[4] He set out to build an orchestra primarily of local professional musicians. He hired a local cellist, Nancy Bidlack, as the contractor for the Bach Festival Orchestra. A fine, experienced musician living in Bethlehem, she was on the music faculties of Lehigh University and Moravian College, and a member of various area orchestras. Church told the Executive Committee "there will be dramatic changes in the orchestra both physical and audible."[5]

There was also general agreement that the soloists had to be upgraded for fear that the more musically discerning members of the audience would lose interest in the Festivals. Two guarantors had established a "Musical Excellence Fund" to aid in subsidizing a higher level of soloists. This fund proved helpful, but soloists had long been selected by a prominent singer, Rose Bampton, and interested Board members who met at her apartment in New York. With the full support of the Executive Committee, this process was changed, and Funfgeld, as conductor, took over selecting the soloists. "Things got much better very quickly," Church stated succinctly.

Hiring a new conductor, replacing the orchestra, and upgrading the soloists went "remarkably smoothly." Revitalizing The Choir proved more difficult. The quality of The Choir had deteriorated over time, and its sound could no longer be compared favorably with the many other fine choirs in America. Also, The Choir was very large, comprising more than two hundred singers at a time when the taste for Bach performance was shifting away from the massive Romantic style. While a large amateur choir was still acceptable in Bethlehem Bach Festivals, it was no longer nationally credible.

Though recent conductors had auditioned only new members, Funfgeld's solution was to audition every singer personally, and members every three years. Church supported Funfgeld's audition plan, "I never heard of a top quality choir that didn't have auditions. I supported him on that." Tom trusted that Greg "would do it in a way that would damage people's egos as little as possible." But, "there is no way to invite people to leave that is very nice. He did it as gracefully as it could be done."

Private ten-to-twelve-minute interviews with each Choir member began in 1984. A year later, Funfgeld reported to the Board "the time has come to audition each member vocally. He found some of the members could not match pitches."[6] Egos were damaged, as Church had predicted. Many angrily resigned. Others were not accepted after they were auditioned. In the fall Funfgeld reported, "13 members were not invited back to the Choir. Resignations from 24 members were received over the summer, and 7 members are on leave. . . . Ten new singers were invited to join . . . a total of 140 members."[7]

Auditions improved both vocal quality and size. The Bach Choir was now able to plan national and international tours and hoped to receive praise and acclaim from notable music critics. Funfgeld and Church's solution, painful as it had been, was necessary for renewal.

The changes were fully in place and the press reaction was positive. After the first session of the 1985 Bach Festival, a reporter wrote an extended review, "Bach Festival: Tradition yields to professionalism," in which he critiqued each innovation:

> Yesterday afternoon and evening saw a few small traditions quietly laid to rest. Gone are the all-white dresses . . . in favor of white blouses and white skirts. Soloists are now free to wear the bright colors most featured singers sport. . . . There is talk that the brass choir prelude to the "B Minor Mass"—set aside last year by Sir David Willcocks—will not be revived.
>
> So the Bach Choir and the festival it supports won't remain the same big, comfortable old shoe we're fond of year after year. What is blossoming in its stead is a more professional organization, one long overdue on living up to its reputation . . . [It] was evident—from orchestra to choir—that the Bach Choir is entering a new and exciting phase . . . Greg Funfgeld's conducting technique has settled down. Gone is the nervous bobbing around at the podium in favor of a rock-solid stick technique and a marvelous expressive cuing and encouragement that drew from the choir a more specific and thus more varied sound. If the choir was in good form, the soloists completed the picture. . . . Soprano Arleen Auger was truly an astonishing revelation . . . At the close of the night session there was again a pause and then a brief burst of applause. There was some grumbling disapproval. This may be one Bach Festival tradition that will die hard.[8]

Funfgeld's next proposal was to expand performances beyond the annual Festival. Even though The Bach Choir was singing the Christmas Vigils at Central Moravian Church, Funfgeld told Church, "It would interest The Choir to have more activity than just the annual festivals." The members were experienced, fine singers and they wanted to rehearse more music, rather than spend a full year preparing for one concert. Funfgeld proposed a Christmas concert.

While Church had given his full support to auditions, his reaction to expanding their schedule was guarded: "I was reluctant. I didn't perceive that much local interest." Additional concerns were raised by members of the Executive Committee: "We are inadequately organized, funded or equipped for any activity beyond the basic Festival. . . . Even if there is no change in the format of the Choir's activities, we still need to consider our organization and office equipment."[9] In the end, however, he and the Executive Committee supported Funfgeld's expansion of the season.

Church and Funfgeld had jumped a fifty-year-old barrier. Choir members were excited to sing more Bach. The Bach Festival Orchestra was delighted to play another Bach performance. Area music lovers wanted to hear Bach more often. The Executive Committee voted "in favor of an extra non-festival concert at Christmas or another time of year."[10]

This expansion of The Bach Choir's offerings beyond the May Festival had laid the ground for celebrating the tercentenary of Bach's birth in 1685 with three programs in addition to The Bach Festival, providing a perfect opportunity for participation by many area choruses. Plans for the celebration were announced in the fall of 1984. Funfgeld would conduct Bach's *Christmas Oratorio* in December 1984, and the *Passion According to Saint John* in March 1985. As part of the regular 1985 Bach Festival, Sir David Willcocks, conductor of the oldest Bach Choir in England, would conduct the *Mass*. Marie-Claire Alain, an internationally acclaimed French organist, would conclude the celebration with an organ recital in the fall of 1985.

Church said that about half of the $90,000 budget would be covered by ticket sales. There was the assurance that "about 1,000 tickets will be available [to the public] for each performance."[11] Then, he asked individuals and businesses to support the expansion with donations.

A local reviewer applauded the soloists and orchestra in his review of the March 1985 performance of Bach's *Passion According to St. John* and wrote of The Bach Choir, "The choir of more than 160 voices was admirably responsive and flexible. Its harmonic balance and purity of tone were very much in evidence."[12]

Before the May Festival, Willcocks responded to a question about the possible difficulty of a guest conductor in Bethlehem, "I very much admire Greg Funfgeld's work. He is a very good musician himself, and I anticipate very little change from what he's doing. He, in fact, came to hear me perform the *Mass in B Minor* in Florida two weeks ago, so we have met and discussed the work in detail, and I think there shouldn't be any difficulty whatsoever.[13]

Two singers commented on the press account they'd read in a later review of Willcock's conducting of the Festival Mass, "Tradition shattered as festival applauds Bach," "It's the best *B Minor Mass* we've sung in my six years with the choir," said an alto. The other said, "It was just an incredible feeling up there. The atmosphere was electrically charged . . . There was a dynamic flow between the conductor and the performers, and the choir and audience—a flow all the way around."[14]

After the Festival, Church reported that the tercentenary celebration was already an "artistic and financial success," even before the organ recital had yet taken place.[15] Marie-Claire Alain's performance in December closed the celebration and capped the "artistic success." A *Globe-Times* writer reported, "Superb," "impeccable" and "excellent according to colleagues in the audience. Ms. Alain amazed listeners with her virtuosity . . . A standing ovation followed the "Fantasia and Fugue in G Minor which ended the program."[16]

The tercentenary celebration led to long-lasting profound changes in the Bach Board. Church knew from the time he had been treasurer that reorganization would need a more active board, no longer one that was basically social. On the one hand, too much responsibility was falling on the president and the conductor. On the other, if the program expansion were to continue, Board members needed to become involved in planning and fund raising. The Board had to return to the kind of organization that had been designed and had governed the second Bach Choir in 1911.

The first step would be to make the Bach Board smaller. When there'd been only one annual Bach Festival and The Bach Choir itself had had no national aspirations, a large Board of prestigious members governed by an Executive Committee had been adequate. That model, however, could not adapt to the changes needed for an expanding yearly program. After Church had reported that the tercentenary celebration was "an artistic and financial success," he was urging the Board members to govern and to finance a very different organization.

Two issues questioning traditions of The Festival faced the smaller Board, whether to allow applause at the performance and whether to eliminate trombones playing a chorale to precede the "Kyrie" of the *Mass*. Willcocks had opposed both inhibition of applause and the use of trombones, but tradition dies hard, and a period of intense discussion ensued.

No applause after the *Mass* was a rule J. Fred. Wolle himself had established. Though applause at the Festival was not totally new in 1985, it had occurred only on rare, special occasions. A local reporter described previous instances in an interview with Alfred Mann following the 1980 Festival:

They don't give many standing ovations at the Bach Festivals. In fact they don't usually give any. Yesterday was the exception. At the conclusion of the *B Minor Mass*, the estimated 1,100 persons who filled Lehigh University's Packer Chapel . . . rose to applaud Dr. Alfred Mann . . . who concluded his decade long choir leadership. "I must say it took me by surprise," said Dr. Mann. "I thought it was such a spontaneous gesture that I could only humbly express my thanks." At the conclusion of last year's festival, there was also applause. But there was a request on the front page: "In keeping with a longstanding tradition we request no applause at the end of the sessions."

Applause at the Saturday morning concerts, however, was permitted. Describing both sides of the practice, reviewing the 1983 Festival, a reporter wrote, "What a relief to be allowed to applaud . . . The Bach Foundation is perfectly correct in prohibiting applause for all but the Saturday morning session—Packer Chapel is a church, most of the selections are deeply religious. But the audience feels frustrated where a really fine piece of work is done and they cannot applaud" when they feel most appreciative.[17]

A month after the 1985 Bach Festival, members of the Board were told that a number of guarantors had written letters "to protest the breaking of the tradition about no applause after the choral portion of Festival."[18] Funfgeld's response was that "he likes a moment of silence at the conclusion of the session but would allow the congregation to applaud if they wish to do so."[19] Applause was discussed again in November. The Board directed Funfgeld to "attempt to continue the tradition of no applause."[20]

Two years later, when "there was discussion of . . . applause after the *Mass*, no change in present practice was authorized."[21] The matter, however, remained contentious. At a Board meeting only two weeks later, members went on record with a decision "no applause [was] encouraged." The decision was not heeded; by 1987, the practice became a moment of silence controlled by the conductor followed by applause.[22]

During the tercentenary, Willcocks had separated the trombone choir and the *Mass*. Funfgeld supported the change. At the 6 November 1985 meeting of the Board," Mr. Funfgeld asked for the Committee's approval to discontinue use of the trombone choir's playing a Moravian chorale before the singing of the Kyrie.[23] The Board approved, yet still two weeks later, "There was some discussion both for and against this suggestion."[24] "A majority" of the members accepted the recommendation[,][25] yet there were those who did not agree. Some still regret its absence.

In the winter of 1985 the Board held its first retreat, an occasion that marked a new phase of Church's presidency. The most pressing problem the Board now faced was how to sustain the growth in The Choir's schedule beyond the annual Festival, but "It was the perception of this group that we are inadequately organized, funded or equipped for any activity beyond the basic Festival."[26] A committee was formed to study funding and assess whether a computer was needed to assist in record keeping. In addition, the purchase of a computer was authorized at the cost of no more than $5,000.

As treasurer, Church had seen that ticket sales and guarantor contributions were not generating enough money to sustain the organization over the long term. Many guarantors were also delaying their payments or defaulting; the guarantor system, the backbone of Choir financial support, was failing. The Choir was losing money, and something had to be done. An immediate solution was to invest a large portion of the cash reserve and add the interest income to operating expenses. Cash reserves had previously been carried over from year to year, but this new income stream stabilized the budget and became standard practice.

The record keeping required to maintain an accurate list of hundreds of guarantors proved beyond the capability of the staff; one told the author that during the early 1990s the list of guarantors used to project income contained eighty who were deceased. Though a computer was purchased in 1985, developing the software necessary to manage the guarantor system took years. While solving the problem was begun during Church's presidency, it was not fully solved until the late 1990s.

Another aspect of the guarantor system that required revision was the guarantors' privilege of early ticket sales and reserved seating. This privilege permitted them to purchase more and more tickets for their guests. As a result, Festival seating was at a premium, and the perception of the area public was that there were no seats available. Local people believed Festival tickets were only available to out-of-towners, yet there were clearly vacant seats in Packer Church. Crucial income was being lost.

The Bach Choir's local image needed considerable sharpening. The various issues involved were summarized in a 1984 feature article in the *Morning Call*:

> A more pressing question is how the choir will satisfy the ever-increasing demand for tickets to performances. This year an estimated 775 guarantors will be competing for the Festival's 2,220 seats . . . which means many ticket requests will not be granted and many non-guarantors will not hear the singers.
>
> The Tercentenary concerts and last year's Musikfest appearances have been designed to appease the non-guarantor. An appearance in Musikfest '85 is probable, said Church, who admitted he was unsure about future additional non-festival performances.
>
> We certainly want to put on more concerts per year, . . . the president noted. "We're concerned about it, but whether it can be made to come to pass is a question we can't answer right now . . . We would like to make public more

tickets than the guarantor system provides." A choir representative agreed that the members want more concerts. First . . . Greg Funfgeld insists that more performances, like more practices, make for better singing. Secondly, more local residents will be able to hear the choir.

It is a community choir and it really doesn't make much sense for a bunch of guarantors to come from out of town when we have plenty of people from the community who want to hear it and can't," said the choir rep. "After all, it is the *Bethlehem* Bach Choir, not a choir from out of town . . . Local concerts will be slightly different from festival performances. Fewer tickets will be sold . . . And everyone who buys a ticket will be given a program rather than having to buy one separately at the stand usually set up outside Packer."[27]

Other financial initiatives begun by Church pointed the way to making the expansion of The Bach Choir possible. He was aware that there were wealthy guarantors willing to contribute more. He therefore approached a number of guarantors and solicited their support. Though he admitted he felt uncomfortable doing this, he was very successful. More important was the realization that many of the guarantors were a willing source for money and support far in excess of their assessed percentage. It was also clear that there was firm local support of The Bach Choir. The next steps in the expansion, a capital campaign and a series of recordings, could be undertaken with confidence.

Starting with the 1985 Festival, Dr. Robin Leaver began contributing highly informed readable program notes. His writings continue to be an important part of a greatly expanded printed program.

The ensuing capital campaign was called "For the Love of Bach." The effort evolved very slowly according to Church, who recalled, "We oozed into it really!" The drive began as a part of a five-year plan developed by the Board following the 1988 Festival. That plan proposed a capital campaign, "with funds from both private and corporate sectors."[28] This was the first time donors who were not guarantors had been considered possible funding sources. The following spring the Board defined its primary objective in the drive: "to create an endowment [so as] . . . to continue to provide high quality soloists and principal chairs in the orchestra."[29] A broad giving category called The "J. Fred. Wolle Heritage Society" was also added to the Musical Excellence Fund. Fourteen instrumental "chairs" were identified. With those decisions, the Board launched "For the Love of Bach."

To assist in managing the campaign, a part-time public relations person and a part-time secretary were hired. There were 105 members in "The J. Fred. Wolle Heritage Society." In the next two years twenty-seven members were added and eight of the fourteen chairs were fully endowed.

On a wall in The Choir office hangs a large plaque with the caption "For The Love of Bach." It contains the names of the various contributors to the capital campaign. Nearby is a cabinet filled with tapes and CDs made by The Bach Choir of Bethlehem conducted by Funfgeld offered for sale. The plaque displays the breadth of the financial expansion of the organization, and the recordings are evidence of The Bach Choir's artistic contribution to national and international Bach recordings.

In 1984 the Bethlehem critics had already raised a pressing question regarding recordings. "Another Bach Festival has come and gone, but inquiries about a Bach Choir album linger on . . . The Choir will mark the 300th anniversary of Bach's birth with great fanfare next year. Will a record be part of the celebration?"[30] It had been more than twenty years since The Choir under Ifor Jones had recorded the *Mass* for the Book-of-the-Month Club. Church had already responded to the press that The Bach Choir was in a "transition stage." He recounted that much change had already taken place, and he emphasized that much was yet to happen. As for a recording, Church explained, "A new conductor wants to make sure it would be his recording, and not left over from his predecessor."[31] Three years later a recording was announced, and Funfgeld told a reporter, "We felt ready for it."[32] Funfgeld assured the Board that the orchestra and the singers were ready and that a new recording of the highest quality would be available for the 1988 Festival.[33]

Church and Funfgeld met with the director of Dorian Recordings, an emerging record company, and planned recording sessions. Six thousand copies titled "Christmas In Leipzig" were ordered. The album included two cantatas Bach had composed for the Christmas season and concluded with the "Sanctus" from the *Mass*. Roland Kushner, The Choir's public relations person, told the press that the recording was expected to cost more than $50,000. Funds would come from three sources: the South Branch Foundation, a family foundation of several of the guarantors; other guarantors; and anticipated revenue from recording sales. "We think it will make money."[34] The recording was ready for the 1988 Festival.

The album sold well. A second recording was made for the 1989 Festival. That recording, *Wachet Auf!*, included two cantatas and a motet. Following the Festival, the board was informed that "Christmas In Leipzig" had sold "over 5,000 copies . . . The profile of the Choir has been raised immensely, and the recording paid for itself. We have received very good reviews from several technical publications."[35] Many more recordings followed, and Funfgeld became recognized as a major Bach interpreter.

At a breakfast retreat, when Thomas Church stepped down, he summarized his time as president. As the Board minutes record:

Church praised Funfgeld for expanding our program. Our orchestra is now of top musical excellence as are our soloists. Salaries have increased, and our recent For the Love of Bach! campaign and Musical Excellence Endowment have been successful. . . . We have come a long way in a short time.[36]

By applying his expert organizational skills, Church had redefined the organization and management and continued the legacy of Bethlehem Steel's contribution to the cultural life of Bethlehem. He then invited Jan Bonge, an experienced fundraiser and musician, to join the Board, and asked her to replace him as president. Bonge agreed, and Church stepped down: "I had been President for ten years. That seemed long enough."

In his self-effacing manner, Church praised Funfgeld, who had raised the musical quality of The Choir, soloists, and orchestra; expanded the season beyond the traditional May Festival; and produced two recordings of "fine quality." Breaking with tradition, he had advocated applause during the choral sections of the Festival and separated the trombone choir from *The Mass*. He'd consistently received the support of the Board's majority, the guarantors, and the audience for these innovations. Funfgeld had masterminded and brought to fruition The Bach Choir's complex celebration of the 300th anniversary of Bach's birth. He had readily accepted help from prominent Bach conductors, other Bach Festivals, and a notable coach in sung-German, Frau Fraunke Haaseman of Westminster Choir College.

Remaining true to his musical convictions, he had reduced the size of The Choir. There were fewer people singing Bach, but the expanded yearly program allowed more people to hear him.

NOTES

1. "Minutes of the Board," 1 September 1982, ABCB.
2. Ibid., 22 June 1983, ABCB.
3. Ibid., 26 April 1983, ABCB.
4. Ibid., 15 November 1983, ABCB.
5. Ibid., 22 February 1984, ABCB.
6. Ibid., 26 June 1985, ABCB.
7. Ibid., 6 November 1985, ABCB.
8. *Morning Call*, 17 May 1986.
9. "Board of Managers Minutes," 27 February 1995, ABCB.
10. Ibid.
11. *Globe-Times*, 18 September 1985.
12. *The Express* [Easton, PA], 18 March 1985.
13. *Call-Chronicle*, 5 May 1985.
14. *Call-Chronicle*, 12 May 1985.

15. "Board of Managers Minutes," 10 May 1985, ABCB.

16. *Globe-Times*, 7 October 1985.

17. *Call-Chronicle*, 19 May 1980.

18. The *Globe-Times*, 22 May 1983.

19. "Board of Managers Minutes," 26 June 1985, ABCB.

20. Ibid.

21. Ibid., 6 November 1985, ABCB.

22. Ibid., 2 November 1985, ABCB.

23. Ibid., 19 November 1985, ABCB.

24. Ibid., 6 November 1985, ABCB.

25. Ibid., 12 November 1985, ABCB.

26. Ibid., 27 February 1985, ABCB.

27. *Morning Call*, 14 December 1984.

28. "Board of Managers Minutes," 13 March 1989, ABCB.

29. Ibid., 13 March 1989, ABCB.

30. *Globe-Times*, 27 May 1984.

31. Ibid.

32. *Globe-Times*, 11 February 1988.

33. "Board of Managers Minutes," 27 February 1985, ABCB.

34. *Globe-Times*, 11 February 1988.

35. "Board of Managers Minutes," 19 May 1989, ABCB.

36. "Board of Managers Minutes," 18 January 1991, ABCB.

Chapter 19

"A More Sophisticated Organization"

1991–1996

Mrs. Jan Bonge was elected the twelfth president of The Bach Choir in June 1991, the second woman to hold the position. She had graduated from Westminster Choir College as an organ major and auditioned successfully as a singer for The Choir soon after she and her husband had arrived in Bethlehem. Church had recruited her to be The Choir's representative on the Board. She had had successful fundraising experience among her fellow alumni. Church felt that The Bach Choir's expanding schedule called for a leader with musical experience (which he felt he himself lacked) as well as managerial talent. She was elected vice president of the Board, and she helped Church develop a new plan for business and guarantor giving.

Bonge recalls that the nomination for president "came out of the blue." She had not sought the position and at first was, "somewhat reluctant to take it." But a musician at heart, she accepted. "Greg [Funfgeld] was conducting . . . I liked his style . . . We had similar backgrounds, and I knew that he had some good ideas of things he wanted to have happen. I thought that maybe I could help."[1]

Bonge injected fresh energy into Church's vision to involve the Board members more directly in long-term planning. At the Board's 1992 winter planning retreat, she led members in developing a five-year plan to take The Choir beyond its traditional Bethlehem Festivals and holiday concerts.

Energized Board members took immediate action and initiated several operational changes. A marketing committee was formed, and the Board's executive secretary was promoted to "executive director" with added responsibilities and additional staff. The committee began work immediately on plans to finance a concert tour to Germany. Also, on the agenda was financing an educational outreach program titled "Bach to School."

Other projects that received prompt attention and required special financing included a request by the conductor to add both a spring concert and Christmas season concert. Another addition was The Bach Choir's acceptance of an invitation to sing at Bethlehem's annual twelve-day summer Musikfest.

One of the immediate needs was an efficient record-keeping system to ensure an accurate source of information for those working on Board projects. Also needed was expert instruction in more efficient fundraising techniques. Board members accepted these challenges and immediately approved the development plan and its prompt implementation. Added to this ambitious five-year plan was a committee for the Centennial celebration of the premiere of the *Mass* to take place in the year 2000. The officers, Board members, singers, and administrative officers were "becoming a more sophisticated organization."[2]

The Bach Choir on the Steps of Central Moravian Church, 2002

J. Fred. Wolle had always insisted that the only way to truly study music was by performing it. Education through participation had been the reason J. Fred. Wolle's and Ruth Doster's singing group had met to study Bach's *Mass*. Subsequent conductors had approached the education of the singers and the public differently, but each had remained true to this basic mission. Ifor Jones and Alfred Mann also had taught both the musical and textual meaning of the cantatas so thoroughly that most choir members had sung their parts from memory and many could sing other parts as well. One seasoned singer was offended when a newcomer asked her why she was not looking at her music. "Because, young man, I know every part by memory!" was her indignant reply.[3] Mann's program notes for each Festival were written to supply additional meaning about the music for interested listeners. Now The Choir's educational mission was extended to young people in schools.

When the author asked Jan Bonge who had started Bach To School, she said, "It sort of grew. It was something I wanted to do."[4] Anthony Villani, chairman of the Bach To School committee, credits Greg Funfgeld for the initial idea. After Bonge became president, the Board formed an educational committee and asked it to design a proposal "to develop an educational program for youngsters in grades Kindergarten through 12."[5] The purpose of Bach To School was to introduce young people to Bach's music and The Bach Choir and to demonstrate Bach's importance using concert/lecture and classroom presentations by choir members. Members of The Bach Choir would volunteer for the assemblies and would visit classrooms. A smaller orchestra would be hired to perform in the school concerts.

A pilot study for Bach To School 1992 had proved encouraging, and the Board endorsed the plan. The concerts began in the spring of 1993. Area foundations, grants from local major corporations, donations from individuals, and contributions from schools covered the costs. More than 65,000 children have heard The Bach Choir and members of the Festival Orchestra sing and play Bach's music.

Funfgeld is a master teacher. He presents Bach with charm, knowledge, and an effective, relaxed manner moving back and forth from his position as a conductor to the role of musical interlocutor. A press reporter described him with an audience of young people:

> Funfgeld broke down each piece into its basic elements and revealed Bach's rare gift for music and composition. He spoke informally with the students and appealed for quiet before the choir sang—a sort of crash-course in concert etiquette.
>
> The youngsters listened intently, some of them stretching forward in their seats to hear the music . . . "What brings us together is our love of this music and our desire to sing and play it," Funfgeld said, pointing out that the choir is made up of people from all walks of life, from an FBI agent to the manager of a sporting goods store.
>
> "Which one is the FBI agent," one boy called out during the question and answer time. Another asked if the choir gets paid. Other questions included: "How do you get in?" and "What made Bach's music so famous?"[6]

Many student responses to the concerts confirmed Wolle's belief in The Bach Choir's mission, Bach for everyone, and Funfgeld's success realizes Wolle's ideal. A middle school girl wrote, "Thank you for playing for us, You were *great*!! I hope my mom will let me come to one of your concerts. I really want to come to one of the Highlights of the Festival 'cause I loved the Glorious Mass in B Minor and I would like to hear it again.—Megan." A third grade boy wrote, "Dear Bach Choir, I like your songs. Can you come to sing at my house? My address is . . . Please come with your friends to my house.—your new fan. Rogelio."

Another boy wrote, "Dear Bach Choir, I want to thank you for the beautiful singing and music you performed for us students at Kids Peace. It took a lot of stress and tension off of me. I could have meditated to it. I really enjoyed myself. I also want to say your choir did do very well up there singing. I usually don't like that music but it was so spiritual and touching. I hope this Bach Choir continues on in the future. Thankfully yours, Gary." From an elementary school girl: "I loved the way you put your voices together to make a wonderful sound. The sound of your voices brought tears to my eyes. Chelsea." A fifth grade boy thanked Funfgeld and The Bach Choir for this "wonderful, and extraordinary lifetime experience! Alex." A seventh grader wrote that "I will be forever thankful for that music because when I heard it, it was like all my problems came and drifted with the music away from me. Jackley."[7]

Greg Funfgeld's teaching in schools is no less heartfelt. After one program: "I looked up and down the street and saw school buses as far as I could see. J. Fred Wolle would be pleased I thought. In fact, Bach would be pleased."[8] He told a *Morning Call* writer, "It's exciting to think that you might be touching little kids and helping them develop an interest in something that will really enrich their lives."[9]

The Board's education committee was concerned not only with audience development, but with the continuity of The Bach Choir itself. The committee authorized a Choral Scholars Program in which young singers from high schools in the Greater Lehigh Valley are selected by their music teachers and presented to The Choir. The best singers are selected each year by jury, ideally one for each voice part. Those chosen become part of The Bach Choir the following season, participating in all the performances.

Under Bonge's leadership the Board proposed a bold plan, a German tour to increase The Bach Choir's national and international prestige; "A trip to Europe represented a major step forward for The Bach Choir of Bethlehem which is a world class organization."[10] Funfgeld added, "The Choir repeats a great deal of material and they require other musical challenges to maintain excellence. A German tour . . . is one way to fill that need."[11] Raising money to finance the German tour now became a major three-year thrust of Bonge's presidency.

The meticulously planned two-week tour took The Bach Choir to cities with symbolic associations. Leipzig, where Bach spent the last third of his life, was the first destination. On the schedule were Bach's birthplace, Eisenach; Munich, where J. Fred. Wolle had studied; Bethlehem's sister city, Schwäbisch Gemünd; and Berching, home to performers in Bethlehem's Musikfest in 1984 and 1989. The final performance in Würtzburg was "to personally thank Mannesmann/Rexroth, a longtime Bach Choir corporate supporter."[12]

On 19 July 1995, 250 people departed Bethlehem, following three years of intense planning. There were eighty-eight Choir members, the thirty-three-piece orchestra, five vocal soloists, the choir executive staff, and many "tagalongs." Every two days Dr. Ellis Finger reported back to Allentown's *Morning Call* and Cynthia Gordon reported to *The Express Times*. Finger wrote of the sights, activities of the group, and the audience responses to various performances. Gordon delved into the personal responses of various members of the tour group.

The Choir's first German tour had been in 1976 when Germany was still divided. In 1995 that was no longer a problem, and one of the members of the orchestra, "recalling two awful border crossing problems the choir had on its 1976 trip, . . . praised the 'smooth entry' into our Berlin quarters this time."[13]

With three years of preparation and rising expectations behind them, formal greetings and intensive rehearsals marked the ensemble's first three days. However, when President Bonge stepped forward in the *Thomas Kirche* and placed flowers on Bach's grave—only at that moment did The Bach Choir trip, "Bach to Germany," truly begin. Probably no other single gesture during her presidency was as memorable and as moving. As she returned to her seat, The Bach Choir and Orchestra burst forth with the cry, "Kyrie eleison." Professor Finger reported:

> After a two hour performance, the Leipzig audience gave the singers, soloists, orchestra and conductor a rousing standing ovation. Flowers and symbolic candles of peace were exchanged. Many of the singers stood quietly in tears, responding to the emotion of bringing this music back to the place of its creation.[14]

The following day, under the headline, "Bach's *Mass in B Minor* from Abroad," *Leipziger Volkszeitung* readers read in German a review of the performance:

The Choir made its first concert trip to Leipzig in 1976. Saturday night in the Thomas Church it launched its second European tour with the *Mass in B minor*, in collaboration with the Bach Festival Orchestra.

The first two "Kyrie" cries rang out with powerful shape. This inner intensity and involvement dominated the entire performance. The musical lines and the articulation of the two "Kyrie" fugues and the "Christe Eleison" duet also left no doubt as to the intensive study by conductor Greg Funfgeld with contemporary performance practices. There his training with Helmut Rilling could be heard.

The performance's flowing tempos also corresponded largely with those used in Peter Schreier's recording with the Leipzig Radio Choir and the New Bach Collegium. And there lay one area of concern; such brisk tempos would have benefitted from a greater suppleness and clarity in the vocal lines, along with greater familiarity with the church's acoustics.

Nonetheless: such jubilantly sung choruses as "Gloria," "Et resurrexit," "Osanna" and such tenderly intoned movements as "Qui tollis," "Crucifixus," "Agnus dei" had an enduring [*sic*] effect. As a whole the performance impressed listeners in a strong immediate manner. Bach himself would never have dreamt of such worldwide spread of his music [to Pennsylvania] and of the power of its return to Leipzig.[15]

In Eisenach the group performed *Easter Oratorio*, Cantata 34, and *Suite No. 3* with a reduced choir and orchestra because the choir loft was not large enough for the whole group. The church where Bach was baptized was filled with townspeople showing, "their appreciation of the Americans who came to the church . . . to share Bach's music. They applauded for many minutes, then waited outside the church to wave farewell to the musicians as they climbed into their buses."[16]

The Mass was performed in the Berching Municipal Hall. Also, Greg Funfgeld's First Presbyterian Church Choir had previously sung there and the Lehigh University Choir as well. "When the Bach Choir performed at Berching on Tuesday, a large American flag was hanging on the wall behind them. The town gave an enthusiastic reception for all the visiting Americans, featuring a choral group that sang among other favorites, Amazing Grace."[17]

Three final large and very different performances remained: Schwäbisch Gmünd, Munich, and Würzburg. The review in the Schwäbisch Gmünd paper praised The Choir:

It was clear that the choir is deeply proficient with the style of Bach . . . Conductor Greg Funfgeld evidently leads the ensemble with a sense of group spirit and common purpose, while also being focused on a high level of accomplishment . . . Throughout the program the musical sound of the singers and instrumentalists steered clear of puritan severity. Voices and instruments were filled with brilliance and exuded joy and an inner religious fervor.[18]

The Bach Choir sang the *Mass* in Munich's Hercules Hall, equivalent to Carnegie Hall. Funfgeld compared the various performances on the tour:

> Each place is special . . . Knowing the significance of Munich as the training ground for our founder, Fred Wolle, and knowing how prominent the *B minor Mass* has been in Munich's concert life, through Karl Richter and his singers, last night's performance was very special . . .
>
> Each time our choir enters a venue, it breathes the musical spirit of our ancestry and, in turn, leaves its own character behind as part of the accumulated legacy of the site. This was certainly true of Leipzig, where Bach led his choirs, and in Eisenach, where he spent the first 10 years of his life. But it's especially true in Munich, where we have now enriched the patina of Barenboim, Maazel, Kubelik, Bohm, and Leinsdorf."[19]

The tour ended with a performance of the *Mass* that displayed not only the depth of Bethlehem's connection to Germany through the music of Bach, but the success of the Church/Bonge initiative involving Lehigh Valley Area businesses in the support of The Bach Choir. The German metal manufacturing company, Mannesmann-Rexroth, with headquarters near Würzburg, was celebrating its two-hundredth anniversary. Its American distribution center was located in Bethlehem, and a company executive was a member of The Bach Choir Board. Rexroth had underwritten portions of the trip's cost, and the concert was a proud acknowledgment of their corporate support.

Finger concluded his series for the *Morning Call*:

> We had performed some of Bach's music to high professional standards in some of the most prestigious churches and concert halls in this homeland of Bach, and the German public had responded with appreciations, respect, and new understanding for the expert care of this composer's music in our region of Pennsylvania.[20]

Bonge reported to the Board later that the German tour "confirmed what we knew. The Choir's ability to communicate well in German was recognized in reviews. It was an emotional experience. From Leipzig to Wurzburg all was done to perfection. The end result was a higher level of performance."[21]

With the German tour successfully completed, Bonge continued Church's plan to vitalize the Board, adding "New members who were willing to work, who knew music, who knew something about an organization." Among those she asked to join the Board was Jack Jordan. In terms of long-range consequences, this was among the significant actions she took as president.

Jack Jordan came to the Board with many years' experience in strategic planning at Bethlehem Steel where he was senior vice president and chief administrator. He was extremely active in community affairs and was committed to making the Greater Lehigh Valley a better place in which to live. In becoming a Choir Board member, he assumed a leadership position at a moment when he knew he could make a difference.

"Jack Jordan is studying and refining the long-range plan," Bonge reported to the Board in 1993.[22] The next year Jordan told the Board that long-range planning "needs more full Board decision-making."[23] Elected treasurer, he continued in charge of long-range planning, using his skills in finance and organization.

At a Board retreat held early in 1995 a comprehensive, ambitious plan, developed mainly by Jordan, was put forward asserting that The Bach Choir needed to redefine and reconsider its philosophy and mission and nearly all its activities.

The number of guarantors must be increased, the staff expanded, core values more clearly defined. Greater community outreach was necessary. The "elitist" image of The Bach Choir, "that we are well-funded and snobbish," must be altered. Its non-guarantor, corporate, and foundation support must be improved. Also, The Bach Choir must be open to, "expanding the Choir's repertoire and venues." Greater focus was needed on Bach To School. Planning for a Centennial celebration of the founding of The Bach Choir and the American premiere of Bach's *Mass* was to begin immediately. Finally, more "prudent budget" decision-making was required and budget making that was more transparent and more open to Board scrutiny. If there was any question about the necessity for an active, working Board before this retreat, there was no question after it.[24]

In less than a month, a Centennial Planning Committee was put in place and a new mission statement was adopted: "to perform the works of Johann Sebastian Bach, to promote and encourage appreciation of the aesthetic and spiritual values of Bach's music through education and performance, and to strive for the highest standards of musical excellence."[25] With that pronouncement, a discussion of changes to the eighty-year-old guarantor system was begun.

A year later at the annual planning retreat in 1996, the Board could see that the Bach organization was becoming a sophisticated enterprise. General topics expressed as concerns the previous year were now given the formal design of "Goals and Objectives." This refinement was directly the result of Jordan's influence and in line with the discipline all forward-looking national organizations were submitting themselves to. Jordan had become ever more forceful and influential in shaping the philosophy and designing the details of The Bach Choir. In this retreat he was offering the Board a precise, rational agenda; they were now to consider the "Goals and Objectives," endorse, and implement them.

Board discussions also centered on two other significant developments: (1) continued computer training and upgrading of the office, and (2) commitment to an extraordinary celebration of the founding of The Bach Choir and the American premiere of Bach's Mass. Finally, because Jan Bonge had indicated she would not be continuing as the president, the Board began a search for her replacement.

Everyone on the Board recognized that an action-oriented Board and an increasingly more active choir required an efficient, rationally ordered, modern office. They advertised for a person to be executive director. Kathy Link was intrigued by the ad. "I was aware that this was a very prestigious organization in the community, and working for it would be a wonderful adventure. I would like this." She was hired to be the executive director with Winnie Erdman as her office manager:

> We did everything. It was soup to nuts. We opened the mail. We sold the tickets. We did the publicity. We handled the money. We did the concert programs. No two days were ever alike. Who were we? Winnie Erdman and I. I often said the best thing I ever did for The Bach Choir was bring Winnie with me . . . hanging immediately over our heads was the . . . the Centennial Celebration."[26]

The Board was told "the Centennial should raise The Bach Choir to a higher level of recognition."[27] The Centennial committee drafted a proposal and prepared to lay its program before the Board. Members were briefed on the overwhelming response to an Easter morning NBC Television appearance of members of The Bach Choir, Greg Funfgeld and Tom Goeman, his assistant and Choir organist. "NBC said that ours is a highly regarded guest Choir."[28] Then, Ellis Finger, chair of the Centennial Committee, presented its centennial proposal, a four-year schedule of concerts, recordings, publications, and meetings.

Everyone was astonished; this was clearly grander in scope than anything The Bach Choir had undertaken before. The estimated cost of over one million dollars was more funding than any previous celebration had required. The Committee received board approval.[29] Sally Gillispie was named cochair of the committee and was soon employed to direct the centennial. No better choice could have been made, as Gillispie had just completed a superlative job directing the sesquicentennial of the City of Bethlehem.

Two months later, Bonge retired as president, but remained fully active as development officer:

> Asked, "Why did you stop?" Jan replied, I had done what I wanted to do. It was time for new ideas . . . we needed an officer that knew things that Jack knew. We needed financial expertise. He was in charge of strategic planning at Steel.

And I asked him if he would become treasurer. He agreed. When I started thinking about giving up my role, I looked around and thought who would be a good
replacement and I spoke to him. He agreed. I was delighted.[30]

Jack Jordan was elected president. The change of administration had gone
flawlessly.

NOTES

1. Jan Bonge in audiotape interview with the author, 14 January 2005, ABCB.
2. "Minutes of the Managers Board," 17 June 1992, ABCB.
3. Martha Luckenbach in audiotape interview with the author, Fall 1982, ABCB.
4. Jan Bonge in audiotape interview with the author, 14 January 2005, ABCB.
5. "Proposal For Bach To School," File: BACH TO SCHOOL, ABCB.
6. "Bach to School," *Morning Call*, n.d., ABCB.
7. "Bach to School Quotes," File: BACH TO SCHOOL, ABCB.
8. Greg Funfgeld in discussion with the author, November 2005, ABCB.
9. "Bach to School," *Morning Call,* n.d., ABCB.
10. "Minutes of the Managers Board," 21 October 1992, ABCB.
11. "Minutes of the Managers Board," 23 January 1993, ABCB.
12. "Bach to Germany Itinerary," File: Bach to Germany, ABCB.
13. *Morning Call*, 21 July 1995.
14. *Morning Call*, 23 July 1995.
15. "Bach's *Mass in B-Minor* from Abroad" [translation], *Leipziger Volkszeitun,*
24 July 1995, ABCB.
16. *(Easton, PA) Express-Times*, 26 July 1995.
17. *(Easton, PA) Express-Times*, 1 July 1995.
18. Ibid., 21 July 1995.
19. *Morning Call*, July 28, 1995.
20. Ibid., 2 August 1995.
21. "Minutes of the Managers Board," 10 May 1996, ABCB.
22. Ibid., 15 June 1993, ABCB.
23. Ibid., 21 September 1994, ABCB.
24. All direct references from "Minutes of the Managers Board," 21 January 1995,
ABCB.
25. "Minutes of the Managers Board," 15 February 1995, ABCB.
26. Kathy Link in an audiotape interview with the author, Fall 2007, ABCB.
27. "Minutes of the Managers Board," 20 January 1995, ABCB.
28. Ibid., 13 March 1996, ABCB.
29. Ibid.
30. Jan Bonge in audiotape interview with the author, 14 January 2005, ABCB.

Chapter 20

"A National Treasure"

1996–2000

The Bach Choir in Packer Memorial Church

Bonge addressed the Annual Meeting of the Corporation on 10 May 1996. She spoke solemnly. "The overall health of the Choir is good . . . There have been necessary changes to enter the '90s. It has not always been easy. Today our Choir stands on firm ground, poised for even better things in the future." John A. Jordan Jr., the nominee for president to succeed Bonge, thanked her for her "extraordinary term as President." The secretary reported, "A rising vote of applause was given for Jan Bonge, for 5 years the 12th President of [T]he Bach Choir of Bethlehem."[1]

At the Board's June meeting, members accepted the proposed slate of officers: Jordan, president; David G. Beckwith and Joan Moran, vice presidents. Jordan said he "hoped to both enhance and preserve the tradition" of The Bach Choir. Bonge "was confident that all would move forward and progress under Jack's leadership."[2] The change of officers was polite and heartfelt. Such respectful ease was made possible because Bonge had chosen her successor very carefully, and early in her tenure had placed him in critical positions on the Board, first as the treasurer and then as the head of strategic planning. Jordan was more than qualified for the position; he required no additional training and had a deep understanding of the organization of The Bach Choir. He became the thirteenth president as a confident, skillful leader.

An admirer of Charles Schwab, Jordan thought "it was pretty neat that I was going to join an organization that Charlie Schwab had been in." Even though Jordan lived in a very different time than Schwab had, there was a close resemblance. Like Schwab, he could now "insure that Bethlehem Steel stepped up its contribution to The Choir . . . In my position I was able to make phone calls to friends of mine . . . who knew how active I had been in the community. They were willing to support me."[3]

Jordan, again like Schwab, worked to have Bethlehem Steel assume an important role in creating a city that was in every sense a superior place to live and to work. He articulated a philosophy that mirrored Schwab's:

> The first thing was to do your job. What you wanted to do outside was your own business. . . . Then in the early 70s that philosophy began to change. . . . It became more important to be active in the community. . . . We didn't have the cash to hand out anymore, but we had people who could benefit organizations in the Lehigh Valley. I played a major role in that change, because I had always believed personally that a key part of a person's life was to be active in work, active in family, active in community.[4]

When Jordan became president, no one knew if maintaining national musical prominence was even feasible in a country with the vast musical riches America enjoyed at the end of the twentieth century. Adding to this uncertainty, there were many, often contradictory, views on Bach performance practices.

Jordan had become president of an enterprise that became much more complex, and much more active, but he envisioned still more:

> I thought the board was too small. I thought it was too cozy. I thought it was ingrown. I thought it had a narrow view of what its role was. I thought it had abdicated its responsibility to the music director. . . . I thought the board was unprepared to make sure that the organization could sustain itself and prosper in the environment that was coming up. . . . I didn't sense any change agents. . . . It was a clearly parochial view; a tight knit club.[5]

He concluded that the Board had to be larger, more diverse, more powerful, more active, and more accountable. "Frankly, my motivation for increasing the size of the board and getting diversity was to give us opportunities to do more. To become national . . . [and] I think it happened."[6]

In Jordan's view, Board members had three responsibilities: Devising and implementing a strategic plan for the organization; exercising a fiduciary responsibility to the public; and, most important, having the right people in the right jobs to manage the organization. Getting people "in the right spots is the solemn responsibility" of the Board and its officers. "Strategy. Finances. People."[7] In a memo to the members of the newly developed Board, he expressed his view of their duties. "In my view that memo was one of the most important things I did." The document encapsulated entirely his organization philosophy. It read in part:

> As we have grown in performance activity and financial resources it has become more and more apparent and important that we should manage our affairs in the highest professional manner possible. We owe this duty to our various constituencies as well as to ourselves. These communities, their membership and your leadership will allow us to accomplish this objective. . . . The very vitality of The Bach Choir of Bethlehem is highly dependent upon us using our insights, our intelligence and our skills to think anew about our mission, our strategic goals and our strategies and tactics to achieve them.[8]

To achieve this professionalism, he began to shift much of the organizational power from the hierarchical command-and-control of the Executive Committee, where it had been previously (something he regarded as fatal in a nonprofit), to other committees, preferring consensus building with a board of the whole discussing and deciding what to do. Fully functioning, purposeful committees became essential in Jordan's organizational design. "Board committees serve many purposes," he wrote in his memo. He emphasized two key committee responsibilities:

1. Ensure that the policies, plans, budgets, etc., approved by the board of managers are being executed effectively and efficiently.
2. Serve as an important source of discussion and debate on issues and subjects that, in turn, become the basis for strategy, policy and budget recommendations to the board to achieve them.[9]

Jordan was well aware that a performing arts organization has two parallel tracks: management of the organization and performance. Addressing the purpose of the artistic director and his relation to the board:

> I wanted the board to take accountability for the management of the organization. That's why the committee structure came into being. It's not Greg's job to fund the organization. . . . The board's job was to insure The Choir could

perform. Greg's job was to make sure that the performances were outstanding. When asked what forces were at work in these changes, he replied: I think that the strategic planning we did, and the desire to make the celebration of the Centennial something very special were triggers in the minds of a lot of people about what might be possible. . . . We could describe a future that everybody wanted . . . with a feeling that we could get the resources to pull it off.

Asked what was unexpected, he recalled with a laugh, "It was unexpected that we could do as well as we did." Summarizing his time as president, Jordan observed, "I always felt as president that I had been entrusted with a treasure of great worth. It was my duty to protect and enhance it and to pass it along to successors better than when I received it."[10] Asked if any of this ever caused him anxiety, he responded, "None whatsoever, because I was convinced that once the board was committed to do something, I was confident it could succeed."

Soon after Jordan became president, Kathy Link resigned as the executive director. David Beckwith was asked to chair a search committee to replace her. Among the applicants was Bridget George, well known in Bethlehem for her active role in theater management. She had the requisite background in both administration and the arts from her undergraduate Oxford education, and was a devoted Bach lover. She became the unanimous choice of both the committee and the Board. Her energetic commitment to The Choir was felt immediately and her creative ideas helped direct the energy released by the celebration of the Choir's Centenary.

Before Bonge resigned, the Centennial Celebration had been defined, its mission articulated, and a committee appointed to design it. Ellis Finger was named chair. Bonge could not have chosen a more competent chairperson. Bonge remained on the Board after her retirement as president and greatly intensified the fund-raising she had begun as vice president. The Board members felt secure that with their genuine support, Jordan, Funfgeld, Finger, and the new staff could lead The Bach Choir back to a position of national musical prominence.

The Board felt the Centennial should honor two events, the founding of The Bach Choir in 1898 and the American premiere of Bach's *Mass* in 1900. The first event, Founders' Day, was planned as part of the 1998 May Festival, featuring a historical sketch in which descendants of early founders formed the cast of characters. A Pennsylvania Historical Commission marker was placed outside J. Fred. Wolle's birthplace opposite Central Moravian Church. Two Wolle relatives, Barbara Martin Stout and Peter Wolle, unveiled the marker, which balanced the bronze plaque directly across the street commemorating the American premiere of Bach's *Mass*. Receptions were held appropriately in the Victorian parlors of Wolle's birthplace, the rooms in which The Bach Choir was reformed when Wolle returned to Bethlehem. Attendance at a dinner included two living past conductors, Dr. Alfred Mann and Dr. William Reese, Ifor Jones's widow, and a number of the oldest living singers. William Reese later wrote a complimentary letter to Greg Funfgeld. "You certainly have created a virtuoso choir. I was delighted with the sound and was able to hear each voice clearly . . . I am deeply appreciative of the invitation to be part of the Festivities."[11]

During the second weekend, The Bach Choir hosted Johannes Richter, superintendent of the Thomaskircke in Leipzig, and Dr. William Scheide, Bach scholar and honorary chairman of The Bach Choir Centennial. To chronicle the centennial, *Bach in Bethlehem*, by Dr. Ralph Grayson Schwarz, became the first history of The Bach Choir published in more than three decades.

Celebrating the Founders highlighted the 1998 Festival. To further honor the Wolle tradition, Funfgeld chose Bach's *Christmas Oratorio* to precede the *Mass*. In his mind it was almost as central to the Bach Festivals as the *Mass*. Ellis Finger understood the meaning of Funfgeld's choice, calling it "Joyous Proclaimings." The Centennial opened with Bach's proclaiming, "Shout ye, rejoice ye, rise up and praise the day!" Expressing Funfgeld's spiritual intention to fuse Bach, Bach in Bethlehem, and the Centennial Celebration, Finger wrote:

> This music documents an incomparable birth and the gathering of those who journey to Bethlehem to offer blessings of praise to the young child. Taking this potent image of infancy and life-giving creation as metaphor, the music . . . bestows blessings on the not-so-distant birthing of our Choir itself, whose work continues to fulfill destiny, ennobling the lives of its home community and its many esteemed visitors with music, cultural birthright, and the enduring legacy of Bach.[12]

A representative of Dorian Records, producer of the CD, expressed particular pleasure in working with The Bach Choir, "Dorian has a great admiration for The Bach Choir which has experienced so much growth under the direction of Greg Funfgeld. We see The Bach Choir as a national treasure, and we recognize the contribution The Choir makes to the appreciation and preservation of the invaluable music of Bach."[13] In *Early Music America* the reviewer, Ted Libbey, wrote that one of the primary considerations of a bid for musical prominence for a large, amateur choir was the emergence of ideals of period performance. Funfgeld had in various ways addressed this concern in his drive to raise the musical quality of The Choir and adjust the group aesthetically to these new standards of period performance. Funfgeld's success was stunning in the eyes of Libbey. "The penetration of 'period' ideas . . . is impressively demonstrated by the latest recording of *The Mass* to come our way."[14] Libbey concluded, "The approach is admirably informed, the music sung and played with a real grasp of period style. . . . It is a remarkable achievement." Following the close of the Festival, Dorian recorded *The Christmas Oratorio* for release during the Christmas season of 1999.

Two very different collaborations took place during the first year of the Centennial Celebration. The Trisha Brown Dance Company performed Bach's *Musical Offering*, melding her company with a chamber ensemble of musicians from The Bach Festival Orchestra that Funfgeld conducted. Brown's dancers brought to the stage Bach's powerful and profound examination of fugal writing, which forms the basis of *The Musical Offering*. In an interview Brown stressed the collaboration. "With Bach, although you will recognize my vocabulary, I had to work very hard to find a distinction between the kind of gestures that I was making so as to be as visible, side by side with his enormous making of music."[15] A local critic writing about the performance stated, "It was not stick-to-the-ribs kind of stuff." A person who also attended the program countered, "It may not have been a "stick-to-your-ribs kind of stuff. More likely it is a stick-to-your-heart-and-mind kind of experience."[16] Finger created a festival symposium around the event with round table discussions of modern dance and musical form, the use of Bach's music in contemporary American choreography, and an exhibition of "Etchings on Johann Sebastian Bach" was on display during the event.

The Centennial's second collaboration was very different. The Third Bethlehem Conference on Moravian Music held at Moravian College later that year honored J. Fred. Wolle. Funfgeld conducted a sing-along for those attending the conference. Cantata *Wachet Auf*, BWV140, was rehearsed and performed for the public with members of The Bach Choir and Bach Festival Orchestra and singers from The Moravian Music Conference. The group combined with the Moravian College Choir to sing an anthem for chorus and bass soloists composed by J. Fred. Wolle.

The guest concert by cellist Yo-Yo Ma was the result of an extraordinary set of circumstances: one personal, one historical. The Centennial Committee was searching for a musician of international prominence, "a great artist," associated with Bach, to participate in the Centennial Celebration; singers, organists and other keyboard players of international renown had been guests in prior festivals and on special occasions. Simultaneously, the Committee was hoping to honor Central Moravian Church, long associated by Bach lovers throughout the world with the Bethlehem Choir and its prominence in the American Bach Movement.

Aiming for a packed house, a program planner suddenly brought forth the idea of the great cellist Yo-Yo Ma to play the complete Bach *Violincello Suites* at Central Moravian Church. A great musician, a soloist, playing Bach in a historic place would be an astounding concert. But would Yo-Yo Ma agree to perform in Bethlehem? Would his concert schedule permit him to accept an invitation? Would the Moravian Church Elders agree to a ticketed performance in the sanctuary?

The Elders quickly said, "Yes," the famous cellist would be welcome in Central Moravian Church. Getting a "Yes" from Yo-Yo Ma was more complicated. However, Ellis, Finger used his thorough knowledge of the concert world and called upon his concert management connections. Once Yo-Yo Ma was aware of the historical importance of Central Moravian Church, the cellist and his agent made dates in late November 1998 available for him to come to Bethlehem. Yo-Yo Ma felt honored by the invitation to join the Centennial, so much so that he agreed to take two days away from his family during the Thanksgiving holiday. Bach concert lovers were so pleased that the concert, set for 21 November, sold out immediately.

The concert, like the *Mass*, would be performed in two parts. Yo-Yo Ma played the first three *Suites* in the late afternoon. In the evening he completed the set. Sitting alone, he spun out Bach's endless musical inventions. The cellist left this moving message to The Bach Choir when he wrote in great humility on the concert poster, "Even as a lower voice tonight I could feel the sustenance your voices brought to those who have sought to be filled over the years. Congratulations on your Anniversary. It is truly a great privilege and joy to be part of your celebrations. Warmest wishes, Yo Yo Ma 11/21/98."[17] The framed signed poster hangs on the wall of the office of The Bach Choir. The next morning Yo-Yo Ma held a public master class at Moravian College. Among the standing-room-only audience were sixty local cellists.

Once the year of guest performances was past, the intent became to showcase The Bach Choir and Orchestra regionally in the Lehigh Valley and Philadelphia and nationally in Washington, D.C., and New York City. The year began with two sets of concerts designed to show the finesse and clarity of the instrumental ensemble and the virtuosity of its singers and conductor.

The works chosen were Bach's *Brandenburg Concertos*. J. Fred. Wolle had conducted Number Two BWV 107 as early as 1903, and individual *Brandenburgs* would be played during later Festivals. This was the first time the demanding challenge of playing all six concertos would be on one program. The first concert, 5 February, performed in Zoellner Center for the Arts at Lehigh University, introduced the instrumentalists to local people who ordinarily would not attend The Bach Festivals. The second concert was played for The Bach Festival of Philadelphia in The Church of the Holy Trinity, a church with a long history of superb musical performances. The ensemble proved itself unquestionably equal to performing six concertos in back-to-back concerts. The performances were enthusiastically applauded by full houses in both places.

The Festival emphasized the Moravian heritage of The Bach Choir with a performance of the *Passion According to Saint Matthew* that Wolle had premiered in 1892. Chamber music by Bach was performed Saturday morning in the *Saal*, the first worship space in Bethlehem, in the historic *Gemeinhaus* of the Moravian Museum. Organist Gerre Hancock played an organ recital that included a four-movement improvisation on the pitches of Bach's name B-A-C-H. This venture proved so successful that it became a frequent Festival offering.

The Bach Choir hoped that singing the *Mass* in Washington's Kennedy Center and New York's Carnegie Hall would restore its national prominence. How vastly different American musical life had become from what it had been in Wolle's time! There were now many Bach choirs singing the *Mass in B Minor* in America. New York was no longer the only center of musical quality, nor were only two or three music critics defining musical taste for the nation. A performance of Bach's *Mass* was no longer national news. Many born after World War II viewed classical music as elitist, suspect, or simply irrelevant. However, Funfgeld also faced issues Wolle and Ifor Jones before him had encountered. A friendly reviewer who discussed these issues wrote:

But just like any historic town, life beneath the surface is more complex. Any population that lives consciously within the walls of its heritage feels the tugs of tradition and innovation. Those same forces have pulled strongly at Bach in the past decades as well, and if the Bach Choir shows no obvious bruises, perhaps it's because this steel town 45 miles north of Philadelphia was already used to negotiating those forces peacefully.

Many of these innovations on "tradition" are welcome. Even the Bach Choir no longer incorporates Moravian chorales into Bach's works. . . . Professional singers, rather than chorus members, now perform the solos. . . . And the chorus, though still not down to the size preferred by scholars of the period, is smaller and more limber than the unwieldy groups of the past.

Conductor Greg Funfgeld, though he refrains from actually using period instruments, adapts the gains of the authenticity movement quite easily. Tempos are suitably brisk, yet allowing plenty of space for ornamentations to breathe. Soloists use vibrato, but not to distraction. The chorus may lack the sheen of a fully professional group, but its precision is no less superb and its way of sweeping a musical line shows much more connection to its material than any professional pick-up group.

As the Bach Choir continues its extended centenary celebration, its Bach campaign remains quite-strong, because its festival sprouted from the town's Moravian roots and has been nourished by the community ever since. Quite, because it holds to an ideal of communal music making that has not aged gracefully in our culture.

For most music lovers today, why devote one night a week to learn a piece yourself when you can hear a professional sing it note perfect? Why support a local production of the *B-minor Mass* when a trip to Tower Records offers more interpretations of the piece than a mid-century listener could ever imagine?[18]

Of immense importance to the celebration of this Centenary was that previously The Bach Choir had performed in Washington and New York by invitation, with Charles Schwab underwriting the New York concerts. Now the halls must be rented and audiences generated. The full weight of fund raising and promotion now fell on the organization.

The Bach Choir had not sung in Washington since 1925, when First Lady Grace Coolidge had invited it to perform the *Mass* for the International Conference of World Fellowship. That had been the first time the *Mass* had been sung in its entirety in the nation's capital. The Bach Choir had sung various times in New York, under Wolle's direction, but it had last performed in Carnegie Hall in 1945 when, Richard Westenberg had conducted the Gala Centennial Concert celebrating Albert Schweitzer. The Bach Choir had also appeared the same year by invitation with the Philadelphia Orchestra under Eugene Ormandy as part of the symphony season.

There was no question that The Choir could sing the *Mass*, convincingly and movingly, if not "authentically." Yet in 1999, even with a smaller Choir, no one knew exactly how out-of-town excursions would be financed. Many believed it could not be done, but that it was done and with great success became proof of the adaptability and vitality of The Bach Choir and its supporters.

A professional publicist was hired to elevate The Bach Choir in the national music scene. Political and social connections already existing in Washington and New York were identified and contacted. Local support groups were organized. Industries, businesses, and foundations were solicited. The executive director, Bridget George, and Funfgeld tirelessly negotiated contracts with the managements of the Kennedy Center and Carnegie Hall. Guarantors were asked for their support.

According to Bridget George, the Board knew that staging a Kennedy Center concert would be expensive. She warned also that the planning would be intricate.[19] Funfgeld met with the conductors of choral organizations, many of whom he knew. Bridget George talked to key congressmen and their wives and to the president of the Kennedy Center to negotiate a lower fee for the hall. Both met with members of the German Embassy and won the support of the Washington German community. They received advertising advice and suggestions about "filling the hall." After the performance an Internet critic wrote:

> Reviews of the concert varied. The most enthusiastic [said] Greg Funfgeld could not be faulted in leading the chorus, orchestra and vocal soloists. A standing ovation by the most appreciative audience was definitely deserved. We hope this long-lived group would make frequent visits to the nation's capital and not wait another two dozen years to supply such inspirational pleasure to music lovers in the nation's capital.[20]

The Carnegie Hall performance was much more difficult to arrange. To a degree, the process that developed in Washington was replicated in New York. Basically the concert had to be self-produced. The choral and political connections in Washington were not the same in New York, though the German Consulate assisted and Mayor Rudolph Giuliani expressed "my best wishes for this special concert and for the continued success of the Bach Choir of Bethlehem in all its future endeavors."[21]

The concert was well attended. Bridget George reported to the Board, "We did extraordinarily well in filling Carnegie Hall both with regular ticket sales and with the complimentary group papering (in excess of 1,000 out of 2,800 seats) normal for a concert such as this and expertly handled by our publicists."[22] The audience response was enthusiastic. There were four curtain calls, and "Greg got his own roar from the crowd in the final curtain call."[23]

The local press review was entirely laudatory. The Allentown *Morning Call* reporter wrote, "The concert will be remembered well into the millennium. It will be regarded as the performance of this magnificent work for others to equal."[24] New York reviewers were less complimentary. One regarded Funfgeld's interpretation of the *Mass* as "quite effective . . . fine performance from the Bethlehem Bach Choir."[25] The *New York Times* critique offered no praise:

> What results . . . is a style that works well at home. In a festival atmosphere awash in community spirits, less well on the road . . . It would be nice simply to laud the Bach Choir's efforts, present and past. But a Carnegie appearance implies a higher standard than was met here. None of this will dissuade a listener from returning to Bethlehem to hear Bach some fine May.[26]

Funfgeld told the board, "It was disappointing, but with all the feedback from colleagues and audience members . . . it almost seemed as if the

NYT critic Jim Oesterich was at a different concert."[27] The board secretary recorded, "President Jordan called for a round of applause for the staff."[28]

The memorial event of the Centennial Celebration was the one-hundredth anniversary of the premiere of the *Mass*, performed to the day, 27 March 2000, in the same location. Replicas of the original tickets were the same price, $1.50 each. The programs were replicas as well, except for the names of the participants. The Moravian Trombone Choir announced the event from the belfry, but it did not precede the *Mass*. While Central Moravian Church had lost its Victorian decor, the structure was unchanged. The gaslights still flickered on the walls, and the acoustics, as always, were superb.

The program was not a reenactment, nor was it meant to be. The organ designed by Wolle's uncle had been replaced. Funfgeld did not conduct from the organ console. The orchestra and soloists were all professionals. The *Mass* was not new to the singers or to the audience.

Other differences were especially interesting. The Funfgeld chorus was larger than Wolle's (twenty-seven sopranos in 1900, thirty-six in 2000; twenty-one altos in 1900, thirty-five in 2000; fifteen tenors, sixteen in 2000; nineteen basses, compared to twenty-six). The chorus in 2000 reflected an aesthetic favoring the two outer voice parts. From accounts of Wolle's frequent changes in tempo, Funfgeld's interpretation was more direct and forward moving. His choir sounded as one voice of blended vocal tone, mature but with little vibrato and emphatically centered pitch.

The soloists in the Centenary performance were international singers, each exemplifying the high level of musicianship Funfgeld had achieved and maintained during his artistic and musical leadership of The Bach Choir. Tamara Matthews and Rosa Lamoreau were the sopranos; mezzo-soprano, Marietta Simpson; tenor, Frederick Urrey; baritone, William Sharp; and bass-baritone, Daniel Lichti completed the outstanding roster.

Wolle's and Funfgeld's orchestras were quite similar in size. Wolle had twelve violins; Funfgeld used nine. Wolle had four oboes; Funfgeld, three. Relative to the chorus, Wolle's orchestra was louder with more prominent violins. Wolle probably had rewritten Bach's high trumpet parts, so that they were an octave lower and therefore easily playable on nineteenth-century trumpets. The current players were all professionals, who played Bach's music as he had written it.

As in Wolle's day, the church was filled to capacity with an audience similarly aware that it was part of an historic event. Following the premiere, the audience applauded Funfgeld, The Bach Choir, the soloists, and the orchestra enthusiastically. Everyone walked out into the night with a feeling of pride.

NOTES

1. "The Bach Choir of Bethlehem, Annual Meeting of the Corporation," 10 May 1996, ABCB.

2. "Board of Managers Minutes," 10 June 1996, ABCB.

3. Jack Jordan in audiotape interview with the author, Fall 2002, ABCB.

4. Ibid.

5. Ibid.

6. Ibid.

7. Ibid.

8. John Jordan to "September 24, 2003, Chairmen and Vice Chairmen, Board Committees 2003–2004, Board Managers," in Jordan Papers, ABCB.

9. Ibid.

10. Jack Jordan, "Re: Draft Chapters," to author, e-mail, 3 June 2005, in Jordan Papers, ABCB.

11. "William H. Reese, May 11, 1998" to The Bach Choir, in "Centennial Album 1998," ABCB.

12. "The 1998 Bach Festival," *The Bach Choir News* 29, no. 2 (Spring 1998): 1, ABCB.

13. Ibid., "News Release."

14. "The Bach Choir's 1998 release of *The Mass*," review in *The Bach Choir News* 30, no. 1 (Fall 1999): 7, ABCB.

15. *Morning Call*, 4 October 1998.

16. *Morning Call*, 9 October 1998.

17. Office of The Bach Choir of Bethlehem. The following morning Yo-Yo Ma held a public master class at Moravian College, Bethlehem, PA.

18. *Newark (NJ) Star Ledger*, 13 May 1999, clipping in ABCB.

19. Bridget George in audiotape interview with the author, ABCB.

20. Bob Anthony, arts critic, World Wide Web (accessed 5 October 1999), Hemsin Associates.

21. "Proclamation," 7 February 2000, archives of ABCB.

22. "Minutes of the Board of Managers,"16 February 2000, ABCB.

23. Ibid.

24. *Morning Call*, 9 February 2000.

25. "The Bach Choir of Bethlehem with the Bach Festival Orchestra," *New York Concert Review* 7, no. 2 (Summer 2000): 4, ABCB.

26. *New York Times*, 9 February 2000.

27. "Minutes of the Board of Managers," 16 February 2000, ABCB.

28. Ibid.

Chapter 21

A Second Centennial

2000–2007

Brochure for One-Hundredth Bach Festival

At its April 2000 meeting, Jack Jordan assured Board members that the long-range plan they had put in place would continue the momentum the Centennial Celebration had generated. Funfgeld, George, and Jordan would work closely within the organization to realize the financial, managerial, logistical, and artistic components of that plan.

A major element would be a tour in the summer of 2003 to introduce The Choir to the United Kingdom. George and Funfgeld traveled to Leipzig and London to begin making the necessary contacts. Funfgeld and George met in London with Nicholas Kenyon, director of the BBC Proms, one of Britain's most prestigious classical music concert series. Kenyon confirmed an invitation for The Bach Choir to sing at the Proms in July 2003, and plans for an eight-concert tour in other cities were settled. With a concert in London's Royal Albert Hall as the climax, the tour would also include a St. Albans International Organ Festival and a Cambridge Summer Music Festival at King's College, Cambridge. On his return, Funfgeld apprised the Board of Managers, "This project will raise the bar of artistic standards for The Choir."[1]

Special fund-raisers were quickly scheduled to help pay tour expenses. The Choir was polled and only two singers out of about one hundred could not participate. By the fall of 2001 George could report to the Board, "Booking arrangements are now completed for eight concerts in spectacular and prestigious settings."[2] The final step was taken by the Board in April 2003 when it approved the budget for the tour and the proposed plan for funding any short fall.[3]

Without question the United Kingdom tour taxed The Bach Choir's personnel and financial resources. But, when the tour was over, there was no question that it had exceeded all expectations. The Bach Choir was not only successful but "both choir and orchestra rose to the challenge magnificently."[4]

During the tour The Choir sang the *Mass* and choral works by Mendelssohn and ventured into performing a difficult and unfamiliar piece by Libby Larsen, a contemporary composer. These works were possible only because of a profound change that had been made in the 2001 definition of The Bach Choir's mission. Including music by composers other than Bach was one of Funfgeld's most important achievements in this period, a vital part of the artistic and educational mission. The Mission Statement was altered:

> The mission of the Bach Choir of Bethlehem is to perform the works of Johann Sebastian Bach, to promote and encourage appreciation of the aesthetic and spiritual value of Bach's music through education and performance, including performance of works by composers who influenced Bach or were influenced by him, and to strive for the highest standards of musical excellence.[5]

Funfgeld and The Choir received rave reviews throughout the United Kingdom tour: Edinburgh, "The Bach Choir . . . worked its transatlantic magic"; St. Albans, the Choir "filled the abbey with glorious sound"; Oxford, its "polished vitality was impressive"; London, it had "endearing sincerity."

Jordan, an inveterate history buff, was reminded of William the Conqueror's invasion of England in 1066:

Our UK tour had a striking similarity to William's effort. Months and months of preparation were required before we were able to depart for England and Scotland. I'm sure you can imagine the countless details associated with taking 250 people overseas for two weeks. We weren't going into battle, but we were going to expose ourselves to sophisticated countries, well-accustomed to very high standards . . . We didn't have to worry about weapons or horses, but we were concerned about preparation of the music . . . hotel and food arrangements, and transportation via airplane and buses . . . While it would be inappropriate to think of Greg and his musicians as conquerors, we certainly can think of them as heroes.[6]

Following the United Kingdom tour, Jordan felt "we have reached a critical juncture in the life of our organization . . . our glorious trip to the UK could, if we are not careful, lead us to complacency and unwillingness to foster fresh thinking and new ideas."[7] Jordan took two decisive actions: he decided to retire as president at the end of June in 2004 with David Beckwith as his recommended successor, and he created a number of new committees for an expanded Board of Managers, including the Strategic Planning Committee.

The Strategic Planning Committee drafted a four-year proposal the Board discussed during a January 2004 retreat. To make a seamless transition to a new Board president, Jordan appointed David Beckwith chair of the committee and the leader of the Board retreat. Beckwith, a longtime vice president of the Board and former member of The Bach Choir, had often been its representative on the Board. He was a past chair of the finance committee. He was the CEO of a major health provider in the Lehigh Valley and had been for many years a leader in area health care.

Working creatively with the legacies of past presidents and conductors, Jordan had built the stability necessary for Funfgeld and The Bach Choir to perpetuate the mission "to promote and encourage appreciation of the aesthetic and spiritual value of the music of Johann Sebastian Bach." Funfgeld had eloquently and persistently articulated his artistic vision for a mature choir singing Bach in the twenty-first century. He efficiently applied the accepted vocal aesthetic of precise pitch and rhythmic articulation, unified tone quality, German language musical pronunciation, and occasional use of period instrumentation. Thus, Funfgeld accommodated to major changes in taste that had occurred in the late twentieth century as a result of recordings, period performance practice, contending views of Bach performance, the increase of concerts by professional choruses, and instrumental ensembles replacing amateur ones. The result was a choir that bore no resemblance to the one conducted by Ifor Jones. The changes set in motion by Church, Bonge, Jordan, and Funfgeld as Beckwith became The Choir's president were complete.

A strategic planning draft was ready for the Board to discuss on 31 January 2004. It addressed the artistic vision, organizational structure, identity and commitment to excellence, investment in scholarship and education, audience expansion, financial integrity and accountability to the public, and investment in human resources. Also proposed were a preliminary study for a new capital campaign, and the celebration of the Centennial of the Bach Festivals in 2007. Monthly noon concerts in Central Moravian Church, free and open to the public, and a plan to collaborate with Moravian College to offer a Bach Institute for teachers sponsored by the National Endowment for the Humanities were included as well. The full plan was accepted, and entirely convinced of Beckwith's capability to lead the organization, the Board elected him president. Deeply emblematic of the social and business influence that resulted from the bankruptcy of the Bethlehem Steel Corporation, Beckwith was the first president not associated with the Steel.

The one-hundredth Bethlehem Bach Festival was the next Centennial celebration held in 2007. The Choir sang *The Passion According to Saint Matthew*, the Taylor 2 Dance Company performed with the Bach Festival Orchestra, and the Baltimore Consort gave a concert in the hall at Moravian College where Wolle had rehearsed The Bach Choir for the first twenty years. An exhibition, "The Bach Choir of Bethlehem—A Visual History," mounted at Lehigh University, was the result of many months of working with the Zoellner Arts Center Gallery.

A key event just prior to the first Centenary had been the hiring of Bridget George as executive director. Now her close collaboration with Greg Funfgeld and their relationship with the exemplary Board of Managers unleashed a flood of creative energy well supported by Winnie Erdman, office manager. The breadth of their actions extends far beyond the annual Bach Festival.

As outreach to area residents, the annual Family Concert offers a variety of arts featuring young people: dance, acting, drawing, composing, poetry, and musical performance. The Bach to School program took Choir and orchestra members into area schools for students to experience Bach's music live. Bach at Noon offers hour-long free monthly programs in Central Moravian Church. In addition to instrumental, vocal, and choral works by Bach, Dr. Funfgeld (who had received an honorary doctorate from Lehigh University in 2007) serves as a skillful guide, demonstrating salient features in the music. The Young Scholars program annually auditions singers for The Bach Choir. Concerts presenting world-class performers such as Yo-Yo Ma and Dave Brubeck have been part of galas open to the public. The repertoire of

FACES OF THE FESTIVAL
A digital photo collage.

A view of one hundred years of Bethlehem Bach Festival: formal, casual, young, old, performers and listeners.

Collage, 2007 (Linda Ganus)

The Bach Choir has been greatly expanded to include works by composers who influenced or were influenced by Bach. In addition original works have been commissioned for special occasions. A Distinguished Lecture series was added to the annual Festival, offering the public the best scholarly thinking on the music of Bach. The outreach broadened as numerous appearances on public and commercial television took place. A highly praised extensive series of CDs was issued. An Archive has been organized which scholars and others interested in the history of The Bach Choir may access freely.

The "backstage" actions of a highly responsive and responsible Board continue to undergird the success of The Choir. Even in difficult economic times, it sustains itself, and sanctions and supports the expansion of its offerings.

When Cheryl Nagel replaced Jan Bonge as development officer, she asked faithful members of the audience: "Tell us your stories!"

> I came first to the Bach Festival at the age of 13 and except for a few years when having babies interfered have been attending ever since. I am now 90 years old.
>
> The Festival was something I always did with my mother, and later my 4 daughters have been added so it is a real family and spiritual resource which is very important to all of us.
>
> I remember Wolle's amazing hands which were almost all that could be seen of him as he was hidden as I remember behind some potted palms.
>
> Alfred Mann is a very close friend, and it was especially interesting for us to hear him conducting.
>
> I miss the wonderful "old timers" who had sung in the Festival for so many years and for whom it was a most important part of their lives; but I have to admit that as the choir became more professional the music has taken off to a new level. It gets "better each year"—at least that's what we have said to each other for the past 71 years!! I fully expect it to continue.

Another person remembered coming to her first Festival in 1937 at age 5:

> My mother would have us sit outside for one half of the *Mass*; inside for the other. Ifor Jones' performances were so intense that even a 5 year old child was totally taken in by their power. Jones was not afraid of great drama; the *Mass* can be great drama. My brother, Paul, then said after the "Sanctus"—"That was hot stuff!" For me no conductor since Jones has been able to communicate the passion of Bach's music so convincingly; powerfully. The "Cruxificus" was slow; agonizing, the Agnus Dei poignant to the point of hurting, the 1st Kyrie stunning,; the "Sanctus" lifted the roof off Packer Chapel; and sent your spirit to the heavens.

A teacher was saved by the Festival and enabled to proclaim the music of Bach for forty years:

> Frustrated with looking at music and contemplating music as a graduate student in musicology at Princeton University, I was seriously contemplating withdrawing from the program. Friends in classics, knowing of the Festival, gently kidnapped me and brought me to the 1960 Festival. The cantatas and especially Ifor Jones' performance of the *B-Minor Mass* changed my life, restored in spirit; I determined to complete the Ph.D. and open the world of Bach and the Festival to students. This I have done for 40 years. The Festival opened other avenues: the Moravian cemetery, the museum with its exquisite piano, convivial gatherings at the tavern. Bethlehem retains a special place in my thoughts. I hope to return soon and experience again the beauty and the glory of the *B-Minor Mass* presented as only Bethlehem can!

The *Mass* took possession of another listener:

> My everlasting memory is the first time I ever heard the Bach Choir. A friend of mine upon hearing that I loved Bach but never had been to the Bethlehem Festival took me to the *B-Minor Mass*. This was during the Ifor Jones era. Hearing the brass ensemble playing the Hymn quietly backstage and sequencing into the Kyrie will remain *the most* thrilling musical moment of my life. As the rest of the performance swept over me I knew I would return year after year—forever. And I have (missing only 2 weekends in the past 39 years.)

Finally, a woman wrote most movingly of her lifelong connection with the Festivals:

> Since my husband's family is from a long tradition of Moravian Church clergy, including his father, who sang in the Bach Choir for 7 years after moving to Bethlehem when he retired from the active ministry, Bethlehem, especially during the Bach Festival weekends, offers rich opportunities for experiences of family, religious, musical, and general American historical significance for me and my grown children.

In the early years of our marriage, we went every year, stayed in the parents' apartment (where the library now stands), had baby sitters from among clergy offspring attending Moravian College, and heard the choir concerts from the cheapest seats available at the Packer Chapel. For me, it was a retreat from the stress of raising two babies a year apart and I drank it all in deeply—being pampered with my mother-in-law's signature meals, "sleeping in" in the mornings while the grandparents "enjoyed" the babies, getting to read an entire book, and having that glorious music to look forward to for two whole days.

At the concerts themselves, I heard all the music with my freshly minted Bachelor of Music background still in my head, but I also worked through all the problems of the previous year that I had carried from home. Sometimes I cried during the singing, sometimes, I got fresh insights through the music of what my life as a young mother and wife was all about, and always I went home refreshed and inspired to face the next year's challenges of family and piano teaching responsibilities.

I guess that's why it is important to be a Festival guarantor and to come back every year that I possibly can. Thank you so much for continuing that tradition.[8]

NOTES

1. "Minutes of the Board of Managers," 20 September 2000, ABCB.

2. "Minutes of the Board of Managers, 14 November 2001, ABCB.

3. "Minutes Board of the Board of Managers," 17 April 2002, ABCB.

4. Giles Woodforde, *Oxford Times* (UK), 25 July 2003.

5. "Minutes of the Board of Managers," 18 April 2001, ABCB.

6. "Letter from The President," *The Bach Choir News* 33, no. 2 (Fall 2003), ABCB.

7. John Jordan to "September 24, 2003, Chairmen and Vice Chairmen, Board Committees 2003–2004, Board Managers," in Jordan Papers, ABCB.

8. "Audience Accounts," file, ABCB.

Appendix A

**BACH FESTIVAL DISTINGUISHED SCHOLAR
LECTURE SERIES**

12 and 19 May 2000. Dr. Robin A. Leaver. No title given.

11 and 18 May 2001. Dr. Joshua Rifkin. No title given.

10 and 17 May 2002. Dr. Johannes Richter. No title given.

9 and 16 May 2003. Dr. Michael Marissen. No title given.

7 and 14 May 2004. Dr. Michael Marissen. No title given.

6 and 13 May 2005. Dr. Michael Marissen. No title given.

5 and 12 May 2006. Dr. Michael Marissen. No title given.

4 and 11 May 2007. Dr. Michael Marissen. "New Perspectives on *The Saint Matthew Passion*."

2 and 9 May 2008. Dr. Christoph Wolff. "Are Bach Oratorios Sacred Operas?"

1 and 8 May 2009. Dr. Michael Marissen. "Hope in Bach's Music."

7 and 14 May 2010. Dr. Michael Marissen. "Bach and Mary."

Appendix B

BACH CHOIR DISCOGRAPHY

Cantata, BWV 78: Jesus, thou wearied spirit (Jesu, der du meine Seele) / Johann Sebastian Bach. [Soprano and alto soloists not listed]; Mack Harrel, bass; Lucius Metz, tenor; Bach Choir of Bethlehem and Orchestra; Ifor Jones, conductor. RCA Victor Red Seal [19--]. 4 sound discs : analog, 78 rpm; 12 in.

Chorale: World, farewell! from Cantata, BWV 27: Wer weiss, wie nahe mir mein Ende!; Motet: Sing ye to the Lord a new-made song (Singet dem Herr ein neues Lied): motet for two choruses; Concerto no. 1 in D minor / Johann Sebastian Bach. Bach Choir of Bethlehem (1st-2nd works); Agi Jambor, piano, Bach Festival Orchestra (3rd work); Ifor Jones, conductor. Recorded in Bethlehem [19--), by Peter Bartok. 1 sound disc : analog, 33 1/3 rpm; 12 in.

Fugue in E-flat major, BWV 552; Passacaglia and Fugue in C minor, BWV 582; Pastorale in F major BWV 590; Toccata in F major, BWV 540/Johann Sebastian Bach. [A reproduction of Mendelssohn's Bach Recital, Leipzig, 6 August 1840; jacket notes by Alfred Mann.] William Whitehead, organist. Recorded at First Presbyterian Church of Bethlehem [19--], by Helffrich Recording Labs. 1 sound disc : analog, 33 1/3 rpm, stereo.; 12 in.

Cantata, BWV 71: God is my king (Gott ist mein König)/Johann Sebastian Bach. Phyllis Curtin, soprano; Lillian Knowles, alto; David Lloyd, tenor; Mack Harrel, bass; Bach Choir of Bethlehem; Bach Festival Orchestra; Ifor Jones, conductor. Recorded at the Bach Choir Festival, Bethlehem, Pa., 25 May 1951, by the Audio Laboratory, Bethlehem, Pa. 1 sound disc : analog, 33 1/3 rpm, stereo.; 12 in.

Mass in B minor, BWV 232 / Johann Sebastian Bach. Lois Marshall, soprano; Eunice Alberts, contralto; John McCollum, tenor; Kenneth Smith, bass; Bach Choir of Bethlehem; Bach Festival Orchestra; Ifor Jones, conductor. Recorded at Lehigh University Chapel, Bethlehem, Pa., [1962], by Peter Bartok, assisted by William Hamilton. The Classics Record Library [1962]. 3 sound discs: analog, 33 1/3 rpm, stereo.; 12 in.

Christmas in Leipzig: Choral music for the Nativity by Bach. / Cantata, BWV 63: Christen ätzet diesen Tag; Cantata, BWV 65: Sie werden aus Saba alle kommen; Chorus: Sanctus, from Mass in B Minor, BWV 232 / Johann Sebastian Bach. Sylvia McNair, soprano; Janice Taylor, contralto; David Gordon, tenor; Daniel Lichti, bass; Bach Choir of Bethlehem; Bach Festival Orchestra; Greg Funfgeld, conductor. Recorded at First Presbyterian Church of Bethlehem, 27 February 1988. Dorian Recordings, 1988. 1 sound disc : digital ; 4 ¾ in.

Wachet auf!: Cantatas, BWV 56 and 140; Motet, BWV Anh. 159. / Cantata, BWV 56: Ich will den Kreuzstab gerne tragen; Cantata, BWV 140: Wachet auf, ruft uns die Stimme; Motet BWV Anh. 159: Ich lasse dich nicht / Johann Sebastian Bach. Henriette Schellenberg, soprano; David Gordon, tenor; Daniel Lichti, bass; Bach Choir of Bethlehem; Bach Festival Orchestra; Greg Funfgeld, conductor. Recorded at First Presbyterian Church of Bethlehem, 27 and 28 January 1989. Dorian Recordings, 1989. 1 sound disc : digital ; 4 ¾ in.

Christmas in Bethlehem: Traditional carols sung by the Bach Choir of Bethlehem, vol. 1. / O come, all ye faithful; Break forth, o beauteous morning light, from Christmas oratorio, BWV 248; Joy to the world; Tomorrow shall be my dancing day; Away in a manger; God to Adam came in Eden; Angels from the realms of glory; O little town of Bethlehem; Behold! In gloomy stable stall, from Christmas oratorio, BWV 248; Lo! How a rose e'er blooming; Wohl mir, das ich Jesum habe, from Cantata, BWV 147; Silent night! Holy night!; What sweeter music; Hark, the herald angels sing; Infant holy, infant lowly; Angels we have heard on high; Jesus Christ the apple tree; Once in royal David's city. Karen Cocca, soprano; Thomas Goeman, organ; Bach Choir of Bethlehem; Fairmount Brass Quartet; Greg Funfgeld, conductor. Recorded at First Presbyterian Church of Bethlehem, October 1994, by Peter Helffrich. 1 sound disc : digital ; 4 ¾ in.

Christmas in Bethlehem: Traditional carols sung by the Bach Choir of Bethlehem, vol. 2. / God rest you merry, gentlemen; Two chorales from Christmas oratorio, BWV 248 (Wie soll ich dich empfangen; Ach mein herzliebes Jesulein); Once he came in blessing; Gloria sei dir gesungen, from Cantata, BWV 140; Il est ne le divin enfant; Ding dong! Merrily on high; Jesus, call thou me; The little road to Bethlehem; Nun seid ihr wohl gerochen, from Christmas Oratorio BWV 248; Brightest and best of the sons of the morning; Mary's lullaby;

Ave Maria; What child is this?; Dem wir das heilig itzt, from Cantata, BWV 129; Good Christians all, rejoice!; Infant holy, infant lowly; See amid the winter's snow. Karen Cocca, soprano; Dennis Bushkofsky, baritone; Donald DeBoer, tenor; Greg Oaten, tenor; Thomas Goeman, organ; Bach Choir of Bethlehem; trumpets and timpani of Bach Festival Orchestra; Philadelphia Brass; Greg Funfgeld, conductor. Recorded at First Presbyterian Church of Bethlehem, February 1997. Dorian Recordings, 1997. 1 sound disc : digital ; 4 ¾ in.

Mass in B Minor, BWV 232 / Johann Sebastian Bach. Tamara Matthews, soprano; Rosa Lamoreaux, soprano; Marietta Simpson, mezzo-soprano; Frederick Urrey, tenor; William Sharp, baritone; Daniel Lichti, bass-baritone; Bach Choir of Bethlehem; Bach Festival Orchestra; Greg Funfgeld, conductor. Recorded at First Presbyterian Church of Bethlehem, May 1997. Dorian Recordings, 1998. 2 sound discs : digital ; 4 ¾ in.

Christmas Oratorio, BWV 248 / Johann Sebastian Bach. Tamara Matthews, soprano; Marietta Simpson, mezzo-soprano; Benjamin Butterfield, tenor; Christòpheren Nomura, baritone; Bach Choir of Bethlehem; Bach Festival Orchestra; Greg Funfgeld, conductor. Recorded at Packer Church, Lehigh University, May 1998. Dorian Recordings, 1999. 2 sound discs : digital ; 4 ¾ in.

The ascension oratorio and two festive cantatas, BWV 11, 51, and 34. / Cantata, BWV 11: Lobet Gott in seinen Reichen; Cantata, BWV 51: Jauchzet Gott in allen Landen!; Cantata, BWV 34: O ewiges Feuer, o Ursprung der Liebe / Johann Sebastian Bach. Ann Monoyios, soprano; Daniel Taylor, countertenor; Frederick Urrey, tenor; Christòpheren Nomura, baritone; Bach Choir of Bethlehem; Bach Festival Orchestra; Greg Funfgeld, conductor. Recorded at First Presbyterian Church of Bethlehem, May 2001. Dorian Recordings, 2002. 1 sound disc : digital ; 4 ¾ in.

Christmas in Bethlehem: Traditional carols sung by the Bach Choir of Bethlehem, vol. 3. / The first noel; There shall a star; The white dove; It came upon a midnight clear; Sweet little Jesus boy; O holy night; In dulci jubilo, from Orgelbüchlein; Schafe können sicher weiden (Sheep may safely graze) from Cantata, BWV 208; While shepherds watched their flocks by night; Fantasia on Christmas carols; Chorale fantasia: In Dulci Jubilo; This little babe; We three kings of Orient are; Silent night, holy night; Go tell it on the mountain. Marietta Simpson, mezzo-soprano; Julien Robbins, bass-baritone; Thomas Goeman, organ; Bach Choir of Bethlehem; Philadelphia Brass; Greg Funfgeld, conductor. Recorded at First Presbyterian Church of Bethlehem, February 2002. Dorian Recordings, 2002. 1 sound disc : digital ; 4 ¾ in.

Christmas in Bethlehem: Traditional carols sung by the Bach Choir of Bethlehem, vol. 4. / Mary had a baby; O come, all ye faithful; A babe is born; Joseph, lieber Joseph mein; Chorale from Wie schön leuchtet der Morgenstern (How brightly shines the morning star), BWV 1; Sir Christèmas; Of the father's heart begotten; Herr, nun lässest du deinen Diener in Frieden fahren; Chorale Prelude: Allein Gott in der Höh sei Ehr; O come, o come, Emmanuel; In dulci jubilo; Joys seven; Stay with us; The three kings; On Christmas night (Sussex carol); Thou shalt know him; O little town of Bethlehem; The angel Gabriel from heaven came; Still, still, still; The rain is over and gone. Marietta Simpson, mezzo-soprano; William Sharp, baritone; Thomas Goeman, organ and piano; Bach Choir of Bethlehem; Philadelphia Brass; Greg Funfgeld, conductor. Recorded at First Presbyterian Church of Bethlehem, June 2006, by George Blood. 1 sound disc : digital ; 4 ¾ in.

Make a joyful noise: The Bach choir of Bethlehem. [documentary film]. PBS-39, 2006. 1 videodisc (58 min.) : sd., col. ; 4 ¾ in.
Mr. Bach comes to call. / Music by Johann Sebastian Bach. Cast: Mark McKenna; Emily Rose Young; Sebastian Rivera; Dale Aumann; Tyler Reighn; Suzanne Edwards; Greg Funfgeld, narrator. Bach Choir of Bethlehem; Bach Festival Orchestra; Greg Funfgeld, conductor. Classical Kids, 2007. 1 videodisc (54 min.) : sd., col. ; 4 ¾ in.

Magnificat in D major, BWV 243; Cantata, BWV 191: Gloria in excelsis Deo / Johann Sebastian Bach; Gloria in D major, RV 589 / Antonio Vivaldi. Julia Doyle, soprano; Rosa Lamoreaux, soprano; Daniel Taylor, countertenor; Benjamin Butterfield, tenor; Daniel Lichti, bass-baritone; Bach Choir of Bethlehem; Bach Festival Orchestra; Greg Funfgeld, conductor. Recorded at First Presbyterian Church of Bethlehem, May 2009. Analekta, 2009. 1 sound disc: digital, 4 ¾ in.

Songs of Hope. / A Dream of Time /Stephen Paulus; Rejoice in the Lamb / Benjamin Britten; Chichester Psalms / Leonard Bernstein; Singet dem Herrn ein neues Lied, BWV 225 / Johann Sebastian Bach. Rosa Lamoreaux, soprano; Daniel Taylor, countertenor; Benjamin Butterfield, tenor; William Sharp, baritone; Bach Choir of Bethlehem; Bach Festival Orchestra; Greg Funfgeld, conductor. Recorded at First Presbyterian Church of Bethlehem, 21, 22, and 23 March 2011. Analekta, 2011 [forthcoming].

Passion According to St. John, BWV 245 / Johann Sebastian Bach. Julia Doyle, soprano; Rosa Lamoreaux, soprano; Daniel Taylor, countertenor; Benjamin Butterfield, tenor; Charles Daniels, tenor; William Sharp, baritone; Christòpheren Nomura, bass-baritone. Bach Choir of Bethlehem; Bach Festival Orchestra; Greg Funfgeld, conductor. Recorded at First Presbyterian Church of Bethlehem, 9, 10, and 11 May 2011. Analekta, 2011 [forthcoming].

Selected Bibliography

PRIMARY SOURCES

Archives

Archives of the Bach Choir of Bethlehem
Heckewelder Place, Bethlehem, PA 18018
A repository of programs, musical scores, visual and audio documents, letters, and records of The Bach Choir of Bethlehem.

Archives of the Moravian Church of Bethlehem
41 W. Locust Street, Bethlehem, PA 18018
The official repository of the records of the Moravian Church in America-Northern Province.

Newspapers

Allentown (PA) Call Chronicle
Allentown (PA) Morning Call
Bethlehem (PA) Daily Times
Bethlehem (PA) Globe-Times (also *Globe Times*)
Bethlehem (PA) Times
Boston Evening Transcript
Brooklyn (NY) Eagle
Cleveland (OH) Herald
Easton (PA) Express
Easton (PA) Express-Times
New York Daily Tribune

New York Herald-Tribune
New York Times
New York Tribune
North American (Philadelphia, PA)
Oxford Times (U.K.)
Philadelphia Evening Bulletin
Philadelphia Inquirer
Philadelphia (PA) North American
Philadelphia Press
Philadelphia Public Ledger
Philadelphia Times
San Francisco Call
San Francisco Chronicle
San Francisco Examiner
South Bethlehem (PA) Globe
Star Ledger (NJ)
The Moravian (Bethlehem, PA)
The Sun (New York)
Washington (DC) Express

Other materials

Ferguson, Dorothy, comp. "Family Anecdotes of Uncle Charlie Robinson," TS in the author's possession.

Houck, Kenneth L. *Bach in Bethlehem: A Musical Tradition*. Bethlehem, PA: Oaks Printing Co., 1979.

SECONDARY SOURCES

Books

Archambault, Reginald D. *John Dewey on Education*. New York: Random House, 1964.

Barzun, Jacques. *From Dawn to Decadence: 1500 to the Present*. New York: HarperCollins, 2000.

Botwinick, Michael. "Foreword," *The American Renaissance 1876–1911*. New York: Pantheon Books, 1979.

Bowen, Catherine Drinker. *Family Portrait*. Boston: Little Brown, 1970.

Campion, Joan. *Bethlehem Pennsylvania: A City of Music*. Bethlehem: Moon Trail Books, 2007.

Chase, Gilbert. *America's Music from the Pilgrims to the Present*. New York: McGraw-Hill, 1966.

Church Music and Musical Life in Pennsylvania in the Eighteenth Century. Lancaster: Wickersham Printing Co., 1972.

Cox, Howard, ed., and Ellis Finger, trans. *The Calov Bible of Bach.* Ann Arbor: UMI Press, 1985.

Crawford, Richard. *America's Musical Life: A History.* New York: W. W. Norton, 2001.

Crist, Stephen A. *Bach in America.* Urbana: University of Illinois Press, 2003.

David, Hans T. *Musical Life in the Pennsylvania Settlements of the Unitas Fratrum.* Winston-Salem, NC: Moravian Music Foundation, 1954.

David, Hans T., Arthur Mendel, and Christolph Wolff, eds. *The New Bach Reader: A Life of Johann Sebastian Bach in Letters and Documents.* New York: W. W. Norton, 1999.

Davis, Ronald L. *A History of Music in American Life.* 2 vols. Huntington, NY: R. E. Krieger, 1980–1982.

Dawson, Mary. *The Programs of the Bach Choir of Bethlehem: 1975–2000.* Bethlehem: The Bach Choir of Bethlehem, 2004.

Gapp, Samuel H. *A History of the Beginnings of Moravian Work in America.* Bethlehem: Archives of the Moravian Church, 1955.

Gerson, Robert A. *Music in Philadelphia.* Westport: Greenwood Press, 1970.

Hamilton, K. *A History of the Beginnings of Moravian Work in America.* Bethlehem: Archives of the Moravian Church, 1955.

Hamilton, Kenneth G. *The Bethlehem Diary, 1872–1744.* vol. 1. Bethlehem: The Moravian Archives, 1971.

Hamm, Charles. *Music in the New World.* New York: W. W. Norton, 1983.

Heintze, James R. *American Musical Life in Concert to 1865.* New York: Garland Press, 1994.

———, ed. *American Music Life in Context and Practice to 1865.* New York: Garland Publishing, 1994.

Hessen, Robert. *Steel Titan: The Life of Charles M. Schwab.* New York: Oxford University Press, 1975.

Horowitz, Joseph. *Classical Music in America, A History of its Rise and Fall.* New York: W. W. Norton, 2005.

Howe, M. A. DeWolfe. *Venite in Bethlehem.* No publisher, ca. 1940.

Hubbard. Elbert. *Little Journey in the Houses of Great Musicians: Vol. Eight.* East Aurora: East Aurora, 1901.

Hutchinson, Ruth. *A City and Its Music.* Bethlehem: *Bethlehem Globe Times*, 1967.

———. *A History of the Bach Choir.* Typescript, 1967.

Johnson, H. Earle. *First Performances in America.* The College Music Society, 1979.

Johnson, Paul M. *A History of the American People.* New York: Harper Perennial, 1997.

Jones, Ifor, ed. "We must through great tribulation," no. 146. New York: G. Schirmer, 1942.

———, ed. "Cantata 78." New York: G. Schirmer, 1941, 3.

————, ed. "Cantata 23." New York: G. Schirmer, 1947.

Kassler, Michael, ed. *The English Bach Awakening: Knowledge of Bach and His Music in England 1750–1830.* Aldershot: Ashgate, 2004.

Knouse, Nola Reed, ed. *The Music of the Moravian Church in America.* University of Rochester, N.Y. 2008.

Larson, Paul S. *An American Musical Dynasty: A Biography of the Wolle Family of Bethlehem, Pennsylvania.* Bethlehem: Lehigh University Press, 2002.

————. *The Programs of the Bach Choir of Bethlehem: The First Fifty Years.* Bethlehem: The Bach Choir of Bethlehem, 1996.

Lawrence, Vera B. *Strong on Music: Volume 2, Reverberations 1850–1856.* Chicago: University of Chicago Press, 1995.

Levering, Joseph Mortimer. *A History of Bethlehem, Pennsylvania 1741–1892.* Bethlehem: Time Publishing, 1903.

Levine, Lawrence W. *Highbrow Lowbrow: The Emergence of Cultural Hierarchy in America.* Cambridge: Harvard University Press, 1988.

Mack, Elmer L. *Why a Bach Choir in Bethlehem?* Bethlehem: privately printed, 1973.

Mann, Alfred. *Bethlehem Bach Studies.* Bethlehem: Moravian Book Shop, 1985.

Mann, Alfred, Irving Lowens, Robert Freeman, Paul Brainard, Gerhard Heraz, and Howard Cox. *Bach in Bethlehem Today: A Conference Report.* Bethlehem: Moravian Book Shop, 1979.

Martin, Edmund F., with David J. Morrison. *Bethlehem Steelmaker.* Bethlehem: BMS Press, 1992, 98.

Martin, John Hill. *Historical Sketch of Bethlehem in Pennsylvania With Some Account of the Moravian Church.* Philadelphia: John L. Pile, 1872.

May, Rollo. *The Courage to Create.* New York: W. A. Norton, 1975, 140.

McCorkle, Donald M. *The Moravian Contribution to American Music.* Winston-Salem, NC: Moravian Music Foundation, 1956.

Mencken, H. L. *A Mencken Chrestomathy.* New York: Alfred A. Knopf, 1978.

————. *Thirty-five Years of Newspaper Work.* Baltimore: Johns Hopkins University Press, 1994.

Musselman, Joseph A. *Music in the Cultured Generation.* Evanston: Northwestern University Press, 1971.

Myers, Richard E. *Sketches of Early Bethlehem.* Bethlehem: Oaks Printing Company, 1981.

Newhard, Nelson James, Sr. *The Newhard Piano Quartette of Bethlehem, Pennsylvania,* Allentown, PA: Lehigh Printing, 1946), 160.

Osgood, Charles G. *Bach Choir of Bethlehem a Brief History.* Bethlehem: no publisher, 1957.

————. *Going to Bethlehem.* Bethlehem: no publisher, 1957.

Reichel, Levin Theodore. *The Early History of the Church of the United Brethren, Commonly Called Moravians in North America.* Nazareth: Moravian Historical Society, 1888.

Roberts, J. M. *Twentieth Century*. New York: Penguin Books, 1999.

Robinson, James. *The Bach Choir*. no publisher, no date.

Russell, Lynes. *The Taste-Makers*. New York: Harper & Brothers, 1949.

Schlenker, Alma H. *Music in Bethlehem*. Bethlehem: Oakes Printing Company, 1984.

Schwarz, Ralph Grayson. *Bach in Bethlehem*. Bethlehem: The Bach Choir of Bethlehem, 1998.

Schweitzer, Albert. *Bach* I. New York: Macmillan, 1905, 262–63.

Smith, Jewel A. *Music, Women, and Pianos in Antebellum Bethlehem, Pennsylvania*. Bethlehem: Lehigh University Press, 2008.

Stebbins, Lucy P. *Franck Damrosch: Let the People Sing*. Durham: Duke University Press, 1945.

Thomas, Kurt, Alfred Mann, and William H. Reese. *[Lehrbuch de Chorleitung.] The Choral Conductor. The Technique of Choral Conducting in Theory and Practice*. English adaptation by Alfred Mann and William H. Reese. New York: Associated. Music. Publishers, 1971.

Thompson, Virgil. *Music Reviewed 1940–1954*. New York: Vintage Books, 1967.

Tranupman-Carr, Carol A. *Pleasing to Our Use: David Tannenberg and the Organs of the Moravians*. Bethlehem: Lehigh University Press, 2000.

Walters, Raymond. *The Bethlehem Bach Choir*. Boston: Houghton Mifflin, 1918.

———. *The Bethlehem Bach Choir: A Historical and a Critical Compendium*. New York: Houghton Mifflin, 1923.

———. *Bethlehem Long Ago and Today*. Bethlehem: Cary Printing Company, 1923.

Weikel, C. H. H. "A Brief History of the Bach Choir Guarantor's Meeting—May 14, 1965." Typescript.

Willistein, Paul. D., Jr. *Bethlehem Pilgrimage: The Bach Past and Present: A Pictorial Account*. Bethlehem: Moravian Book Shop, 1979.

Wolff, Christoph. *Johann Sebastian Bach the Learned Musician*. New York: W. W. Norton, 2000.

Wolle, Francis. *A Moravian Heritage*. Boulder: Empire Reproduction Printing Co., 1972.

Yates, W. Ross. *Bethlehem of Pennsylvania: The Golden Years. 1841–1920*. Bethlehem:

Bethlehem Book Committee, 1976. Articles

"Bach's Music," *The Musical Times*, no. 645 (1 September 1896): 585–87; no. 644 (1 October 1896): 652–57; no. 645 (1 November 1896): 722–26; no. 646 (1 December 1896): 797–800.

"Bach's Music in England," *The Musical Times and Singing Class Circular* 37, no. 646 (1 December 1896): 800.

Blume, Friedrich. "Bach in the Romantic Era," *Musical Quarterly* 50, no. 3 (July 1964): 290–306.

"Comments of a Critic on the Tenth Bach Festival," *Alumni Bulletin of Lehigh University*, July 1915. Scrapbook, ABCB.

Cox, Howard. "The Scholarly Detective: Investigating Bach's Personal Bible," *The Bach Journal of the Riemenschneider Bach Institute* 25, no. 1 (Spring-Summer 1994): 28–45.

Dirst, Matthew. "Doing Missionary Work Dwight's Journal of Music and the American Back Awakening," in *Bach in America*, Stephen A. Crist, ed. (Urbana: University of Illinois Press, 2003), 15–35.

Ehmann, Wilhelm. Trans. by Alfred Mann. "The Romantic A Cappella Tradition," *American Choral Review* 15, no. 2 (April 1973): 5–23.

Hartzell, Lawrence W. "Musical Moravian Missionaries, Part I, Johann Christopher Prylaeus." *Moravian Music Journal* (Winter 1984): 91–92.

Homburg, Herfried. "Louis Spohr und die Bach-Renaissance." *Bach- Jahrbuch* (1960): 64–82; 65–66 for a list of some of these conductors.

Hutchison, Ruth. "A Tribute to Ifor Jones," *American Choral Review* 12, no. 2 (April 1970): 43–46.

Leaver, Robin A. "Bach Studies Approaches to the B Minor Mass," *American Choral Review* 27, no. 1 (January 1985): 1–71.

———. "Introduction Dawn of a Choral Era." *American Choral Review* 20, no. 2 (April 1978): 5–7.

———. "New Light on the Pre-History of the Bach Choir in Bethlehem." *Bach, The Journal of Riemenschneider Bach Institute* (Fall-Winter 1996): 24–34.

———. "The Revival of the St. John Passion, History and Performance Practice," *Bach Journal of the Riemenschneider Bach Institute* 20, no. 3 (1989): 34–49.

———. "A Tribute for Jones," *American Choral Review* 12, no. 2 (April 1970): 1–2.

———. "Two Pupils of Rheinberger and Their Use of the Organ in the Performance of Bach's *St. John Passion*." *The Tracker* 33, no. 2 (1989): 19–23.

Mann, Alfred. "Review," *American Choral Review* (Winter/Spring 1990): 34–35.

Mann, Alfred, and Gustav Reese. "Introduction," *American Choral Review* 13, no. 2 (1971): iii–iv.

McCurdy, Alexander. "Registration that Won Highest Honor." *The American Organist* (April 1955): 115–17.

"Overview of the Performances of Bach's Works from the End of 1904 to the Beginning of 1907" (translation), *Bach-Jahrbuch* (1906): 114–29.

Owen, Barbara. "Bach Comes to America," in *Bach in America*, Stephen A. Crist, ed. (Urbana: University of Illinois Press, 2003), 1–14.

Schneider, Max. "Verzeichnis bis zum 1851 gedruckten Werke v. Bach," in *Bach-Jahrbuch* (1906): 84–113.

Schünemann, Georg. "Die Bachflege der Berliner Singakademie," in *Bach-Jahrbuch* (1928): 138–71.

Steelman, Richard. "A Cantata Performed in Bethlehem in the 1740s," *The Moravian Music Foundation Bulletin* (Fall/Winter 1975): 2–6.

Trautmann, Christoph. "Bach's Bible," *American Choral Review* 14, no. 4 (October 1972): 3–11.

Walters, Raymond. "Bach at Bethlehem, Pennsylvania," *The Musical Quarterly* 21, no. 2 (April 1935): 179–89.

Wilson, Richard Guy. "Cultural Conditions," in *The American Renaissance 1876– 1911*, Michael Botwinick (New York: Pantheon Books, 1979).

Wollny, Peter. "Sara Levy and the Making of Musical Taste in Berlin," *The Musical Quarterly* 77 (1993): 651–88.

Index

About the Author

Paul S. Larson is professor emeritus at Moravian College in Bethlehem, Pennsylvania, where he taught music education, non-Western music, and music history. A longtime resident of Bethlehem and archivist of The Bach Choir of Bethlehem, he has known and worked with many of the people he writes about in this book. He was fortunate to have an academic office in the building where T. T. Wolle, The Bach Choir's first conductor, received his early musical education and where The Bach Choir rehearsed for many years. Active as an author and lecturer in local history, Larson is involved with area cultural and historical societies.